ABNORMAL

ABNORMAL

JU GOSLING^{ju90}

BETTANY PRESS

2011

First published in Great Britain by Bettany Press 2011.
8 Kildare Road, London E16 4AD.

© Ju Gosling 2011

British Library Cataloguing in Publication Data. A catalogue record for this book is available from the British Library.

This book is sold subject to the condition that it shall not, by way of trade or otherwise, be lent, re-sold, hired out, or otherwise circulated without the Publisher's prior consent in any form of binding or cover other than that in which it is published and without a similar condition including this condition being imposed on the subsequent purchaser.

All rights reserved.

ISBN 978-1-908304-15-5

Designed by Tony Malone.

Printed and bound by CPI Group (UK) Ltd, Croydon, CR0 4YY.

CONTENTS

Acknowledgements — iii

INTRODUCTION: Body Blues, or, — 1
The case for claiming that we are a dysphoric society

SECTION I: Hampered by History, or, How did we come to this? — 16

1. Philosophy and Social Control, or, The pursuit of perfection — 19
2. Divine Punishment, or, Failing to live up to God's image — 37
3. Industrial Bodies, or, (Sub)standardising humanity — 51
4. Taking Our Medicine, or, Doctor knows best — 65
5. Victorian Values, or, Delusions of omnipotence — 79

SECTION II: Dividing Ourselves, or, How we created disabled people — 90

6. Stereotypes and Shame, or, The cultivation of the crip — 93
7. Miraculous Medicine, or, What can't be cured must be ignored — 109
8. The Cost of Living, or, The survival of the richest — 125
9. Washing Machines Good/Wheelchairs Bad, — 143
or, Stigmatising technology
10. Dysphoric Designs, or, — 157
Making the world over in a distorted image

SECTION III: Facing Facts or, — 170
Why the human race will never be 'perfect'

11. Science Fictions, or, Ten reasons why science teaches us — 173
that it doesn't have all the answers

12. Designer Babies 1, or, — 201
Why redesigning the human race is not an option

i

13. Designer Babies 2, or, 211
Why we could all live to regret a eugenics-based abortion policy
14. Misunderstanding Evolution, or, 223
The importance of the individual to the survival of the human race

SECTION IV: Alternative Futures, or, 232
Do we really have a choice about changing?

15. The New Ancients, or, Who wants to live for ever? 235
16. Medical Meltdown, or, 241
What will happen if we continue in our dysphoria?
17. (In)Voluntary Euthanasia, or, Better dead than disabled? 251
18. A Different Tomorrow, or, How to heal and live healthily 263

Acknowledgements

As a nurse, my mother Phyllis Gosling initially taught me about science, while always encouraging my interest in the arts. She also taught me the importance of her own version of the 'big society'.

From the 1980s onwards, many people have been instrumental in explaining to me the issues relating to 'abnormal' bodies. These include Keith Armstrong, Sarah Olowe, Linda Bellos, Jenny Morris, Nasa Begum, Brenda Ellis, Petra Kuppers, Mat Fraser, Anne Pridmore, Michelle Daley, Suzanne Bull, Kath Gillespie-Sells, Karen Shook, Rowen Jade, Tara Flood, Rachel Hurst and Peter Wehrli.

Mark Prest, as curator of the *Adorn, Equip* national touring exhibition, encouraged and enabled me to look more deeply at the issues surrounding the design and marketing of disability aids and equipment between 1999 and 2001. (The online version of *Adorn, Equip* is linked from my website at www.ju90.co.uk.) This opportunity was later extended by the Apples and Snakes performance poetry organisation and the Science Museum in 2003, who invited me to make work in response to the objects in the museum's stores. This led me to the Wellcome Collection of antique wheelchairs, from which I created my performance 'Wheels on Fire' (also available on my website).

The City of Graz helped me to reflect on the theories behind the international disability arts and disability rights movements when, as European Capital of Culture in 2003, they gave me an open commission to make a piece of online work. Using a series of tableaux, 'Helping the Handicapped' not only provided an explanation to others of the various theoretical models of disability, but also enabled me to think about them more deeply myself. In 2008 I returned to Graz to produce my installation 'Men in White Coats' for Reni Hofmueller of the ESC Labor gallery, and again this provided me with an opportunity to think, this time about the issues relating to the power that we ascribe to doctors and scientists.

Geza Ziemer of the Zurich Institut fur Theorie der Gestaltung und Kunst provided an opportunity for me to reflect more deeply on the representation of the body within art and culture when she invited me to take part in the Aesthetics of Vulnerability project in 2004/5 along with Raimund Hoghe, Simon Versnel and Milli Bitterli, and the accompanying film by Gitta Gsell assisted in this.

Nicola Triscott and Rob La Frenais of the art-science organisation Arts Catalyst introduced me to hands-on laboratory science in 2005 when they invited me to take part in the SymbioticA course at Guy's Medical School. I am also grateful to Oron Catts from the SymbioticA laboratory at the University of Western Australia for leading the course.

The National Institute for Medical Research (NIMR) opened its doors to me in 2006, and I am grateful to all of the scientists who supported my research and who gave up their time to discuss issues with me and to answer my questions. In particular, Simon Gould curated the project, and Dr Malcolm Logan and Dr Evelien Gevers worked closely with me over an 18-month period to determine how popular perceptions of science impact on our understanding of 'normality' and to develop the 'Scientific Model of Disability'.

The Australian Network for Arts and Technology encouraged me to look more deeply into art-science theory when they invited me to be a keynote speaker at their *Super Human: Revolution of the Species* symposium in 2009. Conversations about the body with Jane Trengrove and artists associated with Arts Access Victoria while I was there greatly enhanced the experience.

The Wellcome Trust funded both the NIMR residency and the resulting tour of the artwork that I created during it, and without them this book would not have existed. Meroë Candy in particular provided feedback and support for the *Abnormal* project from 2006 onwards.

Finally, I could not have written this book without the support, patience and intellectual input of my partner, Julie Newman, and, of course, the company of various furry friends.

DEDICATED TO THE MEMORY OF

Nigel Walton

WHO TAUGHT ME A GREAT DEAL ABOUT BEING HUMAN

&

David Morris

WHO READ IT FIRST

INTRODUCTION

BODY BLUES or, The case for claiming that we are a dysphoric society

Today in the West, our relationship with our bodies has never been less happy or more dysfunctional. We have become increasingly convinced that physical 'perfection' is not only achievable but a duty, and increasingly unhappy when, unsurprisingly, we fail to reach this impossible goal. In fact, our body dysphoria is so wide-reaching that it impacts on every aspect of our lives. The gap between what is real, in terms of what can be scientifically evidenced, and what we believe to be real is now so wide that coming to terms with reality again will be enormously challenging for us all. However, we have everything to gain by doing so, and everything to lose by refusing. At stake is not only our individual happiness, but also the shape of our whole society for the rest of the century and beyond.

'Body dysphoria' is defined as being someone's inability to accept that their body is 'normal', despite all of the evidence to the contrary. It is accompanied by an obsessive interest in the body parts that are viewed as being 'abnormal', and by an overwhelming desire to change these. Body dysphoria is life-limiting, and at its extreme can be life-threatening. Body dysphoria is generally defined as being a psychological disease of the individual. What has been largely overlooked until now is the extent to which, in the 21st century, it is a problem for our (Western) society as a whole. Acknowledging that a problem exists is the first necessary step towards overcoming many psychological conditions. It is essential that we begin to recognise the serious and widespread nature of our society's body dysphoria, and the ways in which it affects us all. Only then can we begin to achieve the changes that are necessary to stop making victims of ourselves.

And we need to do this soon, before our condition becomes so advanced that it becomes incurable.

Our dissatisfaction with our bodies is increasing every year

For evidence of our body dysphoria, we need look no further than the growing normalisation of cosmetic surgery throughout the noughties for people who in fact are already perfectly 'normal'. By the mid-noughties, demand for cosmetic surgery was increasing rapidly in Britain: in one year alone, 2005, the number of operations taking place grew by a third. Breast augmentations, then costing around £4000, increased by more than 50%. 'Anti-ageing' procedures, such as facelifts, eyelid surgery and brow lifts, increased by between a third and a half, with demand from men rising by 80%. All this in just 12 months.

Demand slowed down slightly as the recession began to bite, but still continued to increase year on year. Liposuction was becoming more popular, with the number of operations being carried out rising by 90% in 2006, making it the third most popular procedure behind breast 'enhancement' and eyelid surgery that year; by the end of the noughties, liposuction was still the sixth most popular procedure taking place. Transform, the UK's biggest cosmetic surgery group, reported that over the noughties the total number of procedures taking place in its clinics increased by 400%.

In 2007, the number of facelifts taking place increased more rapidly than any other procedure, rising by 36% compared to the previous 12 months; and by the end of the noughties this was still the fourth most popular procedure among Britons. Breast augmentation, though, continued to be the most popular procedure of them all, with the number of operations performed rising by 32% between 2007 and 2009. Tummy tucks also rose by 30% in 2008 alone, while the number of 'nose jobs' taking place increased by 25% in 2009.

90% of cosmetic surgical procedures were carried out on women, but a growing number of men also opted for surgery, with the number of procedures being carried out on men rising by 21.5% in the last year of the decade alone. According to the British Association of Aesthetic Plastic Surgeons (BAAPS), the number of men having breast reduction surgery increased by over 1000% in the five years between 2003 and 2008, and then rose by another 80% in 2009. Meanwhile, the number of men having brow lifts increased by 60% in just 12 months between 2007 and 2008, and

Introduction

then went up another 51% in 2009. Unlike women, men also have the option to use steroids to change their body shape, and although this is illegal, the number of boys and men using anabolic steroids is estimated to have doubled in the last five years of the decade.

In 2009, 36,482 surgical procedures were carried out in the UK by BAAPS members — an increase of 6.7% on 2008. Since many surgeons are not members of BAAPS, the true number of unnecessary operations taking place is estimated by BAAPS to have been three times higher. Overall, the cosmetic surgery industry in Britain, worth only £143 million in 2002, was valued at £1.2 billion by the end of the decade. And none of the figures above include the increasing number of Britons heading abroad for cosmetic surgery. The 2007 Medical Tourism Survey was the first of its kind. It found that, in 2006, 14,500 people travelled outside the UK for cosmetic surgery, spending a total of £50 million. Overall — including dentistry and elective procedures such as hip replacements — medical tourism from the UK had increased by 25% in just 12 months, and this increase was predicted to continue.

All of this was despite the fact that growing numbers of people who had had cosmetic surgery and dental treatment abroad experienced serious post-operative problems when back in the UK, which they then discovered that they needed to pay privately to treat. A survey of members of the BAAPS in the late noughties found that in the previous year one in eight surgeons had seen nine or more patients who had had problems as a result of having cosmetic surgery abroad. This survey, along with other problems involving overseas cosmetic surgery, received widespread publicity, but did not hinder the rise in the number of people going overseas for treatment, which is continuing into the teens.

Of course, the people who are currently opting for unnecessary cosmetic surgery are still just a small proportion of the population. On their own, they could simply be regarded as people who are seeking surgical solutions to their psychological problems, and who are being exploited by greedy surgeons rather than being referred — in the first instance, at least — for psychiatric treatment. What provides overwhelming proof of our body dysphoria is the number of people who now believe unnecessary surgical treatment to be aspirational and desirable. And we should not forget that as many as one in three Argentinians are now estimated by their tax authorities to have had cosmetic surgery; today's aspiration can be tomorrow's reality.

In 2007, Which? (formerly the Consumers' Association) found that almost five million British adults would consider cosmetic surgery, and this number was likely to have increased still further by the end of the noughties. Women predominated, but a survey by two lifestyle websites found that nearly eight out of ten gay men would consider surgery too. This was of course related to, as well as reflected in, the large number of television programmes about cosmetic surgery that were produced in the noughties, few of which were critical of the procedures being shown. In 2007, an American survey found that 79% of people undergoing cosmetic surgery had been influenced in their decision by 'reality' television programmes.

Among young people — the least likely to 'need' cosmetic surgery — the picture was depressingly similar. In 2009, Girlguiding UK found that nearly a quarter of all young women aged between 16 and 21 who were questioned would consider cosmetic surgery; unsurprisingly, in the same year the number of teenagers having breast implants rose by 150%. This normalisation of cosmetic surgery seems to increase with age: in 2005, a survey of 1000 women by *Grazia* magazine found that half of all British women aged between 25 and 45 intended to have cosmetic surgery once they could afford it.

Similarly, in 2007 a BBC Radio 1 online survey of young adults aged between 17 and 34 found that half of the young women who responded would consider cosmetic surgery. And this was despite widespread fears about the dangers of surgery, with over a third of the women questioned by *Grazia* fearing dying on the operating table. We are much more aware now than we used to be of the dangers of surgery, including the likelihood of scarring; problems with breathing after a 'nose job'; and in the case of breast enhancement — the most popular procedure of all — the need for further procedures in the future. But it seems to make no difference to us whatsoever.

Even more worrying is the fact that the rapidly rising demand and desire for cosmetic surgery reflects far more than our society's anxieties about ageing: dissatisfaction with our bodies is widespread and starts young. When Girlguiding UK asked girls whether they were happy with their appearance, nearly one in five aged between 7 and 11 said 'No'. This proportion almost doubled as girls entered their teens, with nearly four in ten 11- to 16-year-olds being unhappy with the way that they looked, and more than one in ten stating that they were "not at all happy" with their appearance. Our children no longer expect that their bodies will pass muster without outside intervention, and they are increasingly prepared to risk their lives with surgery to change them as they grow older.

Introduction

Cultural images of bodies are increasingly unreal

It is hardly surprising that we feel our bodies are inferior and abnormal when we consider the images that surround us. Women in particular suffer from the fact that clothes intended for the 'ordinary' woman are modelled by women whose bodies most closely resemble men's, making it impossible for all but a tiny minority of women to achieve the figure that is held up as the ideal. Consider this for a moment: female fashion models must be a minimum of 5 feet 8 inches tall, with the average 'supermodel' being 5 feet 10 inches. But according to the 2007 Health Survey for England, 5 feet 10 inches is the average height of English *men* aged between 25 and 34. The average height of English *women* the same age is only 5 feet 4.5 inches, while the average height for all English women over the age of 25 is just 5 feet 3 inches.

Female models must also have breasts and hips that are unnaturally small compared to those of average women, and they must be unusually thin. At the turn of the 21st century, the British Medical Association found that the most-photographed models and actresses of the 1990s commonly had body fat levels as low as 10%, and it is certain that models now are no fatter than they were a decade ago. It may even be that, while average dress sizes have continued to increase, the weight of fashion models has dropped still further. Despite moves in the noughties to ban 'size zero' — UK size 4 — models from catwalks in Madrid and Milan, the British fashion industry refused to follow suit, instead focusing on protecting the physical and mental health of under-age models.

However, the average proportion of fat in a healthy woman's body is between 22% and 26%, double that of the women pictured in fashion shoots. And by the end of the noughties the average British woman took a size 16 dress size, leaving a vast gulf between the representation of women's bodies in fashion advertising, catalogues and magazines and the reality. Probably linked to this is the fact that twice as many women think they are overweight than is actually the case, when being seriously underweight is as dangerous for people's health as obesity. Yet the actresses and models in the images analysed by the British Medical Association were regarded as being aspirational and as role models, particularly by girls and young women.

Increasingly, though, even the bodies of 'role models' are not considered to be good enough by advertisers and magazine editors. Digital airbrushing techniques, once simply used to remove spots and shadows and brighten eyes and so on, are now routinely employed to change the whole shape of women's bodies, making waists thinner, legs longer, and breasts bigger. (And in the case of seriously underweight models, increasing the size of selected parts of their bodies to disguise this fact.) Despite continuing controversy, and despite the intervention of the British Fashion Council to call for a voluntary code, this use of airbrushing has been robustly defended by the publishing and fashion industries, who (rightly) claim that women who view such images prefer them as they are — perhaps to punish themselves for not measuring up, and, since this has become so fundamental to the way in which they live their lives, to support them in their body dysphoria.

Most worryingly of all, airbrushing techniques are routinely used in advertising aimed at the under-16s. In autumn 2009, more than 40 academic specialists in body image from the UK, US and Australia wrote to the Advertising Standards Authority pleading with them to ban airbrushing in these adverts. The British Fashion Council also supported the introduction of a code that would minimise and label digitally enhanced images aimed at the under-16s. In reality, though, such a scheme would be virtually impossible to implement. Since all images are routinely re-touched, all that would happen is that every photo would bear the same mark, which would then become meaningless. Only when we ourselves demand images that are not only aspirational, but also realistic, will anything change.

Unfortunately, the widespread presence of digitally enhanced size zero women's bodies within the images that surround us tells only half the story. Just as relevant is the relative or complete absence of many other body types. For example, in 1999 the over-60s made up 21% of the population. However, only 7% of the people on television — including factual and fictional programming — were from this age group. When older people were shown, it was in very stereotypical and often negative ways. Little has changed since, apart from the growing recognition that women are particularly discriminated against by media employers as they age, and the fact that even older men in the media are beginning to come under pressure to change their appearance or lose their jobs.

Similarly, more than one in ten under-60s are disabled, as is around one in five of the population as a whole. But despite representing such a large proportion of the population, disabled people are virtually invisible within the media apart from as recipients of charity and in documentaries that are essentially an update of the old-fashioned freak show (of which more in Section II). Fat people, Black people, small people and the rest of the diverse range of body types that make up the British population are similarly marginalised, stereotyped or simply invisible.

Introduction

No wonder that a growing number of people from ethnic minorities are opting for cosmetic surgery to make them 'more white-looking'. No wonder that disabled people are not only marginalised within society, but face growing levels of hate crime. No wonder that both children and adults aspire to the unrealistic body types represented in fashion and advertising, when we rarely, if ever, see people like ourselves pictured anywhere at all. And no wonder that people seek an eternally youthful appearance, when to look old is to become invisible and, as we will see later in this book, to be widely assumed to be better off dead.

Our eating habits are increasingly chaotic

Although we aspire to be increasingly thin, we are actually becoming fatter, and more than half of all adults in the UK are now overweight. A quarter of the adult population is classified as being obese, compared to just 15% in 1993. Men and women are equally affected, although women are three times more likely than men to be morbidly obese, and 44% of British women have a waistline greater than the 80cm (37 inch) recommended maximum compared to 32% of men. Obesity brings with it health problems ranging from diabetes, high blood pressure and infertility (for both men and women) to decreased mobility and joint problems. It also significantly increases the risk of certain cancers (oversized waistlines are linked to higher rates of breast, womb, bowel and pancreatic cancer). In the ten years to 2007, hospital admissions relating to obesity rose by a staggering 700%, costing the NHS an estimated £7 billion a year.

Researchers at the University of Oxford analysed the results of 57 separate studies in Europe and North America and found that moderate obesity shortens life by three years, and that serious obesity shortens life by an entire decade. Diabetes UK calculates that diabetes — which is usually obesity-related — is indirectly responsible for one in ten deaths each year in England, and the picture in the rest of the UK is likely to be the same or worse. Obesity can also be inherited, with studies finding that large mothers are more likely to give birth to large babies, who are then more likely not only to be overweight in later life, but also to develop diseases such as arthritis — even if they are by this time of normal weight themselves.

Perhaps it is unsurprising that more than one in eight under-16-year-olds are now obese, with boys slightly more likely to be affected than girls — this compares to only one in ten children at the start of the 1990s. The National Child Measurement Programme found that at the end of the noughties a fifth of all four-and five-year-olds were overweight or obese, rising to a third of ten- and eleven-year-olds; and children as young as three are now receiving medical treatment for obesity. There is some debate about the extent to which these figures will continue to increase, with the Government predicting that, on current trends, half of all children will be obese by 2050, and only a third will be of normal weight. Others question if the rate will increase much, if at all, but the current levels already give extreme cause for concern.

In 2009, the European Congress on Obesity heard that 91,000 under-12s in the UK have high cholesterol; 60,000 under-12s have high blood pressure; and 91,000 under-12s have liver disease as a result of over-eating. Among under-18s as a whole, almost 200,000 have high cholesterol, and more than 200,000 have blood sugar and insulin levels that are associated with diabetes. A growing number of under-18s have Type 2 diabetes, which was unknown in children before 2002, and which is always linked to diet. In all, Britons account for a seventh of all of Europe's overweight and obese under-18-year-olds. If we do not tackle obesity, we will be bringing up the first generation to live shorter lives than their parents.

Unsurprisingly, the fact that our relationship with food is increasingly dysfunctional is equally reflected in the growth of eating disorders associated with extreme thinness. Eating disorders associated with thinness are responsible for more loss of life than any other psychological disorder. This underlines the dangers of having widespread images available that feature size zero women without the balancing effect of images of 'normal' bodies. At least 1.1 million people in the UK are affected by an eating disorder, with young people between the ages of 14 and 25 most at risk of developing this type of illness. In the ten years to 1997, there was an 80% rise in the number of teenage girls being admitted to hospital with anorexia, with a 200% rise in the number of 12-year-old girls being admitted. (Adults are also affected, but are much less likely than young people to be diagnosed and receiving treatment.) The noughties saw the numbers affected continue to increase, and children as young as eight are now being treated in specialist clinics because of eating disorders.

According to the Royal College of Psychiatrists, girls and women are ten times more likely than boys and men to develop anorexia or bulimia, and 90% of young people with anorexia are girls. It is hard not to conclude that this is due to the fact that very few size zero men appear in the media. (For men, a 'manly' body shape is seen to be more desirable, which requires muscle and thus explains the rise in steroid abuse.) However, by the end of the noughties a new 'aesthetic' of male thinness meant that eating disorders among boys and men were rising too. Again, there was a disparity

Introduction

between the 'normal' body and fashion — whereas the average British man had a waist measuring 39 inches, American Apparel's 'Slim Slack' trouser came in a maximum 30-inch waist. Some estimate that as many as 25% of people with eating disorders are now male.

As with cosmetic surgery, the number of people affected by eating disorders still represents a very small proportion of the population — around one in a hundred children of school age has anorexia, with bulimia estimated to be between three and five times more common — but the number of people who are unhappy with their weight is far more significant. This dissatisfaction starts in childhood, and increases with age. Girlguiding UK found that one in twenty of all 7- to 11-year-old girls questioned wanted to be thinner, rising to more than one in ten of all 10 to 11-year-olds. One in five of all 11- to 16-year-old girls questioned wanted to lose weight, and this rose to one in three young women between the ages of 16 and 21. Far fewer surveys have been carried out among young men, but one piece of research found that one in five young men aged between 18 and 25 suffered 'extreme distress' about the appearance of their body.

Worryingly, the girls that Girlguiding UK interviewed may not have been truly representative, and may actually have had higher self-esteem than the majority. A study published in the *British Journal of Developmental Psychology* in 2005 found that almost half of girls aged between five and eight wanted to be slimmer. Despite, or perhaps because of, this a Food Standards Agency report in 2010 found that teenage girls ate more unhealthily than any other population group.

Even the increased interest in healthy eating during the noughties is to be regarded with suspicion. At the end of the 1990s, California doctor Steven Bratman named a new disorder, 'orthorexia nervosa', whereby people become obsessed with the 'purity' of their diet. Originally there were so few sufferers that the condition was lumped in with other disorders, but by the end of the noughties, eating disorder charities reported a significant increase in cases. Orthorexia may not necessarily affect weight, but can still cause malnourishment and extreme stress. At the other end of the spectrum, a diet of processed food can also cause malnutrition, and the number of people eating that has also increased since the turn of the 21st century. Overall, clinical levels of malnourishment soared during the noughties, with estimates that by 2007 up to 3.6 million Britons were suffering from health conditions related to poor diet.

In all, our relationship with food became increasingly dysfunctional during the noughties, hitting a level that has never been seen before. Despite the rise in both obesity and eating disorders, food programmes and recipe books became increasingly popular. However, by the mid-noughties a survey by Mintel found that almost two in five women and one in six men were dieting for the majority of the time, and at the beginning of the teens, the UK diet industry is now worth approximately £1 billion. This is despite repeated research showing that, by and large, diets don't work, because what people actually need to do is make long-term changes to what they eat. And it is despite the side-effects of the new diet pills, which can include uncontrollable diarrhoea.

Our ideas about what is 'normal' are increasingly dysfunctional

Overall, our ideas about what is normal are becoming increasingly separated from reality. Along with cosmetic surgery, the noughties saw a massive growth in cosmetic dentistry, as people became as dissatisfied with their teeth as they were with the rest of their bodies. In 2007, the British Academy of Cosmetic Dentistry found that only one in four people agreed with the statement: "I like my smile and would not change it"; and a third of people questioned said that they were concerned by the way their teeth looked. Nearly a third of women and a quarter of men believed that cosmetic dentistry could improve their quality of life. Teeth whitening, so helpful to people whose teeth had become stained as a result of smoking or medication, became a routine annual treatment for those who could afford it, whether their teeth were already a natural colour or not.

In just a decade, it became the norm for anyone appearing in the media to have their teeth whitened to a bluish tinge. Their teeth, and the teeth of anyone who can afford to copy them, are now unnaturally prominent in their faces, not simply because of their peculiar glow but because they are whiter than their eyeballs. As with size zero body shapes, many young people in particular now regard this unnatural aesthetic as representing what their teeth 'should' look like. And this is despite growing publicity about the widespread increase in tooth sensitivity after whitening, and the possibility of long-term damage to the teeth and gums from repeated procedures.

The noughties also saw a massive rise in the popularity of non-surgical but invasive cosmetic treatments such as Botox and injectable 'fillers', as alternatives to facelifts. The use of these treatments more than doubled in the last five years of the decade, despite the fact that the cosmetic 'benefits' are only temporary. It was also despite well-publicised warnings from the British Association of Aesthetic Plastic Surgeons that 'permanent' fillers remain in the body long term and can cause a range of problems in later life. In the USA, there are just six 'fillers' on the market, because they need to meet the same standards as prescribed medicine and need to be administered by medically qualified staff. In the UK, where we remain without regulation, there are more than 140 fillers on the market, and they are routinely injected by people with no recognisable qualifications at all.

As with cosmetic surgery, in reality only a very small proportion of the population is opting for Botox — although by the end of the noughties, around half a million non-surgical cosmetic procedures were taking place each year. However, people working in the media have been among the most enthusiastic adoptees of non-surgical cosmetic techniques. Again, our ideas of what a normal person looks like are now being shaped by the increasing domination of our TV/cinema screens by people whose faces are immobile and appear to lack all emotion and personality. These people with their whitened teeth and stiffened lips — and, in programmes from the USA, a Peter Pan/Michael Jackson nose — appear bizarre and grotesque, and they are more to be pitied than aspired to. But for viewers, it is their own laughter lines and wrinkles that appear more and more outlandish and abnormal.

Our happiness, and our ability to function, is increasingly at risk

As we have seen, psychiatric impairment in the form of body dysphoria is reaching epidemic proportions, and inevitably this has already had a long-term impact on the physical and mental health of our society. Research published in the British Journal of Industrial Relations showed that, while Britain's wealth rose by 40% between 1993 and 2007, measures of "neurotic symptoms and common psychiatric disorders" showed an increase during the same period. Clearly the reasons for the rise in the number of people who are experiencing emotional distress are many and complex, but the widespread dissatisfaction with something as fundamental to us as our own bodies is bound to have had a significant impact. The additional money that we've had available to spend on fashion, food and cosmetics has certainly done nothing to increase our sense of wellbeing. Rather, millions of people are now suffering from low self-esteem and low self-confidence as a result of our dissatisfaction with our bodies, and this in turn affects our social interactions, our relationships, our life choices and, of course, our happiness.

Even at the beginning of the noughties, research by the Office for National Statistics showed that one in six Britons was suffering from a mental health problem at any one time, with one in four people developing symptoms over a 12-month period. By 2010, analysis of NHS figures showed that one in seven adults was known to the NHS as having a mental disorder during a 12-month period, suggesting that their problems were serious enough to seek medical advice. It is likely that, during the noughties as a whole, the majority of us were affected by a diagnosable mental health problem at some point, whether or not we sought treatment for it. A third of all British women aged over 18 have now taken prescribed anti-depressants at some point in their lives.

It is unsurprising in the circumstances that levels of unhappiness soared throughout the noughties, and that in a 2009 report by the New Economics Foundation into national contentment and wellbeing across western Europe, Britain came third from the bottom. It is also unsurprising that this particularly affected young people: in 2010, 40% of people claiming disability benefits because of mental health problems were under the age of 35. A survey of 2000 young people by YouGov, published by the Prince's Trust in 2009, found that one in ten 16- to 25-year-olds felt that life was meaningless. More than a quarter of those questioned said that they were often or always down or depressed, and almost half said that they were regularly stressed. Similarly, more than half of the students who went for help at university counselling services in the 2006/2007 academic year did so for depression, compared with about a quarter in 2003/2004.

The situation is repeated among younger teenagers and children. Even at the beginning of the noughties, a survey found that 17% of 16-year-olds had serious emotional problems, compared with only 10% in 1986. By the end of the noughties, the Children's Society's Good Childhood Inquiry found that more than a quarter of 14- to 16-year-olds regularly felt depressed. 70% of teachers questioned by the Association of Teachers and Lecturers reported that young people were more stressed than they were in the late 1990s, and pointed to the pressure to look good as being one of the key causes. Girlguiding UK echoed this when they found that half of all the 11- to 16-year-old girls they questioned had been "really stressed" at some point in their lives. Significantly, research commissioned for the Department for Education found that poverty, often imagined to be a key influence on happiness, actually had no statistical impact on the happiness of pupils between the ages of 10 and 15 at all. Comforting though it might be to think otherwise, the cause of our children's unhappiness is not economic.

The facts are chilling. In 2007, more than 113,000 prescriptions for anti-depressants were issued to under-16s. In 2008, a report to the UN found that one in ten British children now has a clinically recognisable

Introduction

mental health disorder. In 2009, a study by the Institution of Engineering and Technology found that British teenagers were the least likely to be optimistic about their future — with less than a third believing that their quality of life would be better than that of their parents — compared with teenagers in other countries surveyed, including the USA. Most chillingly of all, Childline reported that calls from suicidal children had tripled over five years in the mid to late noughties. In 2010, the mental health organisation Sane reported that depression rates among under-14s had doubled in the previous four years, and over the same period had increased by one third in the 15- to 24-year-old age group. Sane claimed that the peak age for onset of depression is now between 13 and 15, whereas in previous generations it was the 20s.

Our teenagers are also among the heaviest drinkers in Europe, particularly in terms of binge drinking and alcohol-related problems, and linked to this must be our position at the top of the teenage pregnancy league. The number of under-age drinkers being treated in hospital rose by 40% in just one year between 2006 and 2007. Researchers are only now beginning to uncover the long-term impact of teenage drinking on the body, but as with obesity, alcohol misuse increases the threat that our children will be the first generation ever to have a lower life expectancy than their parents.

Meanwhile, drug use continues to rise among younger people too, with Britons now taking more 'feel good' drugs such as cocaine than anyone else in the West. The European Monitoring Centre for Drugs and Drug Addiction's 2010 annual report found that 6.2% of Britons aged between 15 and 34 admitted to using cocaine in 2008 (the last year for which figures were available), with 15% of younger people saying that they had tried it at least once in their lives. This compared with 5.4% of Spaniards of the same age, who were the second-highest users; the USA, which previously topped the league table, and which is just across the border from a direct supply, came in third, followed by Canada and Australia. The number of UK death certificates mentioning cocaine doubled between 2003 (161) and 2008 (325).

Our failure to accept our bodies as they are, and our dysfunctional attitudes towards them, have more sinister implications too. As we will see, our social and economic policies are increasingly based on the fictions of body dysphoria and the depression that this engenders, rather than on the scientific realities of our lives. On a more human level, those who cannot begin to measure up to our ideals are stigmatised and excluded and experience increasing levels of abuse. And since the choices that we make now have effects that reverberate through the future and shape the lives of generations to come, the body dysphoria epidemic is impacting on and threatening the future of the entire planet.

Taking the cure

However did it come to this? In order to cure ourselves, we need to understand how we got into this situation in the first place. In the rest of this book, I begin by looking back thousands of years into history, examining philosophy, religion, industry, medicine and politics for the roots of our body dysphoria. I show how we reached the 21st century believing that, despite all of the scientific evidence to the contrary, not only could we become 'perfect', but also we could rely on science to deliver that perfection for us.

Then I look at the impact of these beliefs on disabled people — a group that we will almost certainly all belong to at some point in the future, however unwelcome this thought might be. I show how the vast majority of the problems that disabled people face are socially constructed, rather than being the inevitable result of their impairments, and how eliminating these would improve quality of life for us all.

After this I examine our beliefs about science, contrasting the myths with the reality. I demonstrate how science itself shows us how mistaken we are if we think that we can rely on it, rather than on our own actions, to extend our lives. And I show how science itself proves that permanent youthfulness and physical 'perfection' is unachievable, and that disability and old age will always be with us, exploding some dystopian beliefs about science in the process.

Finally, I look at the different scenarios that the future might hold for us, depending on the actions we take now. I show that a society without body dysphoria is by far the happiest place to live in, as well as being the place where we will live the healthiest and longest lives. And I show that, in any case, living with a disability is vastly preferable to dying. If we refuse to tackle our body dysphoria now, we threaten the future of the whole planet and our own lives will be shortened.

I don't claim to have arrived on this planet knowing all the answers, nor do I pretend to have them today. Having initially trained as a dancer, I found out the hard way how difficult it is to be expected to live up to an unachievable physical ideal; and after being forced to abandon my original career choice because I developed a spinal curvature, I hid my body behind baggy clothing for the next 15 years. I began to come to terms with my own body only after having to wear a spinal brace in 1997, seven years after

Introduction

experiencing a spontaneous spinal fracture at the age of 28 that left me significantly disabled and in chronic pain. At that point I had to choose between hiding my body completely under tent-like garments and revealing it in all its 'abnormality', and somehow I found the courage to do the latter.

I was helped in this by my contact with the Disabled People's Movement, which showed me that there is a different way of looking at disability than as a tragedy, and that being disabled is in fact simply a normal part of the human condition. Now I use a wheelchair, and revel in the independence and mobility that it offers me. If I could change anything in my life, losing my impairments would be a very low priority indeed, and I would not change anything about my appearance. However, my journey towards self-acceptance continues today, and it would be foolish to think that it will ever end.

What I do claim is that the facts in this book will challenge your way of looking at the world, and change it for the better. Read on: you will find them as interesting and useful as I did.

SECTION I

HAMPERED BY HISTORY or, How did we come to this?

Why, when science has never been more able to show us the world as it is, have our perceptions of the world become increasingly dislocated from reality? Why are we so dissatisfied with our bodies, and why do we overwhelmingly produce images that show humans only as being young, healthy and fit? Why, when scientists increasingly understand their own limitations, have we never placed more faith in scientists' ability to remake the world in the way that we would like it to be?

We first need to understand how we got to this point, in order to move away from it and to reconcile our ideas about the world with the reality of our lives for once and for all.

1. PHILOSOPHY & SOCIAL CONTROL
or, The pursuit of perfection

To find the roots of our body dysphoria we first need to look back more than 2000 years in European history, to the worlds of ancient Greece and Rome. Physical appearance was even more important in ancient Greece than it is today, at least for men, while physical fitness was far *more* important and was seen as being inextricably linked to good citizenship. Athletics and gymnastics were central to the Greek culture, not least because they trained the body for war. Men exercised naked, so there was no place to hide an 'imperfect' or 'abnormal' body. Diet books, exercise regimes, personal trainers and worries over how to choose the right gym — all of these originated in ancient Athens. In contrast to today, though, it was men and not women who were most affected by this emphasis on physical activity and appearance, since women were not recognised as being citizens in their own right and also had to remain clothed.

Mathematics and proportions

Unsurprisingly, in Greek culture of the period images of the male nude abounded within society, in both sculptural and painted forms. The Greek sculptor Polykleitos, who worked in the fifth and early fourth centuries BC, was (and is now) ranked as one of the most important sculptors of this period. He developed a theory that the aesthetically perfect body — within sculpture, at least — would be symmetrical and would have body parts that met particular mathematical proportions in relation to each other. He published this theory as his *Kanon* (now lost to history), and accompanied his writing with a statue of a male nude to illustrate his ideas. Polykleitos came from the first generation of sculptors to have a following, and his work continued to be highly influential for at least the next century and a half. About 20 sculptors were listed by the Roman writers Pliny and Pausanias as working in Polykleitos's tradition, with his best-known successors in the fourth century BC being Skopas and Lysippus.

The cult of the male nude was still important by the time that the Roman Empire dominated Europe. Roman men preferred to pose for their statues in uniform rather than being naked, but they collected and copied Greek nudes and spent a great deal of time relaxing naked together in steam baths. Again, it would have been highly difficult to hide an 'imperfect' or 'abnormal' body, particularly given the scanty nature of their army uniform. The links between mathematical theories and theories about 'ideal' body proportions continued during this period, too, with the Roman architect Vitruvius, who lived in the first century BC, having even more influence on later generations than Polykleitos. As an architect Vitruvius wrote primarily about the ideal proportions of buildings, but linked these back to the 'ideal body'.

It is easy to see why our ancestors concluded that a formula could be found to show the 'ideal' proportions of the human body. Within mathematics, there is — usually, at least — only one right answer to a problem or theorem, and this can be discovered by a skilled mathematician. So when maths was applied to the human body, it seemed reasonable to assume that there was only one 'right' answer here too, and that this could be discovered by a skilled artist/scientist.

It is also easy to see why our ancestors believed that this formula would include symmetry. And indeed, microscopic technology has taught us that, within nature, mathematical formulas and symmetry are overwhelmingly present. Symmetry is also important within architecture, not least because it is then much easier to predict the forces that will be acting on a building and thus prevent it from collapsing. However, in reality very few human bodies are symmetrical, and this does not in itself have any negative implications at all.

Long after the fall of both empires, the art world continued to develop theories about 'ideal' body proportions. This search was driven by the need for artists to find ways to explain and teach their craft to their apprentices, as well as to create work that would best please the patrons on whom they depended for financial support. Of course, as every model knows, the proportions portrayed within both two-dimensional and three-dimensional body images have very little to do with the actual body of the model. Rather, they rely on the ways in which the model has posed for the picture or sculpture, and how the 'author' of the image has captured that pose. Artists were most focused on how a body *appeared* within their work, and not on how bodies existed in reality.

Greek ideas of the perfect body continued to be influential within the art world for the next two millennia, particularly during the Renaissance, when there was a rediscovery of and growing interest in Greek art and sculpture, as well as within philosophy and science (of which more later). To give two leading examples: in the early Renaissance, the artist Sandro Botticelli (c1445–1510) stated that to portray the perfect figure the distances between the nipple and navel, between the two legs, and between the navel and the groin must all be equal. As with Polykleitos and his peers, Botticelli believed in the importance of mathematics within aesthetics — today, of course, art and science are seen as being two very different and separate fields. In the same period, Leonardo da Vinci (1452–1519) produced his famous drawing of *Vitruvian Man* (c1485), showing the ideal body according to Vitruvian proportions. Da Vinci was highly interested in body proportions, often relating them to his interest in science and engineering; he wrote about them at length in his sketchbooks.

One formula in particular has fascinated both mathematicians and artists for more than two millennia: the 'golden ratio' (also known as the 'divine proportion' after the three-volume work by Luca Pacioli published in 1509). The golden ratio is an 'irrational mathematical constant', approximately 1.6180339887. Da Vinci was just one of many artists who used it within his work in order to create images that were considered to be particularly aesthetically pleasing. Today, we can see many other examples of art and architecture going back millennia that appear to have incorporated the golden ratio within them. However, whether or not this ratio is an integral part of nature, as many people have claimed, is disputed. Certainly there is no scientific link between the ratio and human intelligence and physical ability, and, as I have already pointed out, there is always a significant difference between the proportions of an image of the body and the proportions of the body of the model who posed to create that image.

The exclusion of the majority

Therefore it is to mathematics — or rather to artists' application of mathematics — that we must look to find the real culprit for our misguided beliefs about the existence of the 'ideal' body. Unfortunately, once you have decided that the 'right' or 'perfect' body exists, you by default create a category in which to put all bodies that lack this perfection — which would be all of them. Compared to the ideal, a body's torso is always too small or too big, too fat or too thin. And even if the torso is regarded as being 'perfect' in its size and shape, the arms and legs can be seen as being too long or too short in relation to it, and the muscles too big or too small. If a body's arms and legs are also 'perfect', then the hands and feet can still be considered to be too big or too small for them. Then the neck can be regarded as being too short for the head; the head can be seen to be too big or too small for the torso; eyes and ears can be too big or too small for the head; the eyes can be set too close together or too far apart… and, of course, if all of the rest of the body matches up to the ideal, its limbs and features may not be exactly symmetrical. Unsurprisingly, there are few bodies on earth that can even begin to match up to this mathematical formula — and then only before the ageing process sets in. By using mathematics to judge the body, then, just about every body on earth instantly became 'wrong'.

Of course, had the study of genetics existed at the time, the 'right' body might simply have been considered as one that is able to support life. Science has taught us that many — perhaps the majority of — potential embryos are unable to support life, underlining the fitness for purpose of all living bodies. From the study of genetics, we also know that our bodies have a 'design' that is good enough, but which is far from ideal. As we have evolved from our ancestors over millions of years, our body parts have adapted for purposes for which they were never originally intended, and this has left them with some innate weaknesses whatever their outside appearance might suggest. In another sense, then, the human body is by its very nature 'wrong', and all of the genetic tinkering in the world would never be able to change this.

For example, the anatomy expert Neil Shubin points out in *Your Inner Fish: A journey into the 3.5-Billion-Year History of the Human Body* that the evolution of the voice box has left us with a mechanism that is vulnerable to a wide range of breathing and swallowing problems. There can be no such thing as a person with a 'perfect' voice box, because the voice box can never be a perfect mechanism for its purpose in breathing and communicating. Meanwhile, the reason that men are prone to hernias is because their spermatic cords were inherited from ancient fish ancestors. Shubin lists many other examples, too, that underline the fact that the body is inherently 'imperfect', but show that it is still fit enough for its purpose by surviving at all.

Crucially, within genetic science the body is seen simply as being a vehicle to allow genes to replicate and survive, and all it needs to do in order to achieve this is to keep living and reproduce. Even someone whose body can't reproduce may still play a part in the survival of their genes, by helping to ensure that their siblings survive to have children, or by assisting with the upbringing of their nieces and nephews, or simply by acting in some way as a force for good on the family structure.

However, as I will discuss in more depth later, in ancient Greece life was believed to be a divine rather than a biological process, with the soul animating the body and later surviving in the spirit world. This belief had a profound effect for generations to come, as we will see later. The body itself therefore had nothing to do with the fact that it was alive, and so deserved no praise for it. This could have resulted in a lack of interest in the body compared with the mind, but as we have already seen, being fit and strong was regarded as a mark of good citizenship in ancient Greece because of the need to be ready for war. The reverse was also true, and people with bodies that were obviously 'imperfect' were regarded as being bad citizens.

In all, once the concept of the 'perfect' body had been created, we had to wait for modern science to come along with the ammunition necessary to destroy it again. Unfortunately, as we shall see later in this book, to date we have used science instead to prop up the concept still further, and so the ancient Greek blueprint for the 'perfect' body remains dominant, with all of its emphasis on proportions and mathematical symmetry.

What science has shown us, and what we choose to ignore, is that in order for us to thrive the necessary balance is found not in the lengths or proportions of our limbs, but in our body mass indexes, and in particular in the proportion of fat within our bodies. Obesity doubles our chances of developing cancer as well as massively increasing our risk of diabetes and heart disease, while under-eating or continually dieting has a range of life-limiting effects, too. Moderate levels of exercise, in contrast, help to prevent cancer — the World Cancer Research Fund believes that 10,000 fewer Britons a year would develop breast and bowel cancer if levels of exercise such as walking were increased. A suitable exercise and diet regime will always have a positive impact on our muscle–fat ratio, and thus on our health and longevity. However, it is easy to see why so few people today are able to adhere to this regime when we are told that we will always be abnormal anyway; that we can never be 'perfect', however hard we try.

Privileging the mind

Away from the art world, over the course of the last two millennia Europeans became progressively less interested in the appearance of the naked body, as they covered it up and became increasingly interested in fashion. At the same time, they began to regard the body as being separate from, and less important than, the mind or soul. As we have seen, this was a concept that had been accepted in ancient Greece, as well as in much earlier civilisations. Philosophers such as Plato (429–347BC) and Aristotle (384–322BC) had disagreed over the extent to which a soul could be said to be the same as a person once the body had died, and by the Middle Ages, Christian philosophers such as Thomas Aquinas (c1225–1274) still reflected Aristotle in believing that once the soul had become separated from the body, it could not be said to be the same as the person it had come from, who consisted of both body and soul. Unsurprisingly, though, this was not a debate that was engaged in by the majority of the population. More important to most people was the belief that the body would be resurrected when Christ returned to the earth in the Second Coming, and that souls would then be reunited with their bodies and ascend into heaven together — of which more later.

With the growth of Christianity it became widely accepted across the developed world that the body was less important than the soul, the soul being immortal. (This belief has been highly convenient for political leaders throughout the centuries, since it has enabled them to conduct battles and wars without running the risk of harming the 'important' part of any human: their spirit.) Greek ideas linking physical fitness with good citizenship were therefore replaced by the belief that spiritual fitness was paramount. Consequently, today only our armed forces are really concerned about the need for physical fitness; it is bodily *appearance* that most concerns us in the pursuit of bodily 'perfection'.

Later, Descartes (1596–1650), popularly regarded as the founder of modern philosophy, developed the concept of the *mind* and the body as being separate entities: the 'Cartesian mind–body divide'. This idea was adopted even by those who rejected religious beliefs and the idea of the eternal soul. Believing that the mind/soul is separate, superior and in some form everlasting has encouraged us to neglect our bodies. For believers, our time on earth is finite and thus is unimportant in comparison to the infinity for which our souls will exist; for non-believers, our bodies have no effect on our minds. This belief in the separate natures of the mind and the body has persisted despite the fact that neuroscientists proved conclusively in the second half of the 20th century that mental processes are directly affected by biological processes. Descartes also regarded the body as being akin to a machine, and this has allowed us in turn to believe that just like a machine it can be repaired and upgraded, and that we simply need to learn how to do this more efficiently in order to achieve immortality on earth.

The impact of Darwinism

Returning to the more recent past, though, the publication of Charles Darwin's *Origin of the Species* in 1859 had what is probably the biggest impact of all on the way in which we view our bodies today. Darwin's theory of evolution was based on 'natural selection', later described by the British philosopher and economist Herbert Spencer (1820–1903) as the 'survival of the fittest'. As with scientists and philosophers before them, Darwin's and Spencer's theories were complex and detailed, while the common understanding of them was highly simplified. In particular, the substitution by Darwin himself of the phrase 'survival of the fittest' for 'natural selection' in the fifth edition of his book in 1869 led to a widespread misunderstanding of his theories that still persists today.

By 'fitness to survive', Darwin first meant that a particular animal, bird or plant was better able to live and reproduce in its immediate local surroundings than one from a different species. In terms of an animal or bird, many factors other than physical strength would affect this 'fitness'. First, it would need the physical attributes required to survive in a particular environment and on the particular diet that was available there — these might include having enough body fat to keep out the cold, or being able to produce the enzymes required to digest the native plant life. Then, it needed to be attractive to the opposite sex in order to have success in reproducing, and this depended as much on its behaviour and personality as on its physical attributes.

Other necessary social attributes included the ability to live in harmony with other members of its species (at least in terms of its immediate family) in order to avoid being killed before it was able to reproduce. It was this last attribute, rather than being strong enough to kill, that was most important to the survival of the species, given that widespread murder would inevitably result in the end of the species sooner rather than later. 'Fitness', then, had little or nothing to do with the 'perfect body', strength or even intelligence, and everything to do with a whole range of other attributes.

Within a species, 'natural selection' would also operate, meaning that over time the species would change and develop, particularly as its surroundings altered owing to the impact of ice ages, droughts and other environmental events. This in turn would affect the diet available at any particular period of time, and so on and so forth, and thus affect how the species developed. For example, a species that had a thick coat during an ice age was likely to develop a thinner coat during a period when the earth was hotter, or it would become extinct, since those with the thickest coats were more likely to die of heat stroke before they could reproduce. Members of the species would also be more likely to choose sexual partners with thinner coats because they would be more physically suited to the new environment, and thus would be more 'attractive'. Over incredibly long periods of time, species would mutate so much because of these factors that they would become one or more entirely different species. All of this 'natural selection', of course, depended on there being as wide a range of attributes to choose from as possible, underlining the importance of continuing diversity within a species.

'Natural selection' involved losses as well as gains. For example, as Neil Shubin points out, 3% of the DNA of all mammals is given over to genes that relate to the ability to smell. However, in humans about 300 of these genes no longer function because of recent mutations, leaving us with an inferior sense of smell compared to most animals. As the ability to smell became less important to us and other functions became more important, 'natural selection' meant that, when it came to a choice, sexual partners favoured other characteristics. (In many animals, of course, the reverse was true, since smell was essential to both successful hunting and surviving hunters.) Again, genetic science shows us that there is no such thing as the 'perfect' body: all genes have benefits and disadvantages, and many have not functioned optimally for millennia.

The birth of eugenics

Leaving aside the widespread controversy surrounding Darwin's theory of evolution that persists today, Darwin's work was quickly appropriated by economists and politicians to give scientific credibility to a very different field: eugenics. Eugenics is based on the idea that a species can be 'improved' by preventing the 'weakest' members of it from living, or at least from reproducing, an idea whose roots can also be traced back to ancient civilisations. Before the late 18th century, though, official eugenics policies had focused mainly on disabled babies, with both the Romans and the Spartans killing those who were deemed to be deformed. Alongside these better-known examples, it is probable that many midwives throughout the centuries helped to ensure that babies who they considered to be incapable of survival, or 'monsters', were 'stillborn', but their motives were generally different and kinder.

However, a more widespread interest in eugenics developed in the West from the end of the 18th century onwards. The Reverend Thomas Malthus (1766–1834) published what was to be an enormously influential theory about the links between population growth, economics and social improvement in his *An Essay on the Principle of Population*, which appeared in several different editions from 1798 to 1826. Overpopulation, particularly by the poor, was regarded by Malthus as holding back society and as being a principle cause of famines and wars. Malthus's work influenced both Spencer and Darwin, with poverty being widely regarded as being biologically determined rather than economically inherited. At this point, of course, science was being used to 'prove' all sorts of long-standing beliefs, including the 'fact' that women were biologically inferior to men. As well as being wealthy, people with the 'perfect' human body were seen as indisputably male, whereas the female body, like poor people, was seen to be 'innately' inferior, and I will discuss the implications of this later on.

This acceptance of 'biological determinism' led eugenicists from the late 18th century onwards to believe that humans could be 'improved' by allowing only the strongest, fittest, sanest and brightest people to reproduce, thus creating humans who were more and more 'perfect'. At the same time, eugenicists felt that humanity would 'degenerate' if disabled and 'morally undesirable' people were allowed to reproduce, something that would also cause widespread economic damage. Deviants from the accepted human 'norm' were viewed as posing a threat to the future of humanity, as potentially undermining all of the evolutionary gains of the past.

In particular, Darwin's theory of evolution sparked fears that if humans were descended from apes, then it would be possible for this process to be reversed, and this belief passed into popular consciousness. 'Deformed' infants were then believed to be 'reverting back' to earlier stages of human evolution. For example, children with what is now known as Down's syndrome were believed by John Langdon Down (1828–1896), the medical superintendent at Earlswood Asylum, to be 'throwbacks' to a 'Mongolian stage' of human development, which is why they were popularly referred to as 'Mongols'. It was feared by some that if people like this were allowed to reproduce, then humans could return to a stage of evolution that even pre-dated apes. In general, eugenicists felt that they could use science to decide who was 'fit' to survive, rather than seeing this as a process that should be left to nature.

Another theory concerned 'freaks of nature': people who might have excessive body hair, or unusual features or sexual organs, or under-developed or missing limbs or body parts. In reality, the physical features associated with 'freaks' largely resulted from poisoning of the foetus while in the womb (food commonly being adulterated, while manufacturing safety standards were very poor); poor nutrition in the womb or in childhood; or the body under- or over-producing a particular chemical, often linked to spontaneous or inherited genetic mutations. However, the Victorians were unable to recognise that apparently wide variations in physical appearance resulted from very small physical differences at a cellular level, and regarded people with differing appearances as being less than human. As is the tendency today, scientific developments sparked a degree of paranoia in the wider community, particularly, but not only (since so many Victorian scientists were gentlemen amateurs), among non-scientists. Many of the eugenic theories that were developed then still enjoy popular currency today, despite science disproving them long ago.

Darwin's cousin Francis Galton (1822–1911) was the major thinker behind modern eugenics. Galton published his book *Hereditary Genius* in 1869, and invented the term 'eugenics' to describe his theory. He did not regard society — social organisation — as being central to the way in which a species survives, preserving as much genetic diversity as possible in order to enable it to adapt to changing circumstances in the future. Rather, he believed that society worked against nature, and enabled many members of the human species to survive who would not otherwise have done so. It was therefore society's duty to ensure that 'nature' prevailed, and that the 'weakest' were, at the very least, prevented from reproducing. Again, this belief remains highly prevalent today despite having no scientific basis in fact.

Darwin himself felt that however scientifically sound eugenics theories might be (from the perspective of what was known at the time), it was impractical to attempt to implement them via social engineering (often referred to as Social Darwinism). Darwin understood that medical and social support for 'the weak' — which included the 'maimed' — would allow them to reproduce, but he believed that sympathy was an innate part of human nature. He wrote that to deny this would be impossible "without deterioration in the noblest part of our nature… if we were intentionally to neglect the weak and helpless, it could only be for a contingent benefit, with an overwhelming present evil" (*The Descent of Man, and Selection in Relation to Sex*, 1882). Eugenicists, though, tended to be rather less sympathetic by nature than Darwin, and like Galton saw society's protection of its 'weaker' members as being unnatural.

Eugenics and racism

Eugenicists also propagated a belief in the superiority of the 'white race' over people from all other 'races', again using evolution to justify themselves. They claimed that white people represented a higher form of evolution than other human beings and that they therefore had a 'duty' to reproduce, whereas the fertility of other peoples should be controlled. They believed that humans could only proceed towards perfection if white people dominated, and that humanity risked returning to an earlier state of civilisation if other populations took over. African and other populations were conveniently regarded as being animalistic, child-like and generally primitive, and not part of the modern human race at all, and as we will see shortly, a vast array of 'sciences' was developed to 'prove' these theories further. Now, only white bodies could be perfect.

Theories of eugenicism and 'survival of the fittest' were subsequently used by Europeans during the latter part of the 19th century and first half of the 20th to justify the widespread slaughter of indigenous peoples throughout the world, as white settlers moved in and took over their land and controlled their natural resources. Indigenous peoples were conveniently regarded as being a different, earlier species of human who were naturally destined to disappear, with colonialism seen as being akin to a force of nature. The fact that many indigenous peoples were not equipped to deal with diseases brought in by colonial settlers was seen to be a further sign of their inability to survive in modern times. All indigenous peoples, then, were 'abnormal'. The fact that they were not regarded as being human was reflected in the declaration that Australia and similar countries were *terra nullius*, or 'empty lands' — indigenous inhabitants didn't count as being people at all.

The belief that indigenous peoples were naturally destined to die out was also used to justify the removal of mixed-race children from their indigenous mothers. If their mothers' tribes were doomed to disappear, then it was only responsible to remove mixed-race children and prevent them from marrying back into their tribes. Rather than take them to their fathers' homes, though (this was clearly unthinkable to those in charge), these mostly illegitimate children were put into institutions where they were forbidden from using their mother tongue and from practising their customs and beliefs. Later, as people became interested in theories of nurture over nature, 'full-blooded' children were also removed from their tribes by British settlers in countries such as Canada and Australia.

Although these policies were largely abandoned by the end of the 20th century, many indigenous families and cultures around the world today are still deeply affected by their impact. Since there was 'naturally' no future in their social and cultural heritage, it was considered to be 'best' to induct these people forcibly into the ruling culture. But because, as 'early' humans, they were 'naturally' inferior, they were seen as mostly suited to being servants and manual and unskilled workers, and as being unable to enjoy or deserve full civil and human rights. As with other 'abnormal' bodies, indigenous peoples were condemned by eugenicists with the cooperation of political bodies, and as with policies regarding women and disabled people, these policies were condoned as being 'scientific' by the population at large. Social and cultural engineering was given a spurious scientific underpinning that sealed the fate of millions. Today, many indigenous communities remain scattered and dispossessed as a result, with unsurprisingly high levels of economic, social, health and addiction problems.

The 'master race'

Eugenic beliefs reached their peak in Nazi Germany in 20th-century Europe. The Nazis, who came to power in 1933, believed in the concept of the Aryan race, a classification invented in the late 19th and early 20th centuries by American researchers to describe a sub-group of Caucasian immigrants. American Aryans originated from western Europe and Scandinavia, and were considered to be the original speakers of Indo-European languages. This originated as a neutral concept, but eugenicists later linked the higher social and economic status of Aryan immigrants to America with their 'natural' superiority. The Nazis therefore believed that Aryan peoples were superior to all other people, and so developed the concept of a master race, with everyone else regarded as being imperfect and as lesser human beings. Being Caucasian was no longer enough to deserve a higher place on the evolutionary ladder.

The Nazis also adopted ancient Greek ideals of the body as part of their push to create a master race of perfect bodies. Following a lull after the Renaissance, a near-obsessive interest in ancient Greece had again developed in western Europe from the 19th century onwards; among other things, this led to the founding of the modern Olympics at the end of the century. The Nazis regarded the ancient Greeks as being Aryans, and therefore as the direct forerunners of the Third Reich. It was not enough, the Nazis believed, to be born 'superior'; as with the Greeks, it was the duty of German citizens to develop and maintain their bodies to as high a standard as possible. This enthusiasm reached its peak in 1936, when Berlin hosted the Olympics and the Nazis invented many of the Olympic ceremonies that persist today — including the torch relay, for which they claimed a history in ancient Greece that did not exist in reality.

Once the Nazi belief system had been developed, the 'least perfect' members of society, disabled people (Hitler's "useless eaters"), were imprisoned, forcibly sterilised and killed from 1933 onwards, having been referred on to the death camps by doctors throughout the country. Disabled people were followed during the late 1930s and the Second World War by millions of Jews, Roma, homosexuals and other people who were deemed by eugenic 'scientists' to be less than perfect. The Nazi death camps are remembered today as the most graphic example of what happens when we decide that some human beings are more worthy, more 'perfect', than others, and determine to influence 'the survival of the fittest' ourselves. However, as we have already seen, indigenous peoples too were victims in their millions, and British settlers were among the key people responsible.

Moving on, it is worth considering another Nazi 'experiment' too when we look at past human rights atrocities and failures caused by eugenical 'science'. At the same time as killing those whom they considered to be the least perfect, the Nazis encouraged those Aryans who were deemed to be closest to the 'ideal' body (including having a 'pure' genetic and racial heritage) to have as many children as possible together with a similarly 'ideal' partner, whether or not they were married. In particular, the *Lebensborn* ('fountain of life') programme was aimed at producing an even more 'perfect' master race in the future. However, its impact was solely to split up families and to cause untold emotional harm.

The programme offered suitable mothers — mostly unmarried, and pregnant by members of the SS — the chance to give birth in one of a network of specially run homes, and then to have their children raised or adopted by the SS, who were considered to be far superior as parents than the birth mothers. Only around 40% of the women who applied to the programme were considered to be 'pure' enough, with qualifications including being able to trace their family back at least three generations, and preferably also possessing blonde hair and blue or green eyes. Later the programme was developed to actively encourage suitable women to meet and have children with SS officers, children who were also handed over to the SS to educate and adopt. During the ten years that the programme existed, about 7500 of these children were born in Germany and 10,000 in Norway.

After 1939 and the outbreak of war, the *Lebensborn* programme was extended to include removing Aryan-looking children from their families in occupied countries and raising them as Nazis. The *Lebensborn* centres were used to 'Germanise' the children before having them adopted by suitable families. If children resisted the process, or were later deemed not to be 'pure' enough, they were sent on to concentration camps. In 1946, it was estimated that as many as 250,000 children had been kidnapped from their homes during the war years, with up to 100,000 taken from Poland alone. However, only 25,000 were ever returned to their families. The rest of the children's families proved to be impossible to trace (often because they were dead), or it was already known that the children had no living relatives left, or the children had been taken away at such an early age that it was believed they had now bonded irretrievably with their new families. Many of the children, of course, were dead themselves. Needless to say, no master race ever emerged as a result of the experiment.

US eugenicists

It is important to remember here that the Nazis did not independently develop policies for perfecting the human race. The first official government eugenics policies were created in the USA at the end of the 19th century, driven by a parallel interest in improving crops and animal breeding. Humans were regarded as being as capable of benefiting from these techniques as race horses, and many of the eugenicists were in fact agriculturists and horse breeders. There continued to be correspondence and collaboration between German and American eugenicists throughout the 1930s. (For example, the notorious Nazi Dr Mengele, who experimented on disabled people in concentration camps, submitted his data to the Rockefeller Institute in the USA as a matter of course.)

Animal breeding was continually used by US eugenicists to show 'parallels' with human reproduction. There was no understanding of the fact that domestic animals had already been so selectively bred through the millennia that much of their genetic diversity had been lost. Two 'weak' human beings would be far more genetically diverse than two 'weak' farm animals, and therefore far fewer predictions could be made about the physical and mental health of their descendants. Meanwhile, science has shown recently that even the success of race horses depends far more on their training from birth than on their genetic heritage. Rather, most human ill health that appeared to the eugenicists to be generational — or linked to the country of descent — was related to poverty. But as we have seen, eugenicists believed that poverty itself was created by biology rather than by capitalism, so regarded this factor as being insignificant.

It was also, of course, American eugenicists who first developed the idea that the 'Nordic race' was superior to all other European ethnic groups. (It being taken for granted at the time that Europeans were superior to every other racial group.) An integral part of American eugenicists' policies was therefore to preserve racial 'purity' and to control reproduction by 'inferior' ethnic groups, while encouraging members of 'superior' groups to reproduce in greater numbers. Owing to these beliefs eugenicists were among the first supporters of family planning policies, including encouraging abortion as well as the use of contraception. (The British family planning pioneer Marie Stopes was a keen eugenicist, however positive the impact of her resulting work may have been.)

Initially, many US states passed marriage laws preventing people with a range of impairments from marrying (and therefore from reproducing). This later resulted in the introduction of blood testing before marriage, with marriage denied if there was evidence of a disease that could be passed on to any resulting children. Then, provision was made in more than 30 states for the segregation and sterilisation of groups deemed to be 'unfit' to reproduce. These included people with mental illnesses and learning difficulties, people with physical and sensory impairments, people with unusual bodies, people who were considered to be morally 'degenerate', or people who were simply very poor. Even people with myopia — short sight — were considered to be suitable candidates for segregation and sterilisation by members of the US Society of Opthamologists.

By the 1920s, governments in countries including Belgium, Brazil, Canada and Sweden were also sterilising disabled people, particularly — but not only — those living in institutions. Often sterilisation was a prerequisite for release from an institution, however short the initial stay. Many of those being sterilised did not even realise until later that the procedure had taken place, since the operations were disguised as being for a variety of other reasons. Today, disabled and older people are still taking legal action across the world as they come to terms with the result of this practice, deeply saddened that they have no family or descendants.

Challenges to eugenics

World opinion was slow to condemn eugenics, even in relation to people whose only 'crime' was being poor or coming from a particular race. However, this all changed following the liberation of the concentration camps at the end of the Second World War. Of course, the camps had been known about since the 1930s, however much politicians tried to rewrite history later. But horrific images on newsreels led to widespread publicity about the experiments that had been carried out on many of the inmates, as well as highlighting the fact that membership of the Jewish or

Roma races was the only reason for the imprisonment and extermination of millions of people. Remembering the victims of the death camps became an integral part of Remembrance Day itself.

After this, it only became acceptable to control the fertility of disabled people, for whom reproduction was seen as undesirable partly because of doubts over their parenting skills. (In the noughties, disabled people were still left campaigning to be included in official holocaust remembrance ceremonies.) People also became more interested in psychology, and in the effects of upbringing on a child's development compared to its genetic heritage, making 'nature' appear less important to the 'improvement' of the species than previously. Committed eugenicists turned to the study of genetics instead, and we will discuss their work later on.

Research scientists have now shown that there is only one race: the human race. Genetic analysis has shown that every non-African still shares a common African ancestor. Modern humans also share genes with earlier humans, particularly Neanderthals, as a result of 'inter-breeding'. Genetic research has also shown that population movement was common in many parts of the world in more recent centuries. This means that beliefs about people from a particular part of western Europe such as Germany sharing an ancestry that was substantially different from other humans were false. In addition to all this, geneticists have discovered that it is genetic 'purity', not diversity, that leads to higher levels of illness and disability among the population.

Of course, eugenicists have only ever formed a small minority of the population, and it would be wrong to suggest here that they have ever existed independently of their critics. While the rationale for the forced sterilisation of disabled people has remained unquestioned until relatively recently, there was always opposition to the idea that a country could be 'improved' by controlling the fertility of its people according to their social or racial group. Only when these beliefs were supported by the armed forces, as in the case of Nazi Germany, were they able to be implemented wholesale.

However, eugenicists have still been enormously influential on popular thinking. Two ideas remain particularly dominant today: that 'weaker people' cause economic ruin by creating a burden on the rest of the society with their uncontrollable 'breeding'; and that the human race could 'regress' as a result of the uncontrolled reproduction of disabled and poor people. As we shall see later in this book, this has led to widespread harassment and abuse of disabled and minority ethnic children and adults, as well as to continued stigmatisation and social disapproval of poor people having families.

But it is the ancient Greek idea that there are 'right' aesthetic proportions that a body needs to meet, as opposed to the reality of a body being 'right' simply because it is able to sustain life, that has had an overwhelming impact on our contemporary body dysphoria. Although science has taught us how difficult it is to create and sustain life, we take the miracle that is our own body for granted and focus instead on the extent to which it fails to measure up to our false ideal. If there is only one 'right' way for our bodies to be, and this is based on a physical appearance and attributes that no one can possess in reality, then we are all left in the wrong — we are all 'abnormal'. No wonder, then, that we feel the need to change our bodies, however hopeless the quest for 'improvement' might be. And no wonder we feel that we have failed to live up to society's expectations of our body, whatever we might do and however hard we might try. Our mission is impossible, and the sooner we abandon it, the better we will feel.

2. DIVINE PUNISHMENT or, Failing to live up to God's image

Along with the histories of science, philosophy and art, we need to look at the role of religion in order to understand fully how we have managed to become so body dysphoric today. Religion was the dominant cultural force in Europe for nearly two millennia, and only began to be less influential with the growth of mass literacy in the late 19th and early 20th centuries. In the 21st century it is still a major and significant cultural force, whether or not we follow a religion ourselves — and whether or not we hold any spiritual beliefs whatsoever. What religion has to say about the body is part of our belief systems, whatever these might be, but often we are completely unaware of where our ideas originated.

To examine the influence of religion further, we need to start even earlier than ancient Greece; we must turn to the Old Testament and to the teachings that are common to Islam and Judaism as well as to Christianity. Religious writing in the Judaic tradition was — and in many cases still is — regarded as being the literal word of God, with God in turn believed to be the Creator of the Universe. It is unsurprising, then, that what religion has to say about the body is fundamental to how we have defined physical 'perfection' and 'abnormality' throughout the centuries, and how we define them today.

Imperfection and sin

At the beginning of Genesis, the first book in the Old Testament and thus common in some form to all Judaic religions, God makes man in His own image (1:26–27). Thus, in the Judaic tradition, the 'normal' body was one that was godlike. Since God was perfect, it was taken for granted that God's body would also be perfect. And so at a stroke, anyone whose body was deemed to be 'imperfect' — the Bible is particularly full of references to blindness, deafness, epilepsy and madness in this respect — was also deemed to be 'ungodly'. People whose bodies were different to the norm also fell into this category, whether they had an obvious impairment or not. God could only have one image, and therefore only people who were average — 'normal' — could be reflecting this. This left many healthy people, such as unusually short people or people with facial disfigurements, also categorised as being ungodly. The idea that healthy people could be nonetheless 'impaired', an idea still prevalent today, originated here.

Much of the Bible tends to be contradictory in its teachings about physical and mental difference and 'abnormality'. In John 9 we have:

> 1 And as Jesus passed by, he saw a man which was blind from his birth.
> 2 And his disciples asked him, saying, Master, who did sin, this man, or his parents, that he was born blind?
> 3 Jesus answered, Neither hath this man sinned, nor his parents: but that the works of God should be made manifest in him.

Teachings like this, in texts such as the Talmud as well as the Bible, were responsible for the enduring idea that providing assistance to disabled people could bring a person closer to God, since they were then able to experience this spiritual manifestation at first hand. Helping disabled people also reflected the work of Jesus, about which more below.

However, there are an overwhelming number of references within all of the major religious texts that link disability with sin, and state that to be disabled is to have been punished by God for your sin or for the sin of a family member. Deuteronomy 28 warns of what will happen to people who break God's laws:

> 22 The LORD shall smite thee with a consumption, and with a fever, and with an inflammation, and with an extreme burning, and with the sword, and with blasting, and with mildew; and they shall pursue thee until thou perish.
> 27 The LORD will smite thee with the botch of Egypt, and with the emerods, and with the scab, and with the itch, whereof thou canst not be healed.
> 28 The LORD shall smite thee with madness, and blindness, and astonishment of heart.

Divine Punishment

To be impaired, then, is also to be guilty of some unspecified crime, and in particular to be guilty of a breach of one of God's most fundamental commandments. This belief unsurprisingly created widespread suspicion of people with any bodily feature or characteristic that was perceived to be less than perfect — suspicion that has echoed down the centuries and is still expressed in a wide range of ways today.

In a critical text within the Old Testament, Leviticus 21 makes it clear that, whether or not they are disabled themselves, anyone who comes from a family line with a member who has an 'abnormal' body is forbidden to take part in key religious ceremonies, including being forbidden to offer sacrifices to God. This seems to have included people who had sustained injuries; for centuries, being wounded in war or being the subject of an accident has been associated with culpable carelessness. Leviticus credits God himself with instructing Moses:

> 16 And the LORD spake unto Moses, saying,
> 17 Speak unto Aaron, saying, Whosoever he be of thy seed in their generations that hath any blemish, let him not approach to offer the bread of his God.
> 18 For whatsoever man he be that hath a blemish, he shall not approach: a blind man, or a lame, or he that hath a flat nose, or any thing superfluous,
> 19 Or a man that is brokenfooted, or brokenhanded,
> 20 Or crookbackt, or a dwarf, or that hath a blemish in his eye, or be scurvy, or scabbed, or hath his stones broken;
> 21 No man that hath a blemish of the seed of Aaron the priest shall come nigh to offer the offerings of the LORD made by fire: he hath a blemish; he shall not come nigh to offer the bread of his God.
> 22 He shall eat the bread of his God, both of the most holy, and of the holy.
> 23 Only he shall not go in unto the vail, nor come nigh unto the altar, because he hath a blemish; that he profane not my sanctuaries: for I the LORD do sanctify them.
> 24 And Moses told it unto Aaron, and to his sons, and unto all the children of Israel.

Many religious references also teach the reader to avoid disabled people in order to avoid being contaminated with their sin. Unsurprisingly, other Judaic texts take a similar line. For example, the Torah states that disabled people are forbidden from serving God: "For each of these disabilities wounds the unblemished character of the House of God." It was not simply because of fear of infection, then, that people whose bodies were regarded as being abnormal were shunned or banished.

The Bible illustrates the fact that the banishment of 'abnormal' people was supported at the highest level. Samuel 2 tells the following story about how King David took over the City of Zion, later to be called David's City, by acquiescing to the citizens' request to banish disabled people:

> 6 And the king and his men went to Jerusalem unto the Jebusites, the inhabitants of the land: which spake unto David, saying, Except thou take away the blind and the lame, thou shalt not come in hither: thinking, David cannot come in hither.
> 7 Nevertheless David took the strong hold of Zion: the same is the city of David.
> 8 And David said on that day, Whosoever getteth up to the gutter, and smiteth the Jebusites, and the lame and the blind that are hated of David's soul, he shall be chief and captain. Wherefore they said, The blind and the lame shall not come into the house.

Divine inequalities

However, as we have already seen, other religious teachings stressed that helping disabled people was an action of which God approved, and that would therefore assist the helper to become closer to God. The effect of this was to encourage people to attempt to distinguish between those who 'deserved' help and those who were 'undeserving', since clearly the latter group should be left to be punished by God. It also created a situation whereby disabled recipients of charity were regarded as being fundamentally different from and inferior to those who were helping them, since — despite John 9 — all disabled people were regarded as being sinners. This was in contrast to the more general teachings of Christ, where it was stressed that, in the eyes of God, all [normal men] were equal.

Even within Islam, we can read about the varying positions of those who follow God and those who turn away from him, with the ungodly seen as being akin to disabled people. For example, in The Holy Prophet:

> 11.24 The likeness of the two parties is as the blind and the deaf and the seeing and the hearing: are they equal in condition? Will you not then mind?

It was obviously taken for granted that disabled people were less equal than people who were regarded as non-disabled. Similarly, in The Thunder:

> 13.16 Say: Are the blind and the seeing alike? Or can the darkness and the light be equal?

Or, in The Believer:

> 40.58 And the blind and the seeing are not alike, nor those who believe and do good and the evil-doer; little is it that you are mindful.

If God does not regard people with 'abnormal' bodies as being equal to the rest of society, it is hardly surprising that even today disabled people do not have equal legal, civil and human rights. It would be more surprising, in fact, if they did.

The power of faith

There are many Bible stories in which Christ healed disabled people, removing their sin at the same time as healing their bodies. See for example Matthew 15:29–31:

> 29 And Jesus departed from thence, and came nigh unto the sea of Galilee; and went up into a mountain, and sat down there.
> 30 And great multitudes came unto him, having with them those that were lame, blind, dumb, maimed, and many others, and cast them down at Jesus' feet; and he healed them:
> 31 Insomuch that the multitude wondered, when they saw the dumb to speak, the maimed to be whole, the lame to walk, and the blind to see: and they glorified the God of Israel.

Faith in God was essential for healing to take place. In Matthew 9:

> 20 And, behold, a woman, which was diseased with an issue of

> blood twelve years, came behind him, and touched the hem of his garment:
> 21 For she said within herself, If I may but touch his garment, I shall be whole.
> 22 But Jesus turned him about, and when he saw her, he said, Daughter, be of good comfort; thy faith hath made thee whole. And the woman was made whole from that hour.

Later:

> 27 And when Jesus departed thence, two blind men followed him, crying, and saying, Thou son of David, have mercy on us.
> 28 And when he was come into the house, the blind men came to him: and Jesus saith unto them, Believe ye that I am able to do this? They said unto him, Yea, Lord.
> 29 Then touched he their eyes, saying, According to your faith be it unto you.
> 30 And their eyes were opened; and Jesus straitly charged them, saying, See that no man know it.

Medicine in the biblical context was literally miraculous. Within Christianity, Jesus is renowned for his miraculous healing abilities, and these were key to his popularity, as recorded in John 6:2: "A great multitude followed him, because they saw his miracles which he did on them that were diseased." Miracles were based jointly on the faith of the person asking for the cure (not necessarily the person who was sick) and Jesus's power to intercede with God. To give just one more example, in John 4:46–54, a nobleman approached Jesus and asked him to come to see his son, who was dying, in order to heal him. Jesus told him there was no need, since his son had already been cured, and the nobleman accepted this and set off alone on his journey home.

> 51 And as he was now going down, his servants met him, and told him, saying, Thy son liveth.
> 52 Then enquired he of them the hour when he began to amend. And they said unto him, Yesterday at the seventh hour the fever left him.
> 53 So the father knew that it was at the same hour, in the which Jesus said unto him, Thy son liveth: and himself believed, and his whole house.

> 54 This is again the second miracle that Jesus did, when he was come out of Judaea into Galilee.

With the development of Christianity also came an emphasis on the redemptive power of suffering, since Christ suffered on the cross in order to atone for the sins of man. Suffering was viewed as a way of atoning for the 'sin' that had led to someone becoming disabled in the first place, as well as a means of coming closer to God, and therefore was a prerequisite to being healed. Just as it is today, suffering was seen as being an inevitable result of having an abnormal body, rather than being caused by the way in which a disabled person was treated within their community and the lack of access to effective pain relief. Since suffering was a 'good' thing, this also gave rise to a belief that the use of painkilling herbs and other means of pain relief was undesirable, and that people should instead 'suffer in silence' until God answered their prayers for healing or took them to heaven.

(It is the religious emphasis on suffering that has led to the irritating — for disabled people — way in which people today are still continually described as 'suffering from' their impairment, however much the 'sufferer' points out that they are not. For example, in 2010 the state-funded Equality and Human Rights Commission (EHRC) put out a call to interview disabled people who were experiencing hate crime. The EHRC listed a long line of impairments that people should be 'suffering from' in order to participate. Yet many of the respondents were in good health. What they were actually suffering from was the crime and harassment they were reporting. Much of what disabled people 'suffer from' (if indeed they are suffering at all) remains invisible even to those charged with tackling it — in this case, the EHRC.)

Within religion, then, prayer and faith were regarded as being of far more importance than any form of healing practice when it came to treating illness, since it was God who actually decided your fate. Within religion, too, people who continued to be disabled rather than being healed through their suffering and the power of their prayers were viewed as being hardened sinners, who lacked faith and so were undeserving of God's healing power. This again was an obvious reason to shun them. Those for whom no amount of prayer worked were regarded as people who would be healed once they went to heaven (if you ignored Bible texts that said disabled people couldn't enter heaven) — in which case they were better off dead.

Death and resurrection

Disabled people were often regarded as being better off dead anyway, and this opinion survives today. Ted Harrison, in *Disability Rights and Wrongs* (Lion Publishing, Oxford, 1995), quotes Martin Luther, the founder of the Protestant Reformation, speaking about a 12-year-old boy with learning difficulties in Dessau. He is said to have advised the prince of the region that: "If I were the Prince, I should take this child to the Moldau River which flows near Dessau and drown him." The advice was refused, so Luther suggested an alternative. "Well then, the Christians shall order the Lord's prayer to be said in church and pray that the dear Lord take the Devil away." After a year's 'prayer', the boy died, although one imagines that prayer alone was insufficient to achieve this.

Even death, though, was not always believed to be enough to enable those with 'imperfect' bodies to enter heaven. The belief in physical resurrection — that our bodies will be recreated whole again at the end of the world — was a central tenet of both ancient Greek religion and Judaism, and was therefore adopted by early Christians and later passed into Islam. Today, the extent to which this is still believed to be literally true depends very much on which branch of these religions you follow. In the past, though, there was widespread acceptance that when Christ came (or returned, according to whether you were Jewish or Christian), the physical bodies of those who had died would be resurrected.

But to complicate matters further, people whose bodies were not formed exactly in the image of God would be resurrected in their original form, and therefore would remain ungodly. This belief often extended to people who had had a limb amputated in later life, unless they were able to retain the limb and later have it buried with them. Some texts suggested that in fact disabled people would be healed at the resurrection, but generally doubts remained that people with 'abnormal' bodies could ever enter heaven, and again these doubts persist in many religious communities today.

The difficulty with all of this — and this is a theme to which we will return again and again — is that disability is a club that we can all join, whether or not we wish to do so. Even today, just about all of us will become disabled to some degree at some point in our lives, with those people who don't develop impairments having a shorter lifespan than the rest of us. Furthermore, any one of us can become disabled at any time, often without warning — two thirds of disabled adults acquire their impairment after childhood, and many disabled children acquire or develop their impairments after birth. And, as we will see later in this book, there is nothing whatever that we can do about it, whatever we believe to the contrary. Accepting cultural and religious customs, stereotypes and myths without subjecting them to some hard questioning in the light of what science teaches us today is therefore going to make all of us very unhappy indeed at some point in our lives.

Witchcraft and demonic possession

For much of the past two millennia, though, impairment rates were much higher than they are in Europe today, when 80% of the world's disabled people live in the developing world. As the example of the developing world shows us, poverty, disease, accidents, war and lack of access to basic health care create a widespread legacy of physical and sensory impairments, learning difficulties and mental health problems, often from youth onwards. In the past, this meant that everyone was affected sooner rather than later by the risks and fears associated with being labelled as 'abnormal' or having an 'abnormal' partner or family member, and these people would blame themselves when this happened.

By the Middle Ages, the widespread belief in witchcraft had brought with it another religious interpretation of disability: that disability was caused by demonic possession or through consorting with the Devil. The belief in possession was common to ancient cultures — for example, it is written about within Sumerian, Akkadian and Chaldean writings — but it is not mentioned in the Old Testament. In the New Testament, however, there are several incidents of Christ healing ill or disabled people by driving out demons, and these have been widely used to validate beliefs in possession right up to the present day. Beliefs equating disability with demonic possession result from texts such as Matthew 9:

> 32 As they went out, behold, they brought to him a dumb man possessed with a devil.
> 33 And when the devil was cast out, the dumb spake: and the multitudes marvelled, saying, It was never so seen in Israel.

Or Matthew 12:22:

> Then was brought unto him one possessed with a devil, blind, and dumb: and he healed him, insomuch that the blind and dumb both spake and saw.

This ability to 'heal' disabled people by casting out demons also extended to Christ's followers — see for example Acts 8:

> 5 Then Philip went down to the city of Samaria, and preached Christ unto them.
> 6 And the people with one accord gave heed unto those things which Philip spake, hearing and seeing the miracles which he did.
> 7 For unclean spirits, crying with loud voice, came out of many that were possessed with them: and many taken with palsies, and that were lame, were healed.

In the Middle Ages, these belief systems became far more dominant in the minds of Christians than ever before. The belief in demonic possession particularly affected the popular perception of people with mental health problems, epilepsy, and learning difficulties such as autism. Overall, though, the equation of disability with evil, and not simply with lack of godliness, became far more fixed than previously, with horrific results. In a 200-year period between 1500 and 1700, between 8 and 20 million people across Europe, mostly women, were put to death as witches. Many of these people were disabled — often because of the ageing process, since the majority of 'witches' were elderly — or had given birth to disabled children. The fear of being viewed as abnormal must indeed have been extreme during these two centuries, particularly for women but also for whole families. No wonder that abnormality became something to disguise or hide, even if today we would simply see most of the impairments that marked people out as 'witches' as being the inevitable consequence of the ageing process.

How must people have felt when they were unable to 'heal' themselves, however hard they prayed; when they were unable to work out what 'sin' they had committed, no matter how hard they thought about it? How must they have felt if they had to hide the fact that they were constantly unwell and in pain, in constant fear of being discovered? Or were in continual mental anguish that they were unable to share with anyone else? Or were unable to hide their or their children's 'abnormality', however hard they tried? When the consequence of exposure would not simply affect their ability to work, as it does today, but could lead to expulsion from their community, and even death?

Modern witches and demons

We actually *do* know something of their feelings, due to disabled people who have spoken out or written about their lives in the late 20th and early 21st centuries — because today, religious communities still hold many of the views about 'abnormal' bodies that they possessed previously. Indeed, it would be hard to see how they could not, particularly given the mass of religious writings produced over the past two millennia that echo the teachings in the Bible, Koran, Torah, Talmud and so on. And to a greater or lesser extent this has an impact on the rest of us, whether or not we are practising members of those religions, since religion contributed so much to our belief systems in the past. Even when theologians interpret texts differently, or look at contradictory meanings, the vast majority of us take a much simpler, hardline message from them.

Within Europe, North America and Africa, Christianity has been overwhelmingly influential, but in any case, the teachings of Judaism and Islam with regard to the abnormal body are so similar to Christianity that there is little real difference in their effects. Other religions, too, incorporate similar beliefs: within Hinduism and Buddhism, for example, where adherents believe in reincarnation, disability is the mark of having sinned in a previous lifetime, or of having chosen to suffer for some spiritual reason, often for atonement for sin. This means that when it comes to the effects of religion on cultural beliefs, migrant communities more or less share the same attitudes to 'abnormal' bodies as the rest of us.

The most disturbing of all the effects of religion today is the impact of beliefs about demonic possession being the cause of abnormality. Across the world, there is a growing tendency for both witch doctors and Christian priests to blame children for their family's difficulties — because they are 'possessed', or are regarded as being witches or wizards. Disability is often regarded as being a sign of possession, particularly when children have epilepsy, autism or similar conditions. Denouncing a child as being possessed or as a witch can result in the child being banished from the family home, leaving them highly vulnerable to starvation and exploitation. Or it can result in the child being subjected to abusive 'exorcism' ceremonies, which in some cases can result in death.

Although such cases are most common in countries like Nigeria, some have also occurred in the UK, and are probably far more common throughout Europe and North America than people realise. Living in east London as I do, I regularly have cards put through my door advertising the services of witch doctors to banish demons and solve all my problems.

Holding these beliefs must impact on the way in which believers regard their own bodies, as well as on their attitude to other people's bodies. And before we dismiss these issues as relating only to developing countries and a few inner-city communities, it is as well to point out that as of January 2011 there were more than 256,000 Google entries for "children+demonic+possession"; which moreover represented an increase of 100,000 in just 12 months. And rather than providing reportage and criticism, all of the leading entries provided 'evidence' for the prevalence of demons possessing children, together with instructions on how to tackle these demons.

As well as showing how widespread the 'problem' is, the availability on the internet of so many texts promoting these beliefs provides spurious credibility for the practice of exorcism and banishment, and so increases the impact of belief in demonic possession still further. The gospel according to St Luke in particular is often quoted by online priests when equating disability with demonic possession, since Luke is regarded as being particularly authoritative because he was a physician by profession. Luke 9:38–42 is quoted as showing that demons cause epilepsy in a child; Luke 11:14 is quoted to show demonic possession as a cause of speech impairment; and Luke 13:10–13 apparently shows demonic possession as a cause of physical impairment.

Whatever our dominant culture, and whatever our social status, our belief systems have been fundamentally affected by more than two millennia of religious teaching: teaching that having an 'abnormal' body marks the owner at best as having sinned, and at worst as being in league with the Devil or being possessed by demons; teaching that disabled people are not the equals of non-disabled people; teaching that disabled people, as sinners, cannot be trusted; and teaching that disabled people should be shunned and segregated. No wonder that we ask what's 'wrong' with a disabled person; no wonder we describe an impaired part of our body as being 'bad'; no wonder that parents of disabled children feel guilty. No wonder that we introduce ever more punitive benefits regimes, and look ever more suspiciously upon disabled people.

We may not be religious ourselves — we may not even have heard or read a religious text during our lifetime — but our underlying beliefs about the body are still affected by religion, which has shaped so many of the beliefs that are prevalent in the world around us. And this extends to beliefs about life after death, whether this takes the form of immortality as a spirit, resurrection or reincarnation. Religion has programmed us to expect to live for ever, so that when we lose our belief in God, we turn to science to fulfil this promise for us instead. As we shall see later, this has had a fundamental effect on our attitude to science, as well as on our body dysphoria.

3. INDUSTRIAL BODIES or, (Sub)standardising humanity

As we have seen, artists, philosophers, scientists and theologians developed their idea of the perfect body over millennia, with a devastating impact on those who were judged to be quite definitely imperfect. However, in reality their ideas had only a limited impact on the average, 'normal' person for much of the period in question, including many whose bodies would today be regarded as abnormal. Only when people became older, or became significantly disabled through an accident or illness, or when other members of their household were disabled, were they affected by the stigma surrounding 'imperfection'.

A key reason for this — apart from the fact that a far greater proportion of the population had some form of minor impairment before the 20th century — was that there was no parallel concept of what a 'standard' body might look like. People who knew that their bodies were not 'perfect' nonetheless thought of their bodies as being perfectly *normal*, since there was no other yardstick by which to judge them. This all changed when the idea of the 'standard' body was developed as a result of the Industrial Revolution, and people were given a new ideal to measure up to. Critically, those without 'standard' bodies began, as never before, to be excluded from the workforce, their families and their communities, which in turn increased the pressure on the rest of the population to conform to the 'norm'.

The impact of industrialisation

Until the 19th century, manufacturing of all kinds had only ever operated on a small scale. Textiles, for example, were made by individual families of workers in their own homes — by what we now describe as 'cottage industries'. Within a cottage industry there were tasks for most members of the extended family who worked there, including very simple manual tasks, and work caring for the youngest and oldest members of the family. Neither being an amputee, nor having a mobility or sensory impairment, nor being unusually short precluded people from working in some role within what we would now call a 'live–work' environment. This was also true of agriculture. In the early 18th century, this meant that most clothing in Britain was made from wool that had been spun and woven by hand within small family businesses. By the end of the century, ways had been found to process cotton more easily, and this became the major export fabric, with Britain displacing India as the main cotton supplier. However, manufacturing of all kinds was still based within small family businesses.

The late 18th and early 19th centuries saw the invention of a number of automated spinning and weaving devices (for example, the spinning jenny) that enabled textiles to be produced on a mass scale within specially built industrial centres — factories and mills. Along with the use of machinery to carry out tasks that were previously done by hand, the work of producing fabrics was deskilled by being separated into individual tasks, each carried out by different groups of workers. Similar developments took place in many other types of manufacturing industries, with new communities forming around the factories and mills.

Industrialisation meant not only that people moved from cottage industries to factories, but also that vast numbers of people who were previously employed within agriculture lost their jobs due to mechanisation, and so had no option but to join the manufacturing workforce. Many workers were forced to leave the weaker members of their families behind them when they moved to the new industrial centres, particularly their older and disabled relatives. This was because the initial impact of the development of factories and mills was to create new distinctions between who was and wasn't able to work.

Many of the people who had worked within cottage industries and agriculture were regarded as being unemployable within a factory setting. There were several reasons for this. First, the equipment was designed to meet the needs of the 'average' body; it was far more difficult for people to adapt the way that they used equipment to meet their individual needs than it had been with traditional forms of manufacturing. Also, time became far more important than before: people who were unable to work as quickly as their neighbours caused a danger to them, as well as holding back production levels. It was now no longer enough to be able to work hard, you had to be able to work at a particular speed and for most of your waking hours. This defined the 'standard' worker as being fit, fast and untiring in addition to having an average body, a definition that persists today.

Conditions were harsh, and only those who were able to sustain a high level of output remained in employment, causing unemployment among many people who would have been employed in the past. Although factory work initially brought with it many new jobs for small fingers, children who were too young to work were now left at home, causing a separation between paid work outside the home and caring for children and the elderly within the home. So the new forms of manufacturing had created buildings, equipment and ways of organising the workforce that were all based around the concept of a 'standard' body, and this of course also affected the products that these industries produced.

Ready-made fashions

One result of the Industrial Revolution was that it became possible to mass-produce clothing. In the past, and for many centuries beforehand, either the women of the household made their own clothing specifically to fit themselves, or — depending on their social and economic status — a seamstress or tailor was employed to make their clothing for them. As a rule, people bought fabric rather than clothes, and the majority of the population wore the same outfits for many years. Since clothes were made individually, there was no difficulty in finding ones that fitted. This was the case even if you had a body that differed considerably from the average. Clothes could be tailored not only to fit any individual body, but also to disguise characteristics such as a spinal curvature or the use of a prosthetic limb.

Initially, little was different apart from the fact that much larger amounts of the same fabric became available than previously. While textiles were produced by increasingly more complicated and efficient machines, clothes were still sewn by hand, so it was easy to make them to fit the customer and there was only a limited role for mass production. This all began to change, though, with the development of the sewing machine by a number of different inventors. Early designs did not take off, but by the mid-19th century the American Elias Howe had patented a number of designs, and eventually one of these became the basis for a range of machines that were also manufactured by other people.

Most famous of all the sewing machine manufacturers was, of course, Isaac Singer, a particularly good businessman whose slogan was "A machine in every home!" But he did not achieve this ambition, and the main reason for this was that the sewing machine came to be used instead to mass-produce ready-made clothing, thus gradually reducing the number of women who made their clothes at home or who had clothes made for them on an individual basis. Had the sewing machine not been adopted in this way, it is likely that fashion would have continued to be something that anybody could follow.

Mass production of clothing was driven by war. Uniforms needed to be 'uniform' and be produced quickly. Sewing machines made this possible, along with the availability of large amounts of the same fabric. But this left uniform manufacturers with the need to sell other types of ready-made clothing in times of peace in order to keep their workshops going, as well as looking for new markets in order to expand. Clearly, profits lay in being able to produce clothing in sizes that would have as large a market as possible — clothing that would fit the 'average' person.

The outbreak of the American Civil War in 1861 led to the first attempts to standardise sizes for men's clothing. Prior to this, the ready-made clothing market had consisted mainly of coats and jackets ('outerwear') and underwear. Uniform manufacture, initially outsourced to home workers, became factory based in order to meet the demand that had been created by the war. Soldiers were measured by manufacturers in an effort to calculate which measurements occurred most frequently, and what tolerances would allow the same-sized garment to fit different bodies. Following the war, these measurements were used to develop the first commercial sizes for men. As a result of this the 'standard' male body was taken to be a body that was young and fit enough to fight, which inevitably also meant tall and thin. Every man whose body did not fit these criteria suddenly became 'non-standard', or abnormal.

Standardisation and sizing

With the development of the ready-made clothing market, the search for new clothes rapidly became, as it is today, something that could leave you feeling demoralised, disappointed and abnormal, rather than making you feel excited by the fabric and design that you had chosen and by the prospect of having something new to wear. Distinctions existed between small, medium and large outfits of course, but as with today, many people found that their bodies were too small or too large, too short or too tall for the ready-made clothes that first became available. To make matters worse, one manufacturer's idea of a 'small' outfit might be another manufacturer's idea of a 'medium' — another issue that continues to be a problem today.

For the first time, buying new clothes became a process that was affected by the size of your body, rather than simply by whether you could afford the fabric and, perhaps, someone to sew it for you. Shoe manufacturing followed a similar path, with the development of a sewing machine that could be used on leather. This made it particularly difficult for people whose feet would only fit custom-made shoes, but who could no longer afford what then quickly became a luxury item. Before too long, clothing choice became further restricted by the growing standardisation of sizes, accompanied by a reduction in the range of sizes that were available.

By the end of the 19th century, the overall concept of standardisation was being widely embraced across manufacturing industries, and this soon became supported by the law. In Britain, the Engineering Standards Committee was founded in 1901, led by James Mansergh. In 1918 it became the British Engineering Standards Association, receiving a Royal Charter in 1929 and changing its name to the British Standards Institution in 1931. Over time, its remit widened to include most aspects of industrial life, including health and safety and the working environment. The development of standards meant that precise mathematical and quality criteria were now laid down for many things that had previously been flexible and built to meet individual needs.

Inevitably, the growth of support for and the belief in the benefits of standardisation had a widespread impact right across society. Of course, notions about the 'average' body had always permeated architecture and engineering, with skilled craftspeople working to traditional measurements, but there had still been a certain amount of variation, particularly within house-building and manufacturing. However, with standardisation many more people found that their bodies were 'non-standard', as they struggled to reach door knobs and postboxes and see out of windows; to get through doorways without banging their heads; to find a seat that was wide or low enough for them to sit on; and so on and so forth. It was obviously in the manufacturing industry's interest to persuade their customers that it was their bodies, not the designs, that were at fault. The alternative would be for manufacturers to lose profits as they designed goods to suit a wider range of body types, which in turn would have increased their costs.

In terms of fashion, the concept of the standard body size reached its peak in the USA in the middle of the 20th century with the introduction of official size standards for women's clothing. The development of the women's ready-made clothing market had taken place more slowly than that of the men's. Men who lived in a household with no women were loath to sew anything themselves, and ready-made clothing was cheaper and easier for them to buy than tailored items. In contrast, sewing was regarded as an 'accomplishment' for middle- and upper-class women, while working-class women were too poor to buy ready-made fashions.

However, in the 1920s the combination of factors such as fashion advertising, increased manufacturing capability, lower prices and the growth of national markets made ready-made clothing more acceptable to the middle- and upper-class female consumer too. This made the need to agree on what constituted a particular size more urgent. Costs to manufacturers were increased because of the high volume of goods being returned because they were the wrong size, while consumers faced additional costs too, because of the need for alterations to take place before new clothing would fit properly.

In 1937, the US Department of Agriculture therefore prepared to carry out a detailed survey of women's bodies in order to develop a standard method of sizing that could be applied throughout the country. The aim was to discover women's key body measurements, measurements that could then be used to predict other measurements. In 1939 and 1940, around 15,000 American women participated in a national survey conducted by the department's National Bureau of Home Economics. This was the first mass survey of women's body shapes ever to take place. Volunteers, who received a small fee for participating, had 59 measurements taken of their bodies while they were dressed only in their underwear — a process that must inevitably have limited the range of women willing to take part. The results of the study were published in 1941 in *USDA Miscellaneous Publication 454, Women's Measurements for Garment and Pattern Construction*.

During the Second World War, further research took place as a result of women's participation in the armed forces. As with the American Civil War, it was important to predict what sizes would be most common in order to speed up the manufacture of uniforms, only this time it was women who were the unknown factor. The Research and Development Branch of the US Army Quartermasters Corps therefore took measurements from 6510 women from the Women's Army Corps (WACs). Again, these women were necessarily young and fit and represented only a tiny proportion of the female population, thus skewing the results. Following the war, a combination of this set of data with that published in 1941 was used by the Commodity Standards Division of the National Bureau of Standards (NBS) to create industry-wide size standards. The aim was to create the smallest possible number of 'standard' sizes that would fit the largest possible number of women without alteration.

Between 1949 and 1952, analyses and calculations were undertaken by the NBS Statistical Engineering Division for the Commodity Standards Division. This complicated mathematical process was ultimately carried out at the request of the Mail Order Association of America. Catalogue shopping had been developed in the USA as a result of consumer demand from the many people who lived far from urban centres, and had grown in popularity as a result of the post-war economic boom. Women had a host of other things to do aside from sew for themselves, but they were also keen to follow fashion and to reflect a 'standard' look. Clearly, however, clothing catalogues could only operate effectively if customers could be sure of the size of the clothes that they were ordering.

The Commodity Standards Division's conclusions and recommendations were presented to the industry for feedback in 1953, accepted in 1957, and published as *Commercial Standard 215-58* in 1958. This lengthy time period underlines the fact that setting size standards was not a simple process. It was never the case that the majority of women's bodies fell into a small number of easily identifiable size categories. Rather, analysts had to decide how to create clothes that could be worn by women with widely differing bodies, all of which might be deemed to be the same dress size.

The impact of standardisation

As with the Greek concept of the 'perfect body', the possession of 'standard' body proportions became as important as size and shape when it came to ready-made clothes fitting. Owing to the development of sizing, women as well as men were now made to feel abnormal if they were unable to fit into 'standard' clothes sizes. To complicate matters further, even if a dress was the 'right' size, it could be too long or too short, too loose or too tight in the bust or across the hips, and too tight or too loose around the waist. Women blamed themselves for not having standard body proportions, for not being 'normal'. In reality, though, the need to create sizes that fit as wide a range of body types as possible made it unlikely in the extreme that any piece of clothing would fit anyone perfectly. Then, as now, a certain amount of luck was involved, and many clothes in the 'right' size would not fit at all.

All this was, of course, in sharp contrast to the custom-made clothes of the past. Women had had centuries of experience behind them of clothing that actually fit them properly, so the experience of buying something new only to make them feel abnormal was a novel one. Now, though, women had a new ambition: rather than wanting to have a dress made that would fit them properly — an ambition that could be achieved by anyone who learnt to sew — they wanted to have a body that conformed to a particular dress size, to be a 'perfect 10' (today, of course, the predominant ambition is to be a size zero). Although fabric is endlessly malleable, while flesh is not, it was the body that was expected to be able to change.

The belief that the body could be changed to fit standard sizes existed despite the fact that dress sizes reflected a large number of body measurements and proportions, with the amount of fat on a woman's body — the only part of the body that someone could actually influence — being just one of these. Significantly, the sizing 'authorities' had actually recommended six variations on each size. Even after years of calculations, they were unable to classify women's bodies any more tightly than this. The first variation would concern height — clothes should be sized as T for tall, R for regular or S for short. Meanwhile, hips should be sized as slender (-), average (no symbol) or full (+). Combinations of these sizes allowed clothes to be grouped as 'misses', 'women's', 'half-sizes' (for shorter women) and 'juniors'.

In reality, the group classification was the only place where size variations were used. The hip standard was seldom used and has disappeared with today's voluntary sizing, with all women made to feel abnormal if their hips are too full or too slender for the clothes that they buy. Height became something that was only referred to within trouser length, and even then most trousers — if there was a choice at all — were, and are, offered only in regular and long sizes, leaving shorter women with no option but to take up the hems of trousers that have not been designed to allow this. Alternatively, shorter women were left with specialist 'petite' ranges — if their bodies were not full in the hips and bust. The only women who were offered choices were home dressmakers, since paper patterns normally provided for the different size variations within them.

Over the half-century since the development of standard sizing, there has been a recognition that 'standard' body shapes have changed owing to alterations in lifestyle, health and diet. By the late 20th century, standard sizes ceased to be dictated by commercial law, and manufacturers were left to adhere to a voluntary code instead, leading to a wide variation in the dimensions of clothes that are apparently the same size. At the same time, research was and is continuing to take place into the development of more accurate and realistic size standards. However, these developments still depend on the concept of the 'standard' body, a concept that science shows us is fundamentally flawed.

The size, shape and proportions of our bodies are affected by many factors: family and racial genetic heritage, diet, health and lifestyle being just some of them. Ultimately, all of our bodies are unique, with even the bodies of most identical twins varying significantly in size and shape by adulthood. In the same way that none of us are 'perfect', none of us are 'standard' either. The quest to become a standard size is an impossible one, but the continuing belief that it is our bodies that are at fault when our clothes don't fit properly is reflected in the fact that, today, when we do actually have the technology to produce custom-sized clothing at a reasonable price, its use is currently limited to a few overseas suit manufacturers.

Standardising appearance

Along with the desire to conform to a 'standard' body type in the 19th and 20th centuries — for many women this was driven by the need to fit into the workplace as much as into dresses — came the increasing desire among women in particular to standardise their personal appearance. Alongside the other impacts of the Industrial Revolution, by the mid-19th century the growth of mass literacy and the invention of cheaper printing technology had led to the rise of the popular women's magazine. And with the women's magazine came the voice of the 'best friend', advising women on all aspects of how to live their lives, and, in particular, about what to look like.

Women's magazines had been published in Britain since the end of the 17th century — the very first women's magazine, *The Ladies Mercury*, appeared in 1693. However, during the 18th and the first half of the 19th century they were priced out of the reach of the majority of the female population. The content, too, had focused more on behaviour and culture than on appearance, with articles on manners and social mores, current affairs, cookery, family life and relationships, along with riddles and puzzles and play reviews. (It is, of course, much easier to follow advice about how to behave or prepare food than it is to follow advice about how your body 'should' look.)

However, in 1852 the first of the truly popular women's magazines was launched by Samuel Beeton. *The Englishwoman's Domestic Magazine* cost just two pence, compared to a shilling (12 pence) for the other women's magazines of the period, and so was affordable by a much wider range of women than previously. The content of the *Domestic Magazine* set the structure for women's magazines that still exists today, with a mixture of fashion, cookery, fiction, personal hygiene, gardening notes, pets and an advice page.

Beeton's magazine was a runaway success, with the circulation reaching 50,000 by 1860, when Samuel relaunched it on better-quality paper and with coloured fashion pictures. It was followed by a host of imitators, many of which were the forerunners of women's magazines today. The magazines were avowedly anti-suffragette and contained little political coverage of any kind, Beeton declaring that: "When we write for women we write for the home." Nonetheless, women became hooked on them, often — as today — subscribing to several different ones. Women's magazines became the key method by which the idea of the 'perfect' body and look was propagated.

Significantly, Beeton and his wife, Isabella (universally known as Mrs Beeton), invented the paper dress pattern as something that could be given away with the magazine, thus contributing to the growth of the idea of a 'standard' women's figure that could be reflected in a pattern. What had even more impact on their readers' ambitions to conform, though, was the role of women's magazines in promoting images of fashionable clothing worn by models. In particular, Isabella Beeton visited the Paris fashion collections twice yearly and reported back to her readers, her reports accompanied by images of the models wearing the clothes.

The first professional fashion model is popularly believed to be Parisian Maria Vernet Worth, who in 1852 modelled the clothing that was being sold by her salesman husband. Professional models were soon being widely used in Paris to display clothes to customers in couture salons, and were therefore the obvious people to display the clothes when they were being sketched or — by the early 20th century — photographed for magazines and newspapers.

These early models were required to have similarly sized bodies (as do today's models) in order that designers could make up just one sample of their work and still be sure that it would fit the model who was displaying it. It seems that initially models' bodies were closer in size and shape to those of average women than they are today, being both shorter and more curvy. However, the use of professional models still introduced the idea of the aspirational body, whereas previously the focus of fashion drawings had been on the clothing or the social status and life of the woman wearing it.

Cosmetic changes

Together with mass-market women's magazines came mass-market advertising, and this also had a part to play in introducing the concept of the standard body being something to aspire to. Advertising works according to a simple formula: first create a need; and then fulfil it. For women, this largely depended on advertisers and editors introducing them to the idea that the natural female body was unworthy, incomplete, defective, deficient and abnormal, and certainly 'below standard'. Then as now, advertising revenue helped to subsidise the cost of magazines for their purchasers, meaning that more people could afford them than otherwise and so increasing circulation. This meant that advertising was an important source of publishers' income, and therefore editorial content was created to support the messages in the advertisements.

According to the magazines, women's skin was now not soft enough without the application of various cosmetic products; their hair was not shiny, straight or curly enough; while perfumes, and later deodorants, were necessary to overcome their body's natural smells. In the 20th century, as it became increasingly socially acceptable to wear make-up and more and more revealing clothing, other 'deficiencies' were discovered, too. Lashes were not dark or thick enough without mascara; eyes did not stand out enough without eyeliner and eye shadow; lips were not red enough without lipstick; and skin looked 'bare' without foundation and powder. (The concept of skin being 'naked' was particularly clever, since nakedness was generally socially unacceptable and also had connotations of the story of Adam and Eve and the links between nakedness and sin.)

The results of all this meant that cultural images of women became increasingly unnatural and unreal, at the same point as being presented as increasingly aspirational. Only by buying and using all of the range of products being advertised could a woman overcome the 'deficiencies' of her natural body and achieve a 'standard' body. Without the 'benefits' of these cosmetic treatments, women's bodies were regarded as being masculine and thus deeply unattractive, as well as being unnatural and abnormal. On the other hand, it was seen as being natural for women to make great efforts with their appearance. Women were regarded as being 'unfeminine' — deficient in their 'natural' qualities — if they failed to follow the fashion to change as much of their appearance as possible with cosmetics in order to meet the 'standard' that had been set for them.

At least it was possible for all women to conform to the standard in terms of using cosmetics. To put it simply, if the advertisers deemed the standard lipstick to be red, then all that was necessary was to have the wherewithal to buy the lipstick and to remember to put it on. In contrast, nothing was going to change women's bodies to meet the standard, however hard they tried through the use of dieting and exercise, since the 'standard' body did not in fact exist. However, by following the trend set by advertisers and aiming for a standard appearance, women's ideas of what their bodies 'should' look like became increasingly separated from reality. Today, these beliefs have become deeply rooted within our society, leaving many women feeling that they have no choice but to alter their bodies in an attempt to meet this false standard themselves.

Most disturbingly, in Britain and the USA — though not so much in mainland Europe — the natural hair on women's bodies was also recast by advertisers as being 'masculine', creating a new market in razors, hair removal creams and waxing products. If evolution had created the 'naked ape', then it followed that body hair was soon destined to disappear completely, with women first becoming completely hairless as they had less hair to begin with. Body hair on women was therefore presented as a sign of being 'unevolved', of nature needing a helping hand — which had the added advantage of disguising the erotic aspects of hair removal. Deodorants were also created for women's genitals, with their natural pheromones being presented as off-putting to men rather than as playing a key role in sexual attraction.

Only today are scientists beginning to realise that hair removal, together with the use of deodorants, may be contributing to the fast-growing levels of infertility within our population. Pheromones, naturally excreted by the body and present on our body hair, are likely to play a key role in the release of other hormones that are essential to the reproductive process, whether or not we are conscious of smelling them. Nonetheless, the vast majority of British women and men today still agree that a woman's natural body hair is highly *un*natural — a sign of being unevolved and ape-like — and is therefore sexually unattractive. A physicality that is detrimental to human reproduction is therefore seen as the only means by which a couple can come together in the first place in order to attempt to create life. Truly, we are body dysphoric.

Slaves to fashion

From the Industrial Revolution onwards, then, the following of trends in dress and appearance became increasingly popular, driven by the development of mass-market popular women's magazines in the 19th century which brought to the forefront fashion and the use of cosmetics. Initially, drawings from Paris fashion collections were copied by women readers and their dressmakers. Then the Beetons' invention of the paper pattern meant that readers could literally create the same designs as each other, often from the same fabric — so long as their bodies could be made to fit the pattern, that is. By the 20th century, with the development of the ready-made clothing market, readers could buy clothes that were identical to those they saw being advertised in their magazines — again, so long as they fitted.

In reality, the rise of the ready-made market made it increasingly difficult to *wear* fashion if you did not — as the majority of women don't — have a 'standard' body. As we have seen, the same market forces that made it possible for women to buy affordable copies of the latest fashions also made it unlikely that these clothes would fit properly — particularly as they were being shown first on models whose height and body proportions were closer to the average *male* figure. Patterns can at least be adapted when clothes are being cut out and stitched from scratch, and these generally were designed to allow for different variations, but ready-made clothes have very little spare fabric within them and so are extremely hard to alter.

However, women were placed under increasing pressure to wear the 'right' designs, and men were not far behind. Rather than blame the manufacturing process for the difficulty or impossibility of doing this, though, the blame was put squarely on consumers themselves for not having 'standard' bodies. The concept of standardisation and the belief that this is a 'natural' phenomenon had by this time been widely accepted. It is entirely unsurprising that at this point our body dysphoria really began to take off.

There are clearly many good reasons for the introduction of standards across the whole range of service and manufacturing industries. There are quite a few very strong arguments for standardising the delivery of professional services such as education and medicine, although there are also good arguments against this. But it is impossible to standardise the human body, and equally impossible even to sort our bodies into 'groups', particularly because we are genetically so much more diverse than domesticated and farmed animals. And indeed, as we will see later in this book, preserving that diversity is essential if the human race is going to continue to survive. Science teaches us without any room whatsoever for doubt that there is no such thing as a standard body. However, even if its approach is to use smoke and mirrors, the fashion world is both more attractive and more convincing.

4. TAKING OUR MEDICINE
or, Doctor knows best

An integral part of our body dysphoria is our unshakeable belief in 'the cure'. We fully expect that, no matter what is wrong, doctors will have a diagnosis and treatment readily available for us. We know that we *should* live our lives in a way that is good for our bodies, but at the same time we believe that this is not really necessary. Medicine, in some form or other, will rescue us when we need it to do so. As a result, we believe that we do not need to take a great deal of responsibility for our own bodies, because the real responsibility lies instead with the medical profession (with God or fate in any case being the ultimate arbiter).

This is not to say, of course, that everyone trusts Western medicine; however, those who do not will usually place their trust in an alternative form of healing instead. In the noughties, sales of herbal and homeopathic remedies in chemists, supermarkets and health food shops doubled, and by the end of the decade the market was thought to be worth £200 million. But whoever we trust, we give our doctors, therapists and healers an enormous amount of power over our lives, often without question. Again, once we look back at history the reasons for this become obvious.

Magic and mysteries

There is no doubt that our overwhelming belief in the power of the modern medical system owes a great deal to the past. It is significant that when we look back 5000 years for the roots of the medical profession, we find a world that combined magical ceremonies and spiritual beliefs with practices that we would still recognise today — with the use of medicines, herbs and surgery occurring alongside rituals and spells. In the ancient world, as in less-developed societies today, healers were given a spiritual/magical status that was superior to that of their patients, and in general they were regarded as being closer to the spirit world than were the rest of society. This made their opinions and their actions unchallengeable, since they took on an aura of spiritual authority whether or not their patients benefited from their healing practices.

We find the first well-documented European medical culture in ancient Egypt (the Egyptian Empire lasted from the 33rd century BC until the Persian invasion of 525BC). Some Asian cultures have medical roots that are at least as old, and shamanic healing practices, including trepanning surgeries, go back further than modern humans have existed. By the time that Asian and shamanic practices were documented, though, many of today's medical practices were already in existence in Eygpt. These included examination and diagnostic techniques, simple surgeries and an extensive range of medicines, many of which have since been proven by modern science to have been more or less effective.

However, spells were as important as medicine in treating the sick, and it is likely that similar belief systems incorporating the supernatural were prevalent elsewhere, too. Healing could only take place when it happened on a spiritual/magical plane as well as on a physical one, and the involvement of someone with the power to intercede spiritually/magically was necessary to the process. This meant that healing could not take place without outside assistance — without an expert. In any case, the Egyptians believed that ultimately people's lifespan and the manner of their death was predetermined by Shai, the god of destiny. The sense of powerlessness over matters relating to our health, and the belief that nothing we could do on our own could ever fundamentally affect it, therefore have their roots at the very dawn of our history.

Alongside the Egyptians, the Babylonians developed diagnostic principles based on the careful examination of their patients and analysis of their symptoms, along with prescriptions for treatment. However, supernatural explanations were provided for many illnesses, and exorcism was prescribed when the use of bandaging and creams proved ineffective. Illness was then believed to be sent as a divine punishment, imposed by demons when someone contravened a rule. Physicians had to learn which of more than 6000 demons might be causing the symptoms, and used divining techniques based on astrological readings, the observation of birds in flight and animal sacrifices in an attempt to find the demonic culprit. The ideas that the patient was responsible for their illness, and that illness was sent as a punishment for transgression, were already firmly rooted in Babylon, along with the belief that doctors were spiritually as well as intellectually superior to the rest of society.

Ancient Greece and the roots of modern medicine

During the same period a more 'scientific' but equally misleading theory about the causes of health and ill health was developed which dominated until the 19th century: the theory of the four humours. It was the Greeks who really founded modern medicine as it exists today, including developing this theory. The four humours comprised black bile (linked to the earth element), yellow bile (linked to the element of fire), phlegm (linked to the element of water) and blood (linked to all four elements), and poor health and disability were believed to result from these fluids being out of balance within the body. Theophrastus, a successor of Aristotle, also linked different personality types to imbalances of the humours, thus aiding diagnosis: too much black bile made people melancholic; too much yellow bile made people choleric; too much phlegm made people phlegmatic; and too much blood made people sanguine.

Again, though, spirituality played a central role, with Apollo's servant Asclepius being the deity who was deemed to be responsible for healing (the serpented staff of Asclepius remains as the symbol of doctors today). Pilgrims who needed healing visited the temples of Asclepius and took part in rituals that included fasting and praying, before the priests were able to interpret their dreams for healing oracles and offer them a range of treatments, mostly dietary. Temple physicians later formed a separate caste, and the first medical school was developed alongside the temple at Cnidus in 700BC. The fame of some of these physicians still exists today, particularly Hippocrates (although much of the knowledge that was later attributed to him is likely to have originated with his colleagues and predecessors).

Hippocrates founded his own medical school at Cos, and the Hippocratic writings provided the basis for the world's medical knowledge for centuries to come. Although, as with the four humours, many Greek theories were later disproved, Hippocrates' findings about lung disease, among others, are still relevant today. Critically, these Greek physicians developed diagnostic principles that were based on the close observation of their patients, and standardised many procedures and approaches. The Hippocratic oath still taken by newly qualified doctors to promise to uphold an ethical code of standards reflects the original oath that newly qualified Greek physicians swore to the healing gods. This original oath included pledges not to perform abortions and euthanasia, to leave surgery to surgeons, and to protect patients.

Belief in religion co-existed with science, with Hippocrates writing: "Before the gods, the physicians bow since they have not superabundance of power." As with the Egyptians, the Greeks also believed in the concept of destiny, with the Fates being the triple gods Clotho, Lachesis and Atropos. Clotho used a spindle to spin the thread of your life, Lachesis (usually pictured with a scroll or globe) measured it, and Atropos (usually pictured with a pair of scales or shears) cut it off at the end. Nobody could challenge them, not even other gods. Divine power, not medical power, was ultimately responsible for how your life ended, and if treatment failed then it was not destined to succeed.

Later, Roman medicine was heavily influenced by the Greeks, with the first Greek doctors appearing in Rome as prisoners of war. Many subsequently bought their freedom and set up practice in the city, while others chose to move to Rome of their own free will. (Prior to this, the profession of physician had not existed in the Roman Empire, with households normally taking individual responsibility for their health.) The Romans developed numerous surgical tools, as well as inventing cataract surgery. The most famous of all their Greek doctors was Galen, who studied anatomy (using the bodies of animals, since the use of corpses was forbidden by law) and carried out operations that were not attempted again until the 19th and 20th centuries.

Owing to religious prohibitions on medical research, Galen's numerous writings formed the basis for much medical knowledge until the 16th and 17th centuries, when the study of human anatomy provided a more accurate understanding of how the body functions. (Galen, for example, believed that the arterial and venous systems were separate, leading to centuries of misunderstanding about the nature of the circulatory system.) Along with Greek medicine, the Romans adopted beliefs in the healing god Asclepius, and made pilgrimages to temples that were surrounded by baths, gardens and other facilities thought to be helpful for healing. Divine healing was believed to take place during sleep, making it clear that spiritual intervention was superior and happened entirely separately from physical and chemical procedures.

As with earlier healing cultures, the availability of an expert was fundamental to more scientific cultures: knowledge that was not possessed by ordinary people was necessary in order to achieve healing. Whether or not the 'expert' had the necessary knowledge to do any good — or even to avoid causing further harm — was almost irrelevant. (Even today, we are discovering that practices that we previously believed contributed to the healing process are in fact counter-productive, or even lethal.) What was of overwhelming importance to our ancestors was the intellectual, social and professional status of the healer, along with the possession of privileged knowledge that was believed to be accurate at the time. And, of course, physicians in Greek, and later Roman, times were closely associated with the gods, which promoted their aura of mysticism and spiritual authority.

Magic, religion and folk medicine

Within Europe, much of the early scientific knowledge was later lost until the Renaissance. Prohibitions on research by the Roman Catholic Church, together with relative poverty compared to the heyday of the Roman Empire, ensured that only Islamic civilisations continued to develop scientific theories and medical practices. For more than a millennium, the Islamic world was dominant in scientific thinking, while in large parts of the old Roman Empire, folk medicine was all that remained. In the following centuries, shamanism continued to bring together magical belief systems with herbs and primitive surgery in parts of Asia and eastern Europe, while African societies had their witch doctors. Again, both types of practitioner had a high social status and were usually involved in the leadership of their communities; they were powerful people who had a link to the supernatural and to spiritual realms which ordinary people did not possess.

Judaeo-Christian societies rejected the use of magic in western Europe, but, as we have seen earlier, religious explanations were often given for medical conditions, including blaming demonic possession for someone's symptoms. This meant that healing was inseparable from religion, particularly given that the scientific medical theories being developed by Islamic civilisations were virtually unknown outside the Italian universities. Even within these theories, however, the Islamic belief that everything that takes place does so because of the will of God reinforced the idea that ultimately what a physician did was of little use compared to divine will.

Christians had a more complex relationship with the idea of destiny, because of their emphasis on free will. Many scientific forms of healing were regarded as being 'un-Christian', and in the 13th century Pope Innocent III declared that all surgical procedures were prohibited by church law. Autopsies were also prohibited, making the study of anatomy virtually impossible and leaving Galen's mistaken theories about the circulatory system to flourish. Men might have free will, but they were still bound by the spiritual authority of the church. Priests and rabbis played leadership roles within their society, and as God's representatives on earth they could not be easily questioned, let alone challenged. 'Free will' was restricted to making 'right' choices (i.e. obeying the church laws), or sinning, and Christians were believed to create their own destiny through these choices. As we have already seen, if a patient did not recover or died, they were likely to be blamed themselves for not praying hard enough, or for having sinned too badly to be forgiven on earth.

The Renaissance was accompanied by a resurgence of interest in ancient Greek medicine, as well as by further medical advances based on observation and experimentation, but in western Europe at least, the majority of ordinary people continued to rely heavily on folk healers of different kinds. Medical knowledge was restricted to the universities and monasteries, with many monasteries having hospitals attached to them. This continued the links between healing and religion, and in particular stressed the necessity of prayer to the healing process. Monks were spiritual as well as medical experts, redoubling their (male) authority.

A woman's place

Male authority was central to medical practice for millennia. Many of the millions of 'witches' who were put to death in the 16th and 17th centuries were likely to have been alternative healers of some kind, particularly herbalists and midwives. The fact that healing had long been associated with spiritual and magical practices probably enhanced beliefs that these women were 'consorting with the Devil'. No doubt the fact that they were women, and that medical knowledge and spiritual leadership were exclusively male preserves, added to the Church's desire to eliminate them. The success of the witch-hunters underlined the widespread acceptance by peoples across Europe that supernatural forces, not natural processes, had the ultimate power over life and death.

Apart from midwifery, rudimentary nursing and work such as cleaning and cooking, women were excluded from medical practice until the mid-19th century, at which point women such as Florence Nightingale and Mary Seacole demonstrated the importance of nursing care to recovery by working in field hospitals during the Crimean War. This led to the founding of the modern nursing profession, with nurses being widely regarded as having a lower social and professional status than doctors, even though they managed (and continue to manage) the day-to-day care of their patients.

Elizabeth Blackwell was the first woman to qualify as a doctor, in America in 1849, and she was slowly followed by others, both in the USA and Europe. In Britain, Elizabeth Garrett was the first woman to qualify, in 1865, after a long struggle for recognition. Blackwell struggled to find employment and had to open her own private practice, eventually founding the New York Infirmary for Women and Children with her sister Emily and Polish immigrant Dr Marie E Zakrzewska, and Garrett also worked exclusively with women. Women doctors continued to be shunned by their male colleagues and by both male and female patients for decades to come. Since women were considered to be biologically and intellectually inferior to men, and this had been 'proved' by science, they obviously could not be as good doctors as men.

At the same time as nursing was developing as a profession, midwives were being superseded by doctors — not always with positive results. Again, the role of the 'expert' was paramount, whether or not they achieved any success. For example, a report into the treatment of ectopic pregnancies in the early 19th century found a survival rate after abdominal surgery of one in six patients, yet one in three patients who were left untreated lived to tell the tale. By the second half of the 19th century, though, midwives were being supplanted by doctors whenever patients could afford this, not least because many midwives were entirely untrained, and maternal and infant mortality rates were high.

Doctors resisted attempts by midwives to train and regulate themselves. Doctors saw themselves, not midwives, as being the 'natural' experts on childbirth and as being best placed to deliver babies. Their successful opposition to the regulation of midwifery took place despite the strenuous efforts of the Trained Midwives Registration Society, which was founded in 1881 and which soon changed its name to the Midwives Institute. The institute, the forerunner of the modern Royal College of Midwives, struggled to convince both politicians and doctors of the importance of midwives to the birth process so long as they were properly trained. Only in 1902 was the first Midwives' Act finally passed, establishing the Central Midwives' Board to oversee the training and practice of midwives and making it illegal for untrained midwives to work.

Women had had thousands of years, then, to learn that they couldn't be experts in their own right unless they adopted what was regarded as being a traditional male role — something that only started to become possible towards the end of the 19th century. But, of course, the vast majority of men were excluded from expert status too. As is the case today, the practice of healing has throughout recorded history been the closely guarded province of an elite, whether this elite has been characterised by intellectual, magical or spiritual expertise; and entry to the profession has often been dependent on the person's pre-existing social status, including the ability to afford to train.

Today, the prohibition against the practice of medicine by non-qualified people is a sensible precaution intended to protect the health of us all. However, it originated thousands of years ago and was really intended to protect the status of healers, whether or not they possessed any useful knowledge and skill at all. No wonder we continue to believe that 'doctor knows best'. No wonder, too, that many people suffer or even die unnecessarily each year in the UK because, even though medical treatment is now free at the point of delivery, they don't wish to 'bother' such a sacred medical figure.

Men in white coats

The perceived links between medicine and religion continued into the 20th century, and only now, in the 21st century, are they disappearing. The medical world as we know it today gradually rejected links with religion in favour of links with science. At the end of the 19th century doctors adopted the scientists' uniform of long-sleeved white coats in order to stress the scientific nature of their discipline in comparison to other types of healers, and thus their superiority. The magical knowledge that doctors now possessed was scientific; and the fact that this was as baffling as magic to the ordinary member of society served to uphold doctors' status. Doctors wished to make it clear that they, and only they, possessed the knowledge necessary to have power over life and death; they, and only they, were the experts.

As we now know, the white coats adopted by doctors were in fact responsible for spreading countless hospital infections over the next century, however useful they were in protecting scientists' clothing from burns and chemicals. Today, the long-sleeved versions are now banned in British hospitals on hygiene grounds. However, in literally taking on the mantle of scientists, doctors were able to take on their semi-godlike status, too (we will look further at scientists in the next chapter). This continued to ensure that doctors were believed to have almost godlike powers, and therefore were as unchallengeable as the shamans, priests and witch doctors who preceded them (and, in some cases, continued to work alongside them).

As for the doctors, they would truly have had to be godlike before they could have resisted the temptation to benefit from the increased social and professional status that white coats gave them. No wonder that today we continue to believe in the ability of doctors to work miracles, whatever the scientific evidence to the contrary. No wonder that we are also easily persuaded by 'doctor-like' alternative healers' promises of cures, however unscientific their claims have proven to be. No wonder that advertisers use men in white coats to sell a wide range of medications, toothpastes and so on.

Of course, we do also have good reasons to believe in the power of medicine, since the last two centuries in particular have seen massive advances in our understanding of the way in which our bodies work, and accompanying advances in how to treat illness. In particular, the understanding that disease was caused by micro-organisms allowed public health programmes to be implemented that had a major impact on reducing the number of people who developed infectious diseases in the first place. Then, as now, scientific understanding together with social action had more of an impact on the health of the majority than medical treatment. However, that is not to say that medical advances were anything other than of major significance.

The understanding of disease mechanisms allowed doctors to prevent the spread of illness among patients, while the use of antiseptic procedures had a major impact on the success rates of surgery, including amputations. Anaesthesia also led to dramatic improvements in surgery, making it much less likely that the patient would die of shock on the operating table as well as making the operation easier for both patient and surgeon. As a result, the number of surgical procedures taking place grew phenomenally, with lengthy surgeries taking place for the first time. (It should be noted, though, that there was considerable opposition to the introduction of anaesthesia on both religious and medical grounds, and that this lasted for some decades.)

The rediscovery and development of vaccinations — first used millennia beforehand in India or China — was also of considerable significance, although these were not developed for widespread use until the 20th century. Then their use made major inroads into the prevalence of common diseases, eradicated smallpox completely and almost totally eliminated polio. The late 18th and 19th centuries also saw the development of a host of medical techniques and inventions such as the hypodermic syringe, which made the intravenous administration of treatments such as vaccines possible.

By the 20th century, the use of scientific imaging and measuring techniques such as X-rays (and later ECGs, ultrasounds, and MRI and CAT scans) made a massive contribution to the diagnosis and treatment of injuries and internal illnesses. Later, the discovery of insulin by Canadian researchers in the 1920s meant that thousands of people then close to death were suddenly able to live near-normal lives. Meanwhile, following Alexander Fleming's (1881–1955) discovery of penicillin in 1928, the development of antibiotics to treat infection during the Second World War led to a dramatic fall in the death rate from infectious illnesses, particularly tuberculosis (TB) and post-operative infections.

After the war, the development of dialysis machines also meant that people with kidney disease could routinely be saved with ongoing treatment. By the late 20th century, organ transplant surgery, including kidney transplants, had become routine, assisted by many other discoveries including drugs to suppress the immune system and prevent the body from rejecting a foreign organ. In all, millions of people who would previously have died were now able to live a normal lifespan. This included many women and children who would previously have died in childbirth, since the combination of trained midwives and doctors, anaesthesia and antibiotics led to a massive decrease in maternal and infant death rates.

It was not simply lifespans that were affected. While better nutrition and hygiene contributed the most to improvements in the physical health of the population as a whole, medicine also made significant contributions to maintaining individual bodies in their optimum condition. Eye surgeons perfected ancient cataract techniques, and, with the development of plastics, contact lenses enabled myopia to become a minor disadvantage rather than an obvious impairment. Corneal transplants and laser surgery also reduced the level of visual impairment, while modern spectacles minimised its impact. Fractures — injuries that we now take for granted will have no lasting effect — had almost invariably had a lasting and disabling impact before the advent of X-rays, and a better understanding of anatomy, made it possible to set and, if necessary, pin bones. Replacement joints followed, radically improving mobility for those fortunate enough to receive them, although long waiting lists and the lack of technology to make them resistant to wear and tear continues to restrict their impact today.

The rise of 'big pharma'

The late 19th and early 20th centuries also saw the development of the modern pharmaceutical industry. Over time, pharmacists gradually moved away from making and dispensing their own drugs, as they had done for millennia, to selling drugs that were mass-produced elsewhere. (Often, of course, these drugs were based on traditional medicines, from throughout the world as well as from Europe.) The development of new products such as insulin and antibiotics drove the expansion of the pharmaceutical industry, and soon drugs companies were conducting their own research in order to expand their markets. Following the Second World War, the industry then underwent a huge expansion, with many new drugs being developed and marketed for mass consumption.

These included treatments for high blood pressure, anxiety and depression, insomnia and inflammatory conditions such as arthritis, as well as the contraceptive pill — a drug that changed attitudes and morality for ever. Related to the Pill was Hormone Replacement Therapy (HRT), a therapy for the previously unmedicalised 'illness' called the menopause. This was initially thought of as a drug that could indefinitely prolong youth for women, based on the assumption that when a woman's body stops producing as much oestrogen as it did previously, the impact of this can be held off by artificially administering more. Only later was it realised that both the Pill and HRT increased the risk of users developing some cancers and heart disease, as well as potentially damaging the environment. Nor had HRT turned out to preserve youth after all, although it certainly reframed cultural views of older women (for better or for worse). However, both the Pill and HRT remain popular drugs today, with many long-term users.

Overall, treatments for 'conditions' that affected a wide percentage of the population were prioritised, since these were obviously the most profitable. We will return to the link between the search for profit and the priorities for medical research later in this book. Suffice it to say now that, as with cosmetics, some drugs were marketed to meet 'needs' that had been artificially manufactured, and for which exaggerated claims were being made.

The plastic body

The period during and following the Second World War also saw significant developments in plastic surgery, driven by the need to treat members of the armed forces who had been horribly burnt in plane crashes and other fires. Plastic surgery had been used as a reconstructive technique in India as far back as 2000BC, but techniques had been developed very slowly, particularly in the West. Rudimentary surgery had been used in ancient Greece and Roman times, for example to repair torn ears, and had also been used occasionally to deal with damaged noses. However, before an understanding of the disease process was developed and anaesthesia was invented, people undergoing surgery ran a high risk of developing an infection, as well as experiencing great pain during and after the operation.

After studying Indian techniques at the end of the 18th and the beginning of the 19th century, though, an increasing number of Western doctors became interested in the possibilities of plastic surgery. Plastic surgery was then used to treat the effects of disease and injury as well as birth conditions such as cleft palate, mostly to improve function but also to 'normalise' appearance. Noses that had been damaged or that had not developed as expected were a particular target, since this affected people's breathing as well as their speech. However, it was war that really drove the invention of new methods and techniques. In the First World War, Harold Gillies, a New Zealander working in London, developed many of the modern surgical techniques in order to treat injured soldiers, and his student and cousin Archibald MacIndoe later continued this work with RAF aircrews in the Second World War. MacIndoe's patients, all of whom had sustained serious burns, became known as the Guinea Pig Club.

After the Second World War, the development of these plastic surgery techniques meant that surgery for purely cosmetic reasons also became increasingly popular. Patients began to opt for unnecessary surgeries, particularly on their noses and breasts, in the belief that they could improve on what was already a normal appearance. The belief in the existence of the 'perfect' body, together with faith in doctors' power over life and death, fuelled a desire for 'improvement' that, as we have already seen, continues to gather pace today. Again, we will return to the impact of these beliefs later in the book.

The creation of life

Doctors were now simply and unsurprisingly regarded as having power over life and death, with religion playing a secondary or non-existent role in this process depending on the view of the patient. Officially, God no longer had any say in the matter at all. However, doctors took on the glamour and authority that had been ascribed to healers from the magicians of early Egypt onwards, and with this a position that had previously been occupied by priests and other spiritual leaders. Science was the new magic, equally mysterious to the uninitiated; and today, with fewer and fewer young people learning much about science at school, there is no sign of this situation changing any time soon.

The godlike status achieved by doctors in the 20th century was helped by the development of infertility treatments, particularly in vitro fertilisation techniques (IVF). Doctors became able to create life outside the womb by bringing together an egg and a sperm in a Petri dish, later implanting the resulting embryo into a woman's womb with a resulting pregnancy success rate that was close to that of nature. Although initially controversial, the technique quickly became accepted, not least because it proved possible to treat large numbers of couples; unlike many more recent experimental therapies, IVF was a treatment that could be successfully 'scaled up' and reproduced in labs across the world. Doctors were literally able to create life where prayer alone had failed.

It is unsurprising that concerns soon grew about the extension of this technology, since doctors' powers appeared to be unlimited. Science was able to prevent conception, or stimulate it. Along with enabling pregnancies in women who would never otherwise give birth, including creating life in a test tube, they were soon able to make post-menopausal women pregnant by using donor eggs and administering artificial hormones to return women's wombs to pre-menopausal conditions. Doctors could also create a biological child for a woman who could not become pregnant herself, if a surrogate mother was used to carry the embryo and give birth. Despite having no basis in fact, it was soon believed that scientists were capable of creating fully formed human–animal hybrids, and able to 'design' embryos to determine their appearance, intelligence and personality. We will return to these myths about reproductive technology and their impact on fertility doctors and patients later in this book.

Today, for reasons that I will discuss further in the next chapter, we confidently expect that medical advances will continue at the same pace as they did in the 20th century. This is despite knowing that many of the most fundamental and all of the most straightforward discoveries have already been made, and realising that further advances will become increasingly complex and expensive. If doctors are unable to cure a disease now, then we confidently believe that scientists will soon find the answers that will enable them to do so. We demand that doctors are able to provide the answers to our problems whether or not these are medical in cause, and we are surprised when they fail. We expect them always to be right, and are shocked when they make mistakes.

Misplaced trust

We also expect doctors to have moral standards superior to the majority, and are amazed when they turn out to be as human as the rest of us. Medical murderers such as the British GP Harold Shipman (one of the most prolific serial killers in history, who is believed to have killed between 250 and 400 of his patients) have been able to commit these crimes with impunity, since no one can believe the evidence against them — including, initially, the police in Shipman's case. The other reason that Shipman was able to get away with his killings for so long was that no safeguards existed against medical murderers, because no one believed that safeguards were necessary. Individual cases of serious medical malpractice had occasionally come to light, but only through the vigilance of relatives, and, of course, many patients were vulnerable simply because they had no families to look out for them. Even then, a number of victims' relatives complained fruitlessly about Shipman, including to the police, before anyone took them seriously enough to investigate.

More than a decade after Shipman was convicted, doctors can still go their entire career without one formal appraisal of their competency, despite promises to change this. It is unsurprising in the circumstances that some doctors have believed that they can get away with a host of other offences, including fraud — particularly, but not only, in terms of misrepresenting research findings and the likely success of private treatments — and theft from patients.

Our belief in the moral and intellectual superiority of the medical profession seems unshakeable. We know doctors to be human, but we still expect them to be magical and/or godlike. We know that health promotion, not medicine, has had the most impact on extending our life expectancy to date, but we still expect that surgery or a pill will save our life and even extend it in the future. We know that we must take responsibility for our own bodies, but we still believe that only doctors have any power over our state of health. Somewhere along the line, we believe that our destiny continues to be predetermined in any case. Inevitably, this adds a great deal to our body dysphoria.

5. VICTORIAN VALUES or, Delusions of omnipotence

For our final voyage back in history to discover the roots of our body dysphoria, we will focus on our belief that given enough time we will be able to understand everything about how the natural world works and then control it, 'perfecting' the human body in the process by developing it from its natural state. This, more than anything, has affected our attitudes to science and the body today. To begin with, though, we need to return to the ancient world again, and to religious teachings about the relationship between humans and nature. This will enable us to understand how science has replaced religion as a belief-system for many of us today.

Humans as godlike beings

At the very beginning of the Old Testament, the first book of Genesis states the following:

> 26 And God said, Let us make man in our image, after our likeness: and let them have dominion over the fish of the sea, and over the fowl of the air, and over the cattle, and over all the earth, and over every creeping thing that creepeth upon the earth.

Looking at the world from this perspective, as people did for thousands of years, immediately set up a separation between humans and the rest of the natural world. According to Genesis, humans were closer to God than to the rest of His creations, and like God they had power over everything else on the planet. This belief is still fundamental to the way in which we organise our world today, and of course is prevalent in Judaism and Islam as well as Christianity.

Abnormal

The fact that having power over nature meant that humans could do what they wished with the natural world, rather than being the stewards or guardians of the planet, is underlined in Genesis 9. God sends a flood to drown most of the population after they become 'ungodly', but deems Noah and his family worthy of saving. God therefore warns Noah to build an ark and to ensure that breeding pairs of 'every living thing' come with him and his family, in order that they can later repopulate the world. After the flood dies down:

> 1 And God blessed Noah and his sons, and said unto them, Be fruitful, and multiply, and replenish the earth.
> 2 And the fear of you and the dread of you shall be upon every beast of the earth, and upon every fowl of the air, upon all that moveth upon the earth, and upon all the fishes of the sea; into your hand are they delivered.
> 3 Every moving thing that liveth shall be meat for you; even as the green herb have I given you all things.
> 4 But flesh with the life thereof, which is the blood thereof, shall ye not eat.
> 5 And surely your blood of your lives will I require; at the hand of every beast will I require it, and at the hand of man; at the hand of every man's brother will I require the life of man.
> 6 Whoso sheddeth man's blood, by man shall his blood be shed: for in the image of God made he man.

So animals, birds, fish and vegetation were there to be killed and/or eaten by humans; but humans were fundamentally different from other living things and were forbidden to kill each other because they were godlike. What made humans godlike were their souls, the spiritual essence of a person that continued to exist after their body died.

(The Bible doesn't categorically state that animals don't have souls; rather, only humans are described as possessing these. However, it has generally been taken for granted throughout history that only humans can expect eternal life on a spiritual plane, and this has reinforced the view that the rest of the living world is there for humans to exploit for their own benefit. From a biblical perspective, animals exist for humans to eat or otherwise make use of their bodies; they may appear to be like us, but this is an illusion because the spirit that animates them dies when their bodies die. Similarly, exploiting natural resources can never endanger us, because these resources only exist to serve our needs.)

The Age of Enlightenment

It was really only in the 17th and 18th centuries that Christians finally began to question whether every word of the scriptures might contain the literal truth. The Age of Enlightenment (sometimes called the Age of Reason when referring in particular to 17th-century developments) marked a new interest in what could be proven to be factually accurate as opposed to being taken on faith, and in the development of knowledge based on reasoning and rationality. This led on from the Scientific Revolution of the late Renaissance, when many of the beliefs about the world that had been based on Greek philosophy and on superstition were proven to be inaccurate as a result of new discoveries in astronomy, anatomy and physics.

At the core of the Enlightenment was a questioning of everything that had previously been taken for granted, including traditional institutions, morals and ideas, while intellectual freedom and democracy were highly prized (though generally not for women and the 'lower classes'). Although belief in God remained largely unshaken, religion — seen as something that was separate and man-made — was blamed for the deaths of millions of people in wars, most latterly the Thirty Years War (1618–48) and the English Civil War (1642–51). The influence of the Church was declining among the population in general; 'dissenting' Christian religions were expanding alongside the Church of England; and it wasn't until the mid-19th century that there was renewed popular interest in traditional Christianity and Dissenters were reabsorbed into the mainstream. In the mean time, across Europe, men (and some women) began to debate a wide range of subjects, in salons, coffee houses, clubs and masonic lodges, and many of today's public institutions were founded during this period.

René Descartes (1596–1650) was a key forerunner of and influence on many of the thinkers who are said to be part of the Enlightenment, since he was as skilled a mathematician as he was a philosopher. As we have already seen, Descartes believed that the body was akin to a machine, a belief that still persists today. Minds — souls — could be affected by the body, but were non-material in essence and therefore continued to exist after death, making the mind far more important than the body. Descartes reinforced the belief that humans are fundamentally different to animals by arguing that only humans have minds/souls. Since animals didn't have minds, they couldn't feel pain, and this convenient theory excused vivisection. (The belief that animals didn't have souls later contributed to the controversy around the theory of evolution, for how could humans have descended from soulless beings?)

Apart from Descartes viewing the body as a machine, Sir Isaac Newton (1643–1727) — one of the most influential individuals in history — developed the idea of the universe itself as being like a machine. The concept of the 'clockwork universe' cleverly brought together religion and science by viewing God as the clock-maker who had built the 'clock' and had set its workings in motion, after which it was governed by the natural laws that kept it ticking. This was not a new idea: the 13th-century scholar John of Sacrobosco (c1195-1256) — who taught at the University of Paris but who may have been English — described the universe as a machine, the "machina mundi", in his introduction to astronomy *De sphaera mundi* (*On the Sphere of the World*, c1230). These concepts encouraged scientists to believe that, like a clock, both the body and the universe could be taken apart, studied, put back together again and improved upon. Today, the roots of this belief are similar to theories of 'intelligent design' and thus have been discredited by science, but as an assumption it remains surprisingly dominant nonetheless. We may or may not believe that God created the machine, but a machine we still believe the body to be.

As with the rest of our romp through history, I don't intend to do more than to summarise some of the key points of the Enlightenment here, generalising wildly in the process. What I want is not to create a potted history of the world or even a history of ideas, but to look at where some of our most deeply held beliefs about the body have come from, and to examine the relationship that these beliefs have to the facts as demonstrated by science today. This is, of course, a process that the Enlightenment thinkers would have approved of themselves. The next philosopher who demands a mention is Francis Bacon (1561–1626). Bacon named "Four Idols" that prevented people from being able to think rationally. The "Idols of the Cave" (*idola specus*) were the assumptions that we acquire from our culture, gender, class, religion, upbringing and education — assumptions that usually go unexamined and therefore unchallenged.

The concept of progress

Many of the ideas that we take for granted today have their roots in Bacon's writings about the world, particularly the idea of 'progress' and the importance of scientific enquiry to the advance of progress. The common concept that society can continue to develop and advance ('progress') became part of popular consciousness for the first time in the 18th century, and had already become dominant by the 19th. By the 20th century, it had become accepted that 'you can't stand in the way of progress', and anyone who tried to do so was frowned upon. (Despite the fact that history had already proved this wrong in the past, with the Church in particular ensuring for centuries that the conditions in which 'progress' could take place were barred by law.) The idea of progress, more than any other idea, continues to affect our thinking about science and medicine — and, by extension, the body — in the 21st century. We take it for granted that society will progress, and that progress will be positive and beneficial for at least the majority of us.

Bacon was also the founder of modern science, in that he believed in the importance of minutely observing the world around us and then basing theory on these observations, rather than developing theory and then searching for 'proof' to justify it. Experimentation was key to this process, as was the need to try to disprove a theory once it had been developed. The gradual acceptance of this method of working enabled scientists to build on the discoveries of the Renaissance — everything from a correct understanding of how our circulatory systems work, to the theory of gravity — and then to 'progress' much more rapidly.

(However, it is important to note that scientists continued to develop theory in parallel with observation, and often selected what to observe as a result of their initial theories. Science itself has never been wholly 'scientific', and in the 20th century approaches to uncovering and testing knowledge were refined again — particularly around the need to attempt to disprove theories alongside searching for evidence to support them.)

Bacon also believed that knowledge needed to be useful; it was only valuable if it could be applied. Bacon rejected the Aristotelian idea that knowledge was valuable for its own sake, and in particular that it was valuable for the way in which it could liberate the soul from the world of the mundane (thus the 'liberal arts'). Whereas the Aristotelian tradition regarded knowledge that related to the economic and social world as being secondary, Bacon believed that knowledge needed to contribute to practical progress to be worth anything at all: "Knowledge is power" (*Meditationes Sacrae*,1597).

The acceptance of this idea meant that science became much more closely related to technological and social development ('progress') than it otherwise would have done — something that we take for granted today. We do not see the sense in scientists researching simply to add to the body of human knowledge: we believe that there must be an easily identifiable 'point' to their research; and this inevitably affects what scientists research and how they present their findings to the public. Medical research scientists cannot simply propose to study the way in which the body functions, but must claim that this can potentially result in a way to control the body for the future benefit of humanity. I will discuss the implications of this pressure on scientists further in a later chapter.

The Industrial Revolution, discussed in previous chapters, was obviously driven by the Enlightenment. The use of reasoning and scientific methodology led to many new discoveries, directed by the belief that knowledge should be useful. Later, when combined with Darwinism, the concept of 'progress' was seen as part of the 'natural' development of humanity, and humanity was believed to be destined to progress to become more and more 'perfect'. The fact that progress was a process that could be reversed, though, contributed to fears that humans could 'regress', and therefore fuelled eugenicists' fears about what could happen in the future if human reproduction was not manipulated and controlled.

Before the idea of progress dominated, it might have been possible to recognise that when past civilisations had collapsed and knowledge had been lost, war, poverty and environmental disasters — but principally war — had been responsible. Now, however, the body itself was seen as a threat to progress. Poverty was seen as being biologically rather than economically determined as well as being a driving force behind war, while 'uncivilised' bodies were regarded as blocking progress in terms of developing the colonies.

Redefining perfection

It is worth pausing here to consider the meaning of the concept of 'perfection' and its links to progress, since this is so relevant to our body dysphoria today. In *Delta of the Metaphysics*, Aristotle defined perfection as having three related meanings: completeness; something that is so good that nothing of its kind could be better; and something that has attained its purpose. Later, in *Summa Theologiae*, Thomas Aquinas regarded perfection as being two-fold: something that is perfect in itself — in its "substance" — and something that is perfect for its purpose. However, for reasons concerning the use of the Latin language, these related and fairly straightforward concepts became confused with another: the concept of excellence, or being the best. Excellence implies comparison with others of its kind, competition, whereas perfection exists on its own.

It is important to point out that in earlier times all humans were considered to be capable of reaching perfection, whether they were 'abnormal' or not. Within Greek society, Plato regarded goodness as being equivalent to perfection, and therefore as being attainable by anyone. The

Victorian Values

Stoics regarded perfection as being a state of harmony with nature, the mind and the self, and therefore again as being a state that anyone could reach. Christians, too, initially believed in the concept of self-perfection of the soul through living according to Jesus's teachings, although by the fifth century they had grown to believe instead that only Christ could be perfect and that perfection was unreachable on earth. Humans, though, still had to strive to lead the best lives that they could if they were to go to heaven.

Therefore, using the initial concepts of perfection, one might say that all human bodies are perfect, in that they are able to sustain life; or one might say that all non-disabled bodies are perfect, while bodies with sensory, physical, mobility, emotional and intellectual impairments are not as good for their purpose as they might be; or one might say that all bodies are capable of achieving perfection because their souls are. But with the more complex definition, perfection is defined by one body or collection of bodies excelling in comparison with the rest. This concept underpinned 19th- and 20th-century ideas about one 'race', one nation, one gender or one social class being more 'perfect' than others, as well as being fundamental to eugenics. It also meant that the vast majority of people were no longer deemed to be capable of being perfect at all, at the same time as perfection becoming a universal goal.

However, 'progress' — the means by which society moved towards perfection — was seen to be driven by imperfection. For some philosophers, imperfection was itself perfect, since it was the means by which perfection was achieved. This has some resonance today with the use of disabled people by scientists to understand how the human body is formed, in order that they can then manipulate it. For example, children with genetic conditions that cause premature ageing are studied to try to discover how 'normal' people can be made to live longer. It is this that drives the research funding into their conditions, however much one hopes that they benefit from the research along the way. These children's 'imperfection' is regarded as being a way to progress towards perfection for others.

Even within the Enlightenment, though, there were two schools of thought about human perfection by the mid-18th century. As we have seen, the idea that became dominant by the 19th century was the idea of progress leading inexorably towards perfection, of civilisation being the most perfect way for humans to live. There was, though, another school of thinkers who instead believed nature to be perfect, and that living close to nature was the most 'perfect' way to live. This was the Romantic school of thought, in which 'primitive man' — the 'Noble Savage' — represented the most perfect form of human being.

The Romantic movement — which included the likes of William and Dorothy Wordsworth, Samuel Taylor Coleridge, William Blake, John Keats, Percy and Mary Shelley et al — prioritised emotion, intuition and imagination over reason; looked to the medieval period and folk art rather than to the future for inspiration; and saw the arts rather than the sciences as being of overwhelming importance. It is unsurprising that, with so many changes taking place around them, nostalgia for the past existed alongside enthusiasm for the future. Along with all of the inventions and technological developments, 'progress' had also led to many people living and working in appalling conditions in the industrial centres and cities, and there was less recognition of the fact that deep poverty could also exist in rural settings. 'Progress' has always involved losses as well as gains, and has many frightening aspects.

One does not have to be cynical to note that business interests were best served by the idea of progress towards civilisation, particularly as countries such as Australia were being declared as *terra nullius* or 'empty lands' by colonisers. Indigenous peoples were not popularly regarded as being 'people' at all. The idea that 'primitive man' actually represented an earlier form of human, and was naturally designed to die out, was far more convenient for politicians and businessmen alike than claiming that indigenous peoples represented the highest form of humanity and were the most perfect. Thus Romanticism proved to be an idea that was less 'fit' to survive than Social Darwinism.

The idea that the human body would become perfected by civilisation also supported the standardisation of the body in the 19th and 20th centuries. If 'natural man' was imperfect, and 'civilisation' of the body marked progress, then the growing importance of fashion and cosmetics, and later cosmetic surgery, was entirely validated. A 'civilised body' was one that progressed as far as possible away from nature, and one that could be easily distinguished from uncivilised bodies. We can see why women in Britain and the USA in particular were so willing to accept that their body hair needed to be removed in order to create a 'feminine' look. Unless you were a Romantic, being 'natural' was to be uncivilised, primitive, behind the times, an opposer of progress — which in itself was deemed to be 'unnatural'.

The rise of the evil scientist

Despite the Romantics, by the end of the 18th century science had become popular as never before. There was a great appetite for science books, even more so than there is today, and many people became amateur scientists, enabling 'progress' to speed up. However, again, it was not all one-sided. Scientists had of course met opposition and disagreement from religious authorities ever since it was possible to distinguish between the two, although often scientific findings were simply explained by theologians in a way that fit their beliefs. Now Romantic philosophers and writers also accused scientists of oversimplification of the universe and God's work, and of ignoring the real beauty in nature.

Largely due to Romanticism, the figure of the evil scientist entered into popular consciousness. This resulted at least as much from the Romantics' fictional as from their non-fictional writings, particularly through ETA Hoffman's (1776–1822) horror fiction and Mary Shelley's enormously popular book *Frankenstein* (1818). Even by this point, scientists had made huge advances compared to the previous millennia, however false some 'science' later turned out to be. The fictional stereotype of the scientist drunk on their own power not only played on but also reflected fears about the omnipotence of scientists and the motives behind their research. Given the difficulties that have been caused by our unquestioning trust in doctors, it is probably a good thing that we learnt to distrust scientists. However, as we will see later in this book, this distrust can also be highly counter-productive.

Knowledge, power and control

The belief that scientists were omnipotent, and thus to be feared, was fuelled by the Victorian conviction that sooner rather than later we would understand everything that there is to understand about the world, and then be able to control it. The roots of this belief lay in Francis Bacon's idea that knowledge equals power. The 18th-century scientist and clergyman Joseph Priestley (1733–1804), who among other things is credited with discovering oxygen, summarised popular thinking about the results of progress as follows in *An essay on the first principles of government: and on the nature of political, civil, and religious liberty*:

Abnormal

> All knowledge will be sub-divided and extended; and knowledge, as Lord Bacon observes, being power, the human powers will, in fact, be increased; nature, including both its materials, and its laws, will be more at our command; men will make their situation in this world abundantly more easy and comfortable; they will probably prolong their existence in it, and will grow daily more happy, each in himself, and more able (and, I believe, more disposed) to communicate happiness to others.

Priestley believed that this progress would eventually bring about the "Christian Millennium", the penultimate or 'Golden' age of life on earth. This belief enabled him — and many other theologians — to reconcile scientific and religious thought rather than seeing scientific discoveries as undermining religion.

It is hardly surprising that, given the speed with which society had changed over the past 300 years, the belief became dominant that learning about how the world works is the precursor to *controlling* it. As we have seen, religion had always taught that the natural world existed for humans to dominate and use, since humans possessed a divine essence that was not shared by other living beings, let alone plants and minerals. Humans, critically, were made in God's image, and God had created everything on the planet; surely humans, then, were destined to shape the world too?

In many ways, the belief that knowledge equals power proved to be true. Huge numbers of discoveries were being made about the world in the 19th century; vast numbers of more or less useful machines and other technologies were invented; and, critically, health was much improved as people finally began to understand how the body worked and, just as importantly, what caused disease. By the 20th century, the speed of development had accelerated still further, fuelled not so much by manufacturing as by communication and defence technologies. We are likely to look back on the 20th century as the Century of Science, as well as the point when for the first time man was able to match the destructive power of nature with the invention of nuclear weapons.

As seen in the previous chapter, medical knowledge and achievements proceeded to rocket ahead during the 20th century, including learning how to create life itself outside the body. Again, in many ways knowledge had indeed proved to be power. By the end of the 20th century, we had not only discovered DNA, but had been able to decode the human genome. Numerous media reports claimed that we would very soon be able to put an end to disease and extend human life almost indefinitely: the 21st century would be the century of the superhuman.

When we look at 20th-century ideas about the future of the body, we can clearly see the continuing influence of Descartes, Bacon et al. Descartes' concept of the body as a machine fuelled the belief that we could control the body still further, as we became skilled in building ever more complex machinery. If a machine goes wrong, it can be mended; if a machine is less efficient than it might be, then it can be improved; and there are always ways to develop machines beyond their initial function.

Plans to extend the body with prosthetics, and to 'improve' the brain with implants, are also the natural extension of ideas about the relentless march of progress towards perfection, and about the 'civilised body' being superior to the 'natural body'. Discussions about 'leaving the meat behind' as human brains are downloaded into computers also reflect a belief in the eternal mind that exists independently of the body, and in the Cartesian mind–body divide. I will discuss the scientific reality of these developments later in this book.

One lesson that we can learn from the Enlightenment is that ideas and perspectives on the world can change. The concepts and beliefs that people had adhered to for centuries, and in some cases millennia, were able to be revisited and changed within decades. Every year, science shows us that some of our assumptions have been wrong, as our means to examine and observe the world become ever more sophisticated. Less frequently, we also change our ideas about the very nature of scientific enquiry. Taking certain things for granted — Bacon's Idols of the Cave — does not make them 'right', or offer the only perspective on life. We need to continue to question, to doubt, to criticise — and to be open to changing our beliefs without being defensive about it. Only then will we be able to tackle our own and others' body dysphoria.

SECTION II

DIVIDING OURSELVES or, How we created disabled people

In the 21st century, the impact of technology and medical advances means that the possession of an 'abnormal' body has never been more irrelevant to the ability to live a 'normal' life (something that I will discuss in detail in Section IV). This is the case whether impairments are present from birth, are acquired during infancy or adult life, or are the consequence of ageing. However, at the same time, concerns about bodies that are less than 'perfect' seem to have gained in urgency rather than diminished.

More than ever, we are concerned to eliminate 'abnormality' in our own bodies and other people's, and to achieve a world where every body is perfect. This is despite the fact that, by the noughties, negative stereotyping of bodies as a result of gender and race had greatly lessened, and Black and female bodies were regarded as being just as capable of perfection as white men's. While people with terminal cancer campaign for access to drugs that will extend their lives for only a matter of weeks or months, those further from death and 'healthy' people argue for euthanasia and state-funded assisted suicide as being preferable to experiencing this level of illness.

In this section I explore how we treat the people who cannot, however hard they try, comply with the demand for 'normality' — a group that the vast majority of us are destined to join at some point in our lives, however unwelcome this thought is to us.

6. STEREOTYPES AND SHAME
or, The cultivation of the crip

How is it that we now live in a world where we have divided people into 'disabled' and 'non-disabled', and disabled people are widely regarded as 'suffering' and therefore better off dead? As we have already seen, in the 19th century there was believed to be a 'natural order', and at the top of this were non-disabled, fit, heterosexual, whiter than white men, with the majority of the population below them. Restoring the 'natural order', and keeping it 'in balance', was the underlying purpose of government, the law and science. This was essential, it was believed, in order to facilitate progress. Therefore, science replaced religion as that which 'evidenced' innate inferiority. At this point, though, disabled people were far less visible than all of the other 'deficient' people.

Deficient females

According to Darwin's *Descent of Man* (1871), 'natural selection' had meant that men had become superior to women in intellect, courage, energy and creative genius, and would always excel over women at art, science and philosophy. Women had evolved to become wives and mothers, roles that were seen as not requiring a great deal of intelligence or creativity at all. Darwin did consider women to be more intuitive and perceptive than men, but regarded this as simply being another sign of their 'natural' inferiority, since he associated these characteristics with the 'lower races' and with a 'lower state' of civilisation. Women were therefore 'naturally destined' to be men's companions rather than their equals, and their role in life was to reproduce and to bring up their families.

These ideas were eagerly developed by other scientists. Girls and women were regarded as being highly emotional by nature, and therefore to be incapable of rational thought and decision-making. 'Scientific' explanations were given to 'prove conclusively' that if women attempted to act like men, they would at best become infertile, and at worst become mentally and physically ill and collapse. As a result of the 'scientific' proof of women's inferiority, women continued to be denied the vote within European democracies. They were likewise believed to be incapable of receiving the same education as boys and men, let alone doing the same jobs.

Girls' education — where they received any at all — was therefore centred around their future role as wives and mothers. The proponents of girls' schooling in the late 19th and early 20th centuries had to argue that the purpose of education was to make women better 'companions' for their husbands, and better able to bring up their children, rather than to benefit them in their own right; only then did girls get an education at all. There was no thought that girls could be educated alongside boys, or could follow the same curriculum. Headteachers had to organise the curriculum in such a way as to protect girls' health, with plenty of time for rest and healthy outdoor exercise. It was only with the introduction of free and compulsory secondary education after the Second World War that British girls began to receive a secondary education alongside boys.

Although council-run 'elementary' schools had always been mixed, girls and boys had been educated separately within these wherever resources allowed, and had had separate entrances into the building and so on. Single-sex schools continued to be common within the state education system until the introduction of comprehensive education in the 1970s, when they dwindled to the minority that still exist today. Even then, it was not until the end of the 20th century that it was proved conclusively that girls could not only achieve the same results as boys in 'male' subjects such as mathematics, but could also outstrip them. Much 'scientific' evidence has since been gathered to 'prove' that boys are not more stupid than girls, but are simply less suited to the same curriculum that was originally developed solely to meet their needs. In truth, the jury is still out.

In the 21st century, many institutions and workplaces continue to reflect historic beliefs about women's supposed greater emotional instability and their inability to make rational decisions by having only a tiny minority of women working in senior positions. In reality, though, both science and history itself have long proved the non-existence of this 'biological inferiority'. Despite this, women's failure to throw off millennia of history and immediately become equal in every way is increasingly being evidenced now to show that the 'natural order' exists after all. And, of course, cultural beliefs about the inferiority of girls in developing countries contribute to the fact that as many as ten million female foetuses are estimated to have been aborted in India in the past 20 years, in addition to selective abortions taking place in other countries.

Racial stereotyping

Even more oppressive than the treatment of girls and women was the use of science in the 19th and 20th centuries to 'prove' that all non-white racial groups (and a fair number of white people) were fundamentally less able as a result of their inherent biology. As we have seen earlier, indigenous peoples were regarded as being earlier forms of humans, 'naturally' destined to disappear. Meanwhile, Africans were regarded as being child-like and of low intelligence but with superior physical strength, and 'naturally' destined to serve white people. Like women, Black and indigenous peoples were 'proven' to be ineducable beyond some very basic skills, and therefore, of course, to be unable to do the same jobs as white men.

Huge amounts of 'scientific' literature were used to prove this 'innate biological inferiority', and it is unsurprising that these beliefs still contribute, consciously or otherwise, to the way in which Black people are treated in Western societies today. It would have been unthinkable to these 19th- and 20th-century believers in racial 'science' that in the noughties a Black man would be elected as President of the United States. They might have been less surprised at the fact that in the noughties people from Black and minority ethnic backgrounds were three times as likely as white people to be admitted as inpatients to British mental health wards, due to a combination of racially biased diagnosis and treatment and the impact of racism on their mental health.

Even today, some social scientists argue that Black people are less intelligent than white people, using the results of IQ tests to 'prove' this. Others point out that these tests are inherently biased, and so any differential in results is meaningless. Although I myself have passed the entrance exams for Mensa (the high-IQ society), I lost any confidence in the testing regime after undergoing a battery of hospital tests at the turn of the millennium to assess the impact on my brain of a serious illness. In a test that asked me how I would find my way home in the event of being lost in a wood, I was given multiple answers to choose from, and was subsequently told that my answer was wrong because I hadn't chosen the option of climbing a tree in order to see further. I looked meaningfully at my wheelchair and then across at the doctor, but my 'failure' was still duly marked down. Whatever spurious intellectual credibility Mensa membership conveys, I am absolutely certain that IQ tests are designed for people from a particular background, culture and upbringing.

Back in the 19th century, as we have already seen, eugenicists also distinguished between different white 'races', with only the Nordic — or, as the Nazis named them, the Aryan — peoples regarded as being 'perfect'. From the 18th century onwards, poor white people had been thought to be biologically inferior too, with their poverty being caused by their inherited characteristics rather than by economics and the social class that they were born into. Eugenicists studying immigrants to the USA similarly concluded that the high incidence of poverty and ill health and the concentration of manual workers among certain national groups were biologically determined. As we have seen, the Nazis seized enthusiastically on this research, resulting in the Holocaust, which was based on the belief that certain white peoples — including Roma as well as Jews — were inferior to others.

Clearly, then, the 'normal' body has been defined for centuries as being male, white, non-disabled and middle or upper class. Being female and/or Black has been seen as equivalent to being disabled; female and Black bodies have been considered to be inherently inferior, and this has prevented equal participation in all areas of society. It was not until the 1970s that discrimination on the grounds of gender and race was outlawed in the United Kingdom. Many white people have also been defined as being impaired by their biology, and thus have not benefited from an education equal to that of others and have been deemed unsuited to a wide range of professions and careers. This might be because they originate from a particular country, or simply because they are poor.

Heterosexuality as the norm

The 'normal' body has, too, been considered to be heterosexual throughout history. Homosexuality (in its widest sense) has been regarded at best as a biological defect, an impairment in its own right, and at worst as a mortal sin and a hanging offence. From the 19th century onwards, psychologists classified homosexuality as a mental illness and, as with other chronic conditions, began to search for a 'cure'. Homosexuals were considered to be deviating from their 'natural' destiny to bond and reproduce with a member of the opposite sex, and were subjected to a wide range of 'therapies' in the name of treatment. It was hard for opponents of homosexuality to decide whether it should be eliminated because it prevents reproduction, or whether homosexuals should be prevented from reproducing anyway in order to prevent their genes from being passed on to future generations.

Treating homosexuals as being mentally ill only changed when decades of research consistently failed to find scientific evidence to support the belief that homosexuality was a psychiatric condition and that heterosexuality was the only 'natural' biological state. Far from being 'against nature', scientists found homosexual behaviour to be widespread in animal and bird populations, too. In the 1970s the American Psychiatric Association and the American Psychological Association finally removed homosexuality from their listing of mental illnesses, and this was echoed by some other countries. It was only in 1990, though, that the World Health Organisation removed homosexuality from its list of recognised diseases.

In the 21st century, a number of countries including the United Kingdom have allowed homosexuals to marry or to legalise their partnerships, and some have enacted legislation to outlaw discrimination on the grounds of sexual orientation. However, transgendered people still have to register for counselling and medical intervention in order to receive any protection under British law at all; they are clearly defined as having a 'medical problem'. Meanwhile, many other countries continue to criminalise homosexual acts, with some enacting the death penalty. Science, as well as religion, is still used to 'prove' that homosexuality is both immoral and a sickness — normal bodies being 'naturally' heterosexual. The gay body continues to be considered an impaired body in many parts of the world, as well as among significant proportions of the populations in countries that have officially rejected this belief as being unscientific.

Science, then, has long been used to justify inequality. At times, science has been used to 'prove' religious beliefs about the body; at others it has been used to maintain traditional divides within society after religious beliefs have become less dominant. However, as science has 'progressed', and as the owners of 'biologically inferior' bodies have asserted their equality, science has instead shown that the principles that governed the world for millennia were untrue. We are all members of one race, the human race, and whatever our gender, cultural heritage or sexual orientation, we can all benefit from the same level of education and we can all — given the opportunity — succeed in every walk of life. Nordic, white, heterosexual men are not biologically superior to the rest of us; being gay, coming from a different ethnic or cultural background or simply being female does not impair our bodies or our minds at all.

Remaining confused

At present, though, we are still in a terrible muddle when it comes to anything that we might term as being disability or ill health. We know that we are all a unique mixture of vulnerabilities, fragilities and strengths — emotional, intellectual and physical. We know that these will vary significantly over our lifetime, as well as being affected by many factors that are external to our bodies. We know that we are all asymmetrical; that we all experience physical and emotional pain which at times can be unbearable in its intensity; that all intelligence and ability to learn is on a continuum; and that none of us can live without physical and emotional support at times. We know — whether we choose to admit it or not — that one day it will be impossible to avoid the realisation that our eyesight, or hearing, or mobility, or our physical, mental or cognitive ability has reached the point at which the medical profession would classify us as being impaired.

We can conclude that the division of people into normal/abnormal, perfect/imperfect, intelligent/incompetent, well/sick, sane/mad, able-bodied/disabled is therefore without meaning. But we are not at all sure of the significance of all this, and are still enthusiastically adopting the view that death might easily be preferable to disability (something that we will explore later in this book). Most of us now believe that there is nothing 'wrong' with being Black, gay or female — so long as we are otherwise 'normal'. But if we are 'abnormal', even being white and male is not enough to put us 'right'. Our laws also reflect this confusion, with disabled people still being denied full human and civil rights (disability discrimination is the only type that can be 'justified' by law), whichever other human category they might also fit into.

Stigmatising disabled people

One particularly unhelpful factor has been that, traditionally, disabled people have been used as a comparator by other groups when fighting for equality; we are *not*, they say, like them. Therefore, women argued that they were *not* emotionally and physically fragile when campaigning for the vote. Likewise, lesbians and gay men argued for the right *not* to be regarded as being mentally impaired when urging their right to equality; and Black people argued that they were *not* mentally deficient when campaigning for civil rights. Later the women's liberation movement of the 1960s and 70s argued for the right *not* to have a disabled child as part of the campaign to legalise abortion, and for the right *not* to provide voluntary care for disabled children and adults in addition to their paid work as part of their struggle for equal rights: disabled people were *not* part of 'normal' families.

Speaking from personal experience, it is virtually impossible for issues that particularly affect disabled women, or disabled lesbian, gay, bisexual and transgendered (LGBT) people, to be discussed openly within the 'mainstream' of these equality movements today. Similar problems have been found within anti-racist organisations. It is as if we can only validate ourselves by comparing ourselves favourably to someone else; it is not enough simply to be ourselves. The fact that we are only comparing like with like seems to go unnoticed.

Attitudes towards disabled people have been reinforced by language. While language that reflects negative beliefs about people from Black and minority ethnic backgrounds has largely been consigned to the rubbish bin, the online Dictionary.com reflects all dictionaries when it includes the following definitions of the word 'lame':

> *–adjective*
> 3. weak; inadequate; unsatisfactory; clumsy: *a lame excuse*.
> 4. Slang. out of touch with modern fads or trends; unsophisticated.
> *–verb (used with object)*
> 5. to make lame or defective.
> *–noun*
> 6. Slang. a person who is out of touch with modern fads or trends, esp. one who is unsophisticated.

As for the term 'blind', it states the following:

> *–adjective*
> 2. unwilling or unable to perceive or understand: *They were blind to their children's faults. He was blind to all arguments.*
> 3. not characterized or determined by reason or control: *blind tenacity; blind chance.*
> 4. not having or based on reason or intelligence; absolute and unquestioning: *She had blind faith in his fidelity*.
> 5. lacking all consciousness or awareness: *a blind stupor*.
> 7. hard to see or understand: *blind reasoning*.
> *–verb (used with object)*
> 22. to deprive of discernment, reason, or judgment: *a resentment that blinds his good sense.*

> 36. without guidance or forethought: *They were working blind and couldn't anticipate the effects of their actions.*

And 'deaf':

> –adjective
> 2. refusing to listen, heed, or be persuaded; unreasonable or unyielding: *deaf to all advice.*

How have our beliefs about impairment, succinctly described above, impacted on those whose bodies or minds have been defined as 'abnormal' in the recent past? And how do these beliefs continue to resonate and affect people who are still being defined as 'abnormal' today? How have we created a false category of 'inferior' humans, and how, as with other 'inferior' humans, can we use science to consign this category to history as well? After all, our gender, race and sexual orientation are dictated, more or less, by birth, and if we change the way in which we are classified, it will be as a result of our own wishes. But, as I will continue to stress, any of us can find ourselves suddenly placed in the 'disabled' category without any notice or warning, however much we wish that this didn't happen. Does this reclassification or acquirement of an impairment really change anything so fundamental about us that we are suddenly no longer worthy of equality with the rest of society? Does it, in fact, actually change anything at all other than our treatment by other people?

The impact of stereotypes

It is unsurprising, given the religious and cultural beliefs about 'imperfect' bodies which have existed for millennia, that we have always regarded disabled people with suspicion and as being potentially threatening. As we have already seen, both mental and physical impairments have been regarded as signs of sinning, either in this life or in a previous existence, and the inferiority of people with impairments has been taken for granted. Often this has gone further, with disabled people being regarded as possessed by demons, or as consorting with the Devil. Why, though, do we retain so many of these suspicions and beliefs today?

A key factor has been popular culture, responsible for these teachings entering our consciousness through a wide range of different media in addition to religious writings. For millennia, storytellers have drawn on religion and relied on the shorthand of body type and appearance to denote character, with physical impairment being used to signify varying degrees of evil as well as inferiority. As a result, rather than being based on scientific evidence, our laws and policies towards the 'abnormal' have always been rooted in popular stereotypes. The impact of storytelling has meant that disabled people have provided the perfect scapegoat for centuries of policymaking, and this in turn has affected our beliefs still further. If religious leaders, storytellers, scientists *and* politicians repeatedly say that something is so, then we pretty much end up taking it for granted.

A range of academics, disabled and non-disabled and from a number of different disciplines, have now produced so much research into the representation of disabled people within popular culture that its accuracy cannot be doubted. (The example of film holds true also for theatre, television and online media, and so will suffice here.) Martin Norden (for the British Film Institute) has pointed out that in the development of cinema, disability provided a convenient visual shorthand for films that were by necessity silent, building on stereotypes that were already present in literature and which had no doubt predated the written word. This explains why a third of all films made before 1919 featured disabled characters, a proportion that was never reached again after sound and, later, colour offered other options for telling stories.

Disabled characters were included mostly for amusement value in early films (people with learning difficulties were the butt of many jokes), or to create fear by denoting evil. Stereotypes identified by Norden in the early period of cinema also include the disabled person as a complete innocent and/or pitiable; the disabled person bent on revenge for their 'suffering'; and, perhaps unsurprisingly, the disabled criminal fraudster. Equally unsurprisingly, more than a third of these films featured the disabled character eventually being cured, either through medicine, divine intervention or chance. Norden points out that in reality many of the impairments portrayed were in fact incurable. The overwhelming belief in the existence of a cure for everything despite all scientific evidence to the contrary was already well established by the early 20th century.

After the Second World War, these familiar images were joined by stories about disabled ex-servicemen, as films about social issues became popular at the box office. Here the disabled character — the 'crip with a chip' [on their shoulder] — needed to change their own attitude to their body and their community, rather than other people's reactions to them changing, and cures also featured heavily. Since impairment was viewed as defining disabled people, it was portrayed as being of overwhelming importance to them and, inevitably, as being overwhelmingly negative in its impact on their lives.

Later these films were replaced by stories of disabled people triumphing over the supposed tragedy of their lives, often with the help of non-disabled people, and often resulting in at least a partial cure. Again, disabled characters' own attitude was seen to be at fault when they had problems; and the fact that they were often outcasts was linked to the fact that their personality had been affected in some way by their impairment rather than to society's treatment of them.

Away from social cinema, disabled characters continued to be the baddies in everything from Bond movies to horror films. Norden points out that films such as *The Hunchback of Notre Dame* (the title says it all), *Treasure Island* (with the one-legged pirate Long John Silver) and *Peter Pan* (with the one-handed pirate Captain Hook) were continually being remade. Disabled baddies might be bent on revenging themselves on society for their impairment, and/or have become evil as a result of the impact of their impairment on their personality. Baddies might also be pretending to be impaired, or pretending to be good, the latter plot creating surprise when, at the end of the film, they were uncovered as the murderer. This reinforced the popular stereotype of disabled people as being untrustworthy, and potentially criminal.

Medical films continued to be popular at the end of the 20th century and the beginning of the 21st, particularly those made for daytime television, and 'real life' stories were preferred. Again, disabled characters generally needed to change their attitude with the help of a non-disabled person, and again cures often resulted. Overwhelmingly, characters 'triumphed over tragedy', whether this resulted in walking again or in mastering a new skill such as flying a plane. 'Supercrips' were common, managing to achieve things that non-disabled people could only dream of once they had first rid themselves of the inevitable chip on their shoulder.

Acting disabled

As the 20th century came to an end, these stereotypes continued, but there was a broadening of representation, and occasionally characters appeared within the mainstream who 'just happened' to be disabled. These roles, though, remained rare, and, as throughout the history of cinema, were usually played by non-disabled people. Since disabled people are widely regarded as being second-class, it has been hard for many producers and directors to believe that disabled actors are competent to take on even minor roles themselves, however good their professional training has been.

Even the 21st-century US hit TV series *Glee*, which supposedly focuses on the talents of minorities, features a wheelchair user played by a non-disabled actor, and who, unsurprisingly, dreams of being able to get out of his wheelchair and dance. The same even holds true of biographical films about disabled characters, the most famous, of course, being *My Left Foot* (1989), which told the life story of writer Christy Brown and starred Daniel Day-Lewis. All of this has the unfortunate effect of conveying the message to audiences that disabled people are incapable of acting well enough to play themselves, reinforcing any stereotyping that the character and plot conveys, and undermining any positive message.

Significantly, actors with genetic impairments such as Down's are most likely to play themselves today, since it is impossible to convince a sophisticated audience that a non-disabled person can be that 'abnormal'. This is beginning to convey the fact that people with learning difficulties are more able than other people imagine; but given that 90% of women opt to abort a Down's pregnancy, there is clearly a long way to go. Equally, people with other learning difficulties such as autism continue to be portrayed by non-disabled actors, as in *Rain Man* (1988) with Dustin Hoffman.

Deaf actors are now more likely than non-disabled actors to play sign language-using characters; however, in both television and film there has been a tendency for directors to cast hearing-impaired actors who can lip-read and speak English rather than actors whose first language is Sign, "to make it easier for the director to communicate [with the actor]". This has had the effect of making a fluid, sophisticated language appear clumsy and rudimentary, with some hearing-impaired actors actually learning British Sign Language (BSL) from scratch for the part. (Similarly, having non-disabled people play wheelchair users makes wheelchair use seem much more problematic and clumsy than it really is.)

As social issues returned to the cinema in the late 20th century, euthanasia also emerged as a theme. Disabled characters had been either killed or cured within popular literature from the foundation of the novel onwards, and this had later been echoed in film and on television. Disabled characters had also been portrayed as being burdens on those around them, whether this was the family members caring for them or the rest of society who paid for care. The message that people with significant impairments were better off dead had therefore been underlined from the early days of cinema. In tackling the subject of euthanasia, films such as *A*

Day in the Death of Joe Egg (1971) and later *Million Dollar Baby* (2004) simply propagated this message further.

Of course, there are positive examples of films that tackle disability issues and stories of disabled people's lives, and a small number of these films actually feature disabled actors. However, cinema — and television, theatre and online media — has overwhelmingly spawned the ideas that 'normal' characters aren't disabled; that disabled characters are either naïve or untrustworthy; that impairment is of overwhelming importance in the lives of disabled people and inevitably impacts on character; and that disabled people can't act. And all of these stereotypes build on those that were already present in literature.

Implicit stereotypes

Other stereotypes of disabled people are implicit in the representations described above too, all of which are far removed from the reality. Since 'normal' characters aren't disabled, it logically follows that disabled people don't lead 'normal' lives, with all of the wide-ranging implications of this. Since disabled people are the objects of pity, it follows that they can't be considered as equal to the rest of society. Since disabled people are the objects of care, it follows that they aren't carers themselves. Since 'deserving' disabled people are sweet and naïve, child-like and subject to victimisation, it follows that they need protecting. Since disabled people don't know how to behave appropriately, it follows that they need controlling. Since disabled people are untrustworthy — because of their naivety as well as their potential criminality — and out to revenge themselves for the tragedy of their lives, it follows that they need identifying and containing. And for all of these reasons, it follows that disabled people are incapable of benefiting from the same level of education as everyone else, and will hold back 'normal' children in the classroom.

Since disabled people don't have sex, it follows that they are not sexual. This is despite the fact that past segregation of disabled people was intended to ensure that they did not have sex and reproduce; disabled people's sexuality was always recognised by policymakers. However, it is now widely believed that disabled people are asexual and effectively genderless, rather than sexual activity simply being undesirable and unsuitable for them. When disabled people *are* represented as having sex, it is usually portrayed as being freakish and exoticised. Or it is problematic, perhaps only possible through the intervention of science. Or it is seen as inherently abusive, since if disabled people are child-like and natural victims, then they are incapable of giving informed consent and in any case will only attract perverts. So it follows that sexual relationships among and with disabled people should not be facilitated, but rather discouraged.

It follows, too, that disabled people don't have normal relationships, and so are not parents either. And, of course, if disabled people are child-like and need looking after themselves, then it follows that they are incapable of parenting in any case. It follows that disabled people should be prevented from having relationships, particularly when they have learning difficulties. It follows, too, that disabled people should be prevented from having children, and if not, should have their children removed and brought up by someone else.

Since some disabled people can be brave enough to triumph over the tragedy of their lives, it follows that others could if they tried harder. Since disabled people have chips on their shoulders, it follows that their complaints should not be taken seriously. Since disabled people's problems are due to their 'abnormal' bodies, it follows that any difficulties they experience can only be dealt with by a cure in any case. Since disabled people are obsessed with their impairments, it follows that they are selfish and self-centred. Since disabled people hate being disabled, it follows that their overwhelming desire is to be non-disabled. And since disability is biological — even if that is characterised simply by the possession of a defective personality that results in someone 'failing' to get better, or by being clumsy enough to have an accident — it follows that non-disabled members of a disabled person's family are equally undesirable as workmates, playmates and partners. And if disabled people don't appear to fit into any of the other stereotypes above, then it follows that they must be lying about being disabled in the first place.

Stereotypes and the media

These stereotypes are reinforced by charitable images, whose impact is magnified by the fact that they are often the only images of disabled people to appear within advertising and print media. A vast number of charities were set up in the 18th and 19th centuries to help the 'deserving poor', of which more later. By the 20th century, certain stereotypes proved to be particularly effective at raising funds. Disabled children and adults were pictured as being equally pathetic and pitiable, suffering bravely but horribly as a result of their conditions, and in dire need of help and support from non-disabled people to triumph over the tragedy of their lives and if possible to obtain a cure. It may or may not be needless to say that the vast majority of charity workers, both voluntary and professional, were not classified as being disabled themselves.

Apart from charitable images and images of people experiencing mental illness as being violent and dangerous, 'factual' television programming today tends to highlight one overwhelming image of disabled people: as freaks. People with unusual bodies have been put on display throughout history, as have 'lunatics' (people used to visit the original Bethlem asylum — known also as Bedlam — and pay to watch the inmates). However, this did not become part of mainstream popular entertainment until the end of the 18th century. By the middle of the 19th century, though, freak shows had become popular in Europe as well as America, both as independent attractions and as part of travelling circuses and fairs. Their popularity was linked to the growth of interest in science and evolution, with people who had unusual bodies being seen as 'throwbacks' to earlier forms of human, as well as being regarded as 'freaks of nature'. Often, the 'entertainment' simply consisted of people carrying out 'normal' daily activities, such as washing and shaving.

Today, disabled people are seen as being equally 'freakish' whether or not their bodies appear to be 'different'; they are viewed as representing a category of human being that will soon disappear as science develops cures for them. As with the freak show, television documentaries often focus on disabled people going about their normal daily lives, as well as showing their interactions with the medical system since their lives are believed to centre around their conditions. Huge amounts of scientific detail are provided about someone's diagnosis, symptoms and the impact of these on their life — detail that is inevitably selected and framed according to the programme makers' beliefs. Despite this effort to achieve scientific credibility, many disabled people simply regard this type of programming as 'crip porn'.

Freak-show television has largely replaced the 'triumph over tragedy' programming of the late 20th century, although a combined sub-genre has developed, whereby disabled people are placed in extreme situations while we watch them cope. In 2010, Channel 4 integrated all three clichéd forms when it branded its Paralympic marketing campaign "Freaks of Nature". The initial programming consisted of a series of documentaries which focused on athletes' medical conditions and intimate details of their bodies along with their sporting prowess: this was described as being "exciting new science". When challenged, Channel 4 described this activity as "widening the audience for disability sport" — freak shows have always been able to attract viewers in large numbers. In contrast, the BBC, who had previously held the contract, had always taken care to report Paralympic sport in exactly the same way as the rest of its sporting coverage. 'Progress' certainly can't be taken for granted.

The impact on the individual

Freak-show television adds to the perception of disabled bodies as public bodies, with other people feeling entitled to ask personal questions about them whenever they wish. This is a prelude to judgement — finding out 'what's wrong' is a means of determining whether someone falls into the 'deserving' or the 'undeserving' category. As I discovered for myself, being asked 'What's wrong with you?' by complete strangers is one of the first things that disabled people become familiar with when they start to use a cane or a wheelchair. Finding out that an answer is expected is the second, with any anger expressed at this intrusion being put down to the ubiquitous 'chip' rather than being seen as justified. (It is probably necessary to note here that successive scientific studies have found disabled people to be neither more nor less 'well adjusted' than anyone else.)

It is unsurprising in the circumstances that the vast majority of disabled people have never recognised themselves in the portrayal of disabled characters within popular culture and media imagery. And further, that most people who would be defined as 'disabled' under current legislation do not identify with the term at all. Often disabled people wish to avoid other disabled people at all costs, since they have absorbed the negative stereotypes along with the rest of us, and also wish to avoid being 'outed' by association. Despite the myth that people who share the same medical diagnosis will experience their condition in the same way and will be similarly affected by their symptoms, in fact even these groups have little or nothing in common, and only a minority will want ongoing support from each other. Sign language users, the only group who do form traditional communities, do not consider themselves to be disabled in any case, but rather to be a language and cultural minority. Since they have a non-oral language, the fact that they cannot hear appears irrelevant to them.

The reality is that we are all 'normal', and that impairment and illness are simply normal aspects of the human condition: one in ten Britons of working age and one in five of all Britons are officially regarded as being disabled. Instead of being united by their impairments, people who form the 'disability community' share the same experience of social exclusion and isolation. Fellow 'sufferers' are the only people who can be relied upon to recognise and treat each other as being 'normal', as well as having a good understanding of how to meet each other's access needs. This is why issues surrounding disability rights cut across the whole range of learning difficulties, physical and sensory impairments and mental illness. As with any equality movement, disability rights campaigners are concerned with the way in which they are treated as a result of their bodies. Otherwise they believe that they have as much — or as little — in common with everyone else as they do with other disabled people.

Impairment may be a negative experience, or it may not: one person's tragedy is another person's opportunity and yet another person's normality. All sudden and unexpected changes in life are traumatic, but this trauma is not normally expected to last for the rest of one's life and to change fundamental aspects of one's character, as impairment-related trauma is believed to do. And in reality, of course, most people who acquire an impairment later in life do adjust sooner rather than later — even if many redevelop self-esteem and self-respect only by reassuring themselves that they are 'not really disabled at all', since their personalities and lives bear no relationship to the stereotypes that surround them. Indeed, many people with non-standard bodies and appearances are perfectly healthy, and are not 'suffering' as a result of them.

It is unsurprising, though, that people mostly *do* react traumatically when they suddenly receive a disability diagnosis, and may well go on to internalise the lessons that society teaches them about themselves as well as distancing themselves from others with the same label. As the stereotypes discussed above show, disability is overwhelmingly associated with negativity, with disabled people regarded as being unfit even to portray their own lives in theatres and on film and television, and often regarded as being better off dead. No wonder that we find it hard to recast 'abnormal' bodies as being equal, and no wonder we are so anxious to avoid being labelled abnormal ourselves.

7. MIRACULOUS MEDICINE
or, What can't be cured must be ignored

As we have seen, disabled people have been publicly identified by their supposed medical condition from the early days of modern medicine. This is linked to the fact that the 'abnormal body' has been central to the development of medicine since the 19th century, with the restoration of 'normality' being medicine's overwhelming aim. Any body that has not been regarded as normal has been regarded as 'diseased' — as having 'problems' that can be medically classified, and that require medical intervention and supervision whether or not they can be 'cured'. This category has included people who simply happen to have been born deaf or blind, with fewer limbs than usual or with an extra chromosome (people who are to all intents and purposes perfectly fit and healthy), as well as people who are ageing.

From the 19th century onwards, our overwhelming belief has been that, sooner rather than later, medicine will be able to cure these 'diseases', at which point formerly diseased people will join the rest of us as we move towards a state of immortality. If a cure is not possible, then we believe the further development of foetal testing and genetic medicine will ensure that 'diseased' babies are no longer born. At no point have we considered instead that 'abnormality' will have any part in our future, let alone be integral to it. In the mean time, as we have seen, we continue to view disabled people through a range of stereotypes, clouded further by suspicion.

Blaming the victim

Our belief in the ever-present cure has been fuelled by medical advances in the 19th and 20th centuries which meant that many people lived who would previously have died, and many people remained fit and healthy who would otherwise have had a lifetime of poor health. While improvements in nutrition, hygiene and housing had the biggest effect on the health of the population as a whole, medicine had a huge impact on the lives of many individuals and their families and friends. As we have seen, doctors seemed literally to have power over life and death, and to have no limits.

In the space of a few decades over the middle of the 20th century, treatments or cures were discovered for a wide range of conditions that would otherwise have led to an early death. No wonder we find it hard to accept that there are limits to the power of scientists and doctors, even when they have already accepted their own; medicine in the past two centuries appeared to be literally miraculous. In the noughties, when new developments had slowed down, media reports still promised us daily that new cures were just around the corner, reassuring us that science had lost none of its power.

Given all of this, it is unsurprising that, during the same period, people who did not 'get better' were increasingly equated with fraudsters, or with people who simply did not try hard enough to triumph over the tragedy of their condition. Illness has long been regarded as an expression of character; as we have seen, the theory of the four humours which persisted for nearly two millennia delineated four types of character, each of which reflected an imbalance in the relevant humour. This was not always seen as pejorative. For example, in the 19th century tuberculosis was popularly regarded as a disease that only delicate, sensitive people — in the parlance of the four humours, 'melancholic' people — developed. As Susan Sontag pointed out in *Illness as Metaphor* (1978), 19th-century literature abounds with descriptions of painless, beautiful, passive, resigned deaths from TB. Romantic novelists saw TB as conveying glamour on its sufferers — and, of course, they regarded the acceptance of death as being more 'natural' than the pursuit of scientific cures.

Although by this time scientists had already replaced the theory of the humours with the concept of abnormality, deviation from the 'norm', this did not stop them from continuing to believe in a relationship between character and illness. However, scientists took a less rosy view than the Romantics, blaming the victim instead of praising them. Until Robert Koch discovered the tubercle bacillus in 1882, tuberculosis was believed by scientists to arise from a combination of circumstances, including biological heritage and "depressing emotions".

In all, from the 19th century onwards, theories were developed to suggest that a wide range of illnesses were effectively caused by the possession of a 'weak' character, or by the repression or expression of emotions. The perceived separation between the mind and the body also led to the belief that if someone's will was strong enough, they could overcome any illness: the mind could control the body and dictate what happened to it. This belief still persists today despite being contradicted by numerous scientific studies.

Often, of course, images of people 'triumphing' over their conditions were very partial, as were images of 'fraudsters'. As we have seen, in the late 19th and early 20th centuries, both charities and popular culture presented images of 'cures' that did not in reality take place. The modern athlete who runs for miles on prosthetic legs may in fact have appalling problems with blistered and bleeding stumps and spend much of the time at home using a wheelchair, but this is not seen in the photograph of them triumphantly crossing the finish line. The person with cancer who fundraises for charity may spend most of their day in bed, but this is not visible at the televised award ceremony. Meanwhile, the person who is spotted out shopping occasionally with apparently nothing the matter with them may be housebound, and indeed bed-bound, the rest of the time.

The paucity of images of disabled people, though, and the stereotypes that abounded, meant that these and other issues seldom, if ever, came to light. Disabled people themselves have always been put under extreme pressure to show how well they are 'coping' and to hide any difficulties that might spoil their 'triumph', and this makes it even harder to see the reality of their lives. Disabled people buy into stereotypes just like everyone else, and are highly reluctant to disclose any difficulties that might suggest they are less able to manage than the 'supercrips'.

The problems with categorising and classifying people

It did not help that many disabled people had unglamorous, and indeed often unclear, diagnoses. From the beginning of medical practice onwards there was an emphasis on categorisation and classification of medical conditions, as with the Babylonian doctors who had to decide which of more than 6000 demons were responsible for causing their patient's symptoms. This emphasis on categorisation reached its peak in the 19th century, as medicine became increasingly scientific. Doctors were encouraged to observe symptoms, discover causes and note similarities and to share these findings with their colleagues, and this contributed a great deal to medical 'progress'. Photography played an important part in this process, contributing to the belief in the disabled body as a public body and acting as the forerunner to the 'medical' documentary.

However, although these classifications appeared to be clear and distinct, in fact they were constantly changing. Conditions that were originally thought to result from the same cause turned out to have completely separate causes; conditions that were originally thought to be completely different turned out to have the same cause; and conditions thought to result from one cause turned out to result from quite another. Often conditions that were originally thought to have psychological causes turned out to be physical in origin, while occasionally conditions that were thought to have physical causes turned out to be psychological. Sometimes conditions were reclassified as not being health problems after all, as with the example of homosexuality. This process, of course, continues today.

For patients, this just compounded the confusion caused by doctors' failure to find a cure for them. It is hard to understand why, when you have been taking your medicine for years as prescribed by an 'expert', it can suddenly turn out to have been useless beyond having had a placebo effect, and that the cause of your condition is something entirely different from what you had previously understood it to be. It is equally hard to understand why in many cases doctors are not concerned with finding out the cause of your condition at all, but only with treating the symptoms of it, leaving you without a convenient label at all. And it is particularly hard to understand why, when doctors seem to have power over life and death, they cannot find a successful treatment, let alone a cure, for a condition that appears to be straightforward and simple in comparison, and which has a disproportionate impact on the way that you live your life.

The classification system has always caused other confusions, too. Someone whose condition has a single cause may see multiple doctors, each specialising in a different area, to treat their symptoms, none of whom look at the patient's health as a whole. Or, particularly with less glamorous diagnoses, someone with several different symptoms may see just one doctor who has no expertise in treating any of them. In both these cases patients miss out on valuable treatment, and as a result are more impaired than they need be.

By middle age, if not before, disabled people may also have multiple conditions that are variously labelled 'mental illness', 'physical illness', 'disability', and quite possibly 'learning difficulties' as well. Since the classification system dominates, local strategies for meeting the needs of disabled and older people are separated out into these four strands and more. Individuals are left to decide which category they best fit into — or more often are categorised by the authorities — while the needs that they have as a result of their other conditions go unmet.

Despite these innate limitations, medical classifications have dominated the treatment of 'abnormal' people, by society as much as by medical professionals, and continue to do so relentlessly today. Indeed, medical diagnoses are seen to define individuals, encompassing everything about their life and personality: individual identities are replaced by medical identities such as 'arthritics', 'epileptics', 'diabetics' and so on and so forth. Administrators use diagnoses to determine what benefits and services are provided to disabled people, while the law uses diagnoses to determine who is protected by anti-discrimination legislation. Members of the public want a diagnosis when they ask, 'What's wrong with you?', since they believe that this information is vital to enable them to classify and thus to understand a disabled individual themselves. This impression has, of course, been reinforced by the various charities that grew up around medical classifications, since it is necessary to portray a 'community' of people with a specific impairment who have particular needs defined by that impairment in order to attract funding to target that group.

It is unsurprising that some groups of disabled people who do have straightforward diagnoses have adopted these to describe themselves, particularly people with spinal injuries: "I'm a T4 incomplete" or "C3 complete" (referring to the vertebra that has been fractured). This is despite the fact that, as with all medical conditions, every individual with a spinal impairment will be affected differently by it. The reality is that knowing an individual's medical classification will tell you nothing about their experiences or needs, whatever the beliefs to the contrary. However, everything about the way in which we treat disabled people within our society is based on the assumption that diagnoses are infallible and all-encompassing, and disabled people find it easier to comply with this where possible than to try to explain otherwise.

The medical model of disability

Classifying and labelling people according to their medical diagnoses have several unfortunate results. First, a person's individuality and personality becomes hidden behind their impairments: 'normal' people, as well as the medical profession, tend to treat everyone with a common impairment in the same way. This means that the bulk of disabled people's lives become invisible, while their medical condition is regarded as being overwhelmingly important to them and thus worthy of focusing their lives around, whatever the evidence to the contrary.

Then the individual needs that do arise from an impairment become invisible too, since everyone who shares an impairment is wrongly believed to have the same experiences. One effect of this is that non-medically qualified administrators rely on medical records to determine benefit and support service levels, rather than on an individual's actual circumstances. Then people who have a different diagnosis but whose needs are the same — perhaps for wheelchair access, or for a particular type of seating — are left out when charitable provision is being made for the group who are being targeted as a result of their medical label. Finally, of course, the lack of visibility — and the perceived unimportance — of individual experiences allow stereotypes to flourish unchallenged.

The emphasis on medical categorisation also reinforces the belief that any difficulties that disabled people experience in society result directly from their medical conditions, from their diagnosed 'abnormalities'. In this context, disability is seen as being a personal problem that can only be relieved by a medical expert: neither the disabled person themselves nor anyone else can act to change their experiences of the world. This is a perspective known as the 'medical model of disability'.

To give a simple example, in viewing life from this perspective we would see a wheelchair user's inability to get up some steps into a building as being the direct result of their imperfect body; only a doctor can achieve change, if they can find a treatment that will allow the person to walk. Looking at the same case from the perspective of a 'social model of disability', it is the environment that becomes the issue: the failure of the architect, planning authorities, builder and operator of the building to provide an alternative means of entry such as a ramp or a stairlift. This is something that all of us can work to change, rather than waiting for possible but improbable advances in medical treatment. Viewing life from a social model of disability perspective enables disability to be viewed as something that is artificially created by the rest of society, and that can just as easily be altered. Or, in other words, from a medical model viewpoint, the person with the impairment causes problems for society; whereas from a social model viewpoint, it is society that causes problems for the person with the impairment — that causes the 'suffering'.

The medical model of disability also affects how money is spent on treatments. Overall, technological treatments and drug therapies — prescribed by doctors and often associated with more glamorous medical classifications — are regarded as being more effective than lower-tech treatments that are provided by 'lesser' medical professionals. Spending money on treatments that will not save lives or effect cures is also seen as pointless and a waste of money, particularly given the poor public image of the recipients.

Therefore, talking therapies may improve the quality of life immeasurably for people with mental illness, and ongoing physiotherapy may have similar benefits for people with mobility problems — but pills are much cheaper. Talking to patients, or providing hands-on therapies for their bodies, is neither high-tech nor sexy, and is not seen as having anything to do with power over life and death (even when, in reality, these therapies can save lives). This leaves millions of people who have chronic conditions such as back pain or depression with far higher levels of impairment than they would otherwise experience.

Experimental medicine

Of course, it was not always like this. Before the medical profession reached the conclusion that some conditions were effectively not worth treating beyond drug therapies, and that in some cases people were better off not being born, a great deal of experimentation had taken place. The Cartesian concept of the body as a machine went hand in hand with an assumption that it could be 'fixed' so long as its workings were understood sufficiently, and experimentation was the means to achieve this understanding. Experimentation also enabled doctors to learn much more about the workings of the body and to apply this knowledge to 'normal' people, people who were more cost-effective to treat. Disabled people, in this context, were then seen as being irretrievably broken — a state which, as we have already seen, was often blamed on disabled people themselves for having defective personalities and for 'not trying hard enough' to get better.

Modern hospitals, as distinct from the infirmaries run by religious orders, were developed from the 18th century onwards and were always sites for experimentation. In addition to charging fees where patients could afford it, infirmaries were initially supported by charitable donations and Poor Law funds, and later by insurance payments, employers' contributions and other contributory schemes. With the development of 'indoor relief', infirmaries were also developed as part of workhouses, and were then gradually taken over by local authorities in the 1930s. In the Second World War all infirmaries were incorporated into the Emergency Medical Service, and afterwards they were absorbed, often reluctantly, into the National Health Service. Alongside these, some wholly private institutions operated, but the wealthy were more likely to be treated at home until the introduction of medical technologies made in-patient treatment preferable.

Perhaps it is unnecessary to state that the purpose of the infirmaries was to find a way to effect cures, to return people to a state whereby they were able to work rather than being a 'burden' on the rest of society. This included attempting to standardise otherwise already healthy bodies in order to meet the demands of the workplace. As we have seen, in the context of Enlightenment beliefs, science was the engine by which progress would be driven, resulting in economic growth, and doctors had to ensure that they worked within this paradigm. Inevitably, this meant that the emphasis was soon on treating and curing people with acute conditions; there was little interest in continuing to alleviate the condition of people with chronic illnesses or impairments once it had been established that no cure was possible. This approach, of course, continues to be taken by health providers today.

However, the medical profession did not give up easily. A great deal of experimenting took place before it was accepted that a wide range of conditions would not respond significantly to medical intervention, and in the process successful treatments were found for many other conditions. Experimentation was made easier by the fact that, for reasons which we have already touched on, the patients being treated were largely poor and disempowered, so it was simple to make them accept that 'doctor knows best'. Infirmary regimes were developed that involved stripping patients of their clothes and possessions, controlling everything about their day and restricting visitors to once a week at most, making it impossible for patients to argue. If they did, though, doctors had developed a wide range of 'therapies' to control behaviour, the use of which was not restricted to asylums.

Certain conditions were particularly attractive to doctors seeking to develop cures: these tended to be conditions that affected the ability to work in the modern industrial environment. Eye conditions were the first focus of specialist hospitals, but orthopaedics later became dominant. Significantly, both of these areas were ones where surgery became the dominant medical profession. This followed centuries of separation between surgeons and physicians, when surgeons were given a much lower status. Discovering how to use surgery to effect cures, then, was a way of boosting surgeons' professional status, and today their relative position compared to physicians has been completely reversed as a result.

The growth in surgical possibilities was of course related to the discovery of antiseptic techniques and anaesthesia, which made surgery far safer and more effective as well as far less unpleasant for the patient. This enabled surgeons to develop operations to 'correct' birth impairments such as club foot — a condition that often made it difficult for someone to find work; and for most of the 19th century, orthopaedic surgery was focused mainly on conditions of the feet.

However, surgery was only part of the picture when it came to orthopaedic treatments. Although fractured limbs had often been amputated in the past, the development of techniques to set bones made surgery far less necessary, and treatment was focused on rehabilitating limbs afterwards. Despite this expertise, though, the British Medical Association estimated in 1935 that 37% of people who sustained fractures remained disabled by these for the rest of their lives. Access to treatment was too expensive for many, and charities remained largely interested in children, while family doctors remained ignorant of correct bone-setting and splinting techniques. Rehabilitation was also restricted to the hospitals, which further limited the chance of making a full recovery from a fracture, and improvements really only took place as a result of the Second World War, of which more below.

(People who had sustained fractures were, of course, also regarded as being careless for having had an accident in the first place. In order to believe that disability can never happen to us, we have to believe that the disabled person is themselves to blame; this also perpetuates the idea that no victim can ever be innocent of sin. This seems always to have been the case, as John Williams-Searle shows in his study of late 19th-century American railroad workers. Blaming the victim fuels our anger at the 'compensation culture' today; we continue to believe that the real person at fault is the victim rather than the person who caused the accident, so they should fund the cost of the consequences themselves. This in turn fuels the scorn heaped on 'health and safety' regulatory measures.)

Alongside surgery and the treatment of fractures, from the 19th century onwards orthopaedic hospitals offered a wide range of therapies. Again, these were aimed at 'normalising' people with conditions that might result from poor nutrition — particularly rickets — as well as treating injuries, illnesses and birth conditions in order to get people into employment. Treatments included 'fresh air therapies' (the patients often being made to sleep as well as live outside), massage and physiotherapy, electrical therapies and exercise regimes. Patients often spent months or years in treatment, although few real improvements might result. However, in order to continue to attract funds, exaggerated claims were made for success rates in 'curing cripples' and getting them into the workplace.

Abnormal

By the 20th century, though, orthopaedic medicine and related neurological practices were driven by war rather than the desire to cure impairments that had existed since childhood. The majority of servicemen who were injured in the First World War had conditions that affected their mobility, with spinal cord injuries from gunshots and aircraft crashes, as well as fractures and amputations. This led to a huge rise in demand for orthopaedic services in an attempt to make injured servicemen economically independent, and preferably 'normal' again. By 1936 there were 40 orthopaedic hospitals in the UK, and 400 orthopaedic clinics. 'Rehabilitation' — physiotherapy, occupational therapy and the like — was an important part of their regimes.

It was only in the latter half of the Second World War, though, that rehabilitation was widely introduced into all hospitals, not just for orthopaedic patients but for everyone who could potentially benefit. Unfortunately, this helped to put the onus for the success or failure of a cure even more squarely on the patient than it had been in the past. If a patient failed to get better, it was not because the doctor had failed to cure them, it was because they had not worked hard enough at their rehabilitation. This reinforced the stereotype of disabled people as being lazy, and left the power of the medical profession unchallenged. In the process, many people's bodies were damaged further, since exercise can often be counter-productive to a wide range of conditions. (As a trained dancer, I remember my own frustration at later discovering that exercise had a negative impact on my spinal condition. I had grown up believing that the more you exercised, the fitter you became, and that any obstacle at all could be overcome by hard work.)

From the end of the war onwards, another specialism developed that was related to orthopaedics: the treatment of spinal cord injuries and other damage to the central nervous system. Again, surgery to normalise bodies as much as possible was combined with rehabilitation aimed at returning people to living as 'normal' a life as possible despite any lasting impairments that they might have. Mechanical engineering soon became part of the equation too, and was used within prosthetics as well as in attempts to return the power of walking to paralysed people. Many children with 'abnormal' limbs had these amputated to make prosthetics easier to fit, in the belief that these would function better than their own bodies.

Classifying and curing children

After the Second World War, concerted efforts were made to redirect resources at the wholesale cure of 'crippled children', using the skills that had been developed on veterans. Children, it was believed, were more amenable to being cured than adults, since their bodies were still growing. Children were also more attractive to charitable donors than adults, and had thus been used to target donors since the 19th century. The charities for 'crippled children' sought funds by stressing that every child could potentially be cured, made 'normal', and therefore could be made economically independent with medical help. Donors were needed since the majority of 'child cripples' were poor, often with conditions that had resulted from poverty such as rickets, rather than their poverty being caused by acquiring their impairment, as was more often the case with adults. The fact that the majority of child patients were poor made them ideal material for experimentation, as well as encouraging a culture where abuse was common.

Long-stay hospitals provided education for child patients alongside therapies, and this helped to establish the principle of segregation within education. Segregation of 'abnormal' children had already been established with the foundation of charitable schools for blind and Deaf children at the end of the 18th century, and this helped to gain acceptance of the principle that disabled children should be taken out of the mainstream. But at the point when the first schools for blind and Deaf children were founded, many children did not attend school at all, and very few children with any kind of impairment received an education. However, Enlightenment values dictated that blind and Deaf children could be brought closer to God and — of course — made economically independent if they were provided with education and training, the children all initially coming from the 'deserving poor'. In order to raise funds, charities stressed the 'tragedy' of sensory impairment, and how this could be overcome, not by medicine, but by education. Education would enable children to become Christians, as well as enabling them to learn how to earn their own living.

Medicine might not have played a significant role in the blind and Deaf schools of the 19th and 20th centuries, but normalisation certainly did. From the middle of the 19th century onwards, Deaf children were increasingly forbidden from learning and using their mother tongue — sign language. Instead they were forced to try to learn to lip-read and speak, without any supporting information in sign language about how to do this. As with indigenous children, they were routinely punished for using their own language. Lip-reading and oral language were presented as being skills that could be acquired by anyone if they tried hard enough, so any failures were, once again, put down to Deaf children's laziness and defective personalities.

Exaggerated claims continued to be made for lip-reading and oralism in the 20th century, resulting in many Deaf children being left without any language in which they could be truly fluent. It was not until 2003 that the British Government recognised British Sign Language as a language in its own right, and this made people realise the importance of teaching all Deaf children to sign, whether or not this accompanied oralism and lip-reading. This was followed in the teens with research that showed that teaching non-hearing impaired infants to sign actually improved their acquisition of oral language.

The growth of 'special schools'

Returning to the past: following the establishment of schools for children with sensory impairments, children with learning difficulties — 'idiots' — were the next targets of 19th-century educators. This followed French interest in the impact of different teaching techniques, principally exercises, on developing 'normal' brain activity in 'idiots'. These exercises were, of course, intended to effect a cure, or at least an improvement, in a child's condition, and, again, the child could be blamed for not trying hard enough if this failed to work. Again, most of the pupils were from the 'deserving poor', and again this left them open to being studied and experimented on as well as being abused.

'Idiots' became particularly interesting to scientists as theories of evolution became more popular, and opinions were often divided as to whether conditions resulted from genetic 'throwbacks' to earlier forms of humanity or were caused by a physical condition. As Black people, women and homosexuals were considered to be 'mentally deficient' in addition to people with learning difficulties, research findings relating to disabled people were considered to have a wider relevance, too. The Victorian 'science' of phrenology also meant that researchers were keen to study facial types and the shapes of pupils' heads, in order to determine how to identify 'idiots' more easily. (Phrenology was based on the belief that character could be determined from studying the structure of the skull, and was linked to the belief that poverty and criminality were biologically determined.)

By the turn of the 20th century, researchers had concluded that the 'mentally deficient' were definitely abnormal, and this meant that their condition was re-categorised as being a medical problem or disease. As a result — and unlike the schools for children with sensory impairments — the medical profession was given control rather than educators, in institutions for children as well as for adults. Therapies therefore became central to what soon became termed 'special schools', with education taking second place.

Medical control was given further impetus by the fact that children with physical impairments or long-term health conditions — children defined as being innately 'deficient' — were increasingly also sent to special schools. Blind and Deaf children were often thought to be intellectually limited as a result of their conditions, so they ended up in special schools, too; it didn't help that specialist schools for blind and Deaf pupils tended to be boarding establishments that were not available throughout the country, and to which working-class children had very limited access.

From the authorities' point of view, this expansion of 'special school' provision was primarily in order that disabled children did not 'hold back' or 'upset' the rest of their peers. However, the availability of medicalised therapies also made the schools attractive to administrators, since the prospect of a 'cure' was once more on offer. There was a clear advantage to the state if disabled children grew up to become 'normal' adults. As a result, after the Second World War the number of children attending special schools more than doubled, in addition to another 20,000 pupils who had previously been provided with education by the health system.

This expansion was despite the fact that the teaching provided in special schools was based on the assumption that every pupil would be limited in their ability to learn. Since all children with significant impairments were by now regarded as being unlikely ever to work beyond a manual job, it seemed pointlessly expensive to offer a more demanding curriculum than the least able could manage. Given the hope of a 'cure', though, therapy seemed more important than education, so pupils were regularly withdrawn from classes to receive 'treatment' — a practice that continues in the 21st century. No wonder that the campaign to end segregation was founded and is led by former pupils.

A change of focus

Only towards the end of the 20th century did it become apparent that medical science and engineering had their limits, something that I will discuss further in the next section. The medical profession, depressed at the successive failures of 'treatments' for people with spinal cord injuries or whose bodies had been damaged by thalidomide, lost interest in experiments that could, in any case, only benefit a small proportion of society. At the same time, medical research had become almost completely separate from medical practice, with most research now taking place at the cellular level in laboratories far removed from medical establishments.

Meanwhile, cost-cutting by successive governments meant that long hospital stays were replaced by day surgeries and home nursing. In the early 1980s, Prime Minister Margaret Thatcher in particular denied that citizens could have a responsibility towards each other unless they were a 'family member' — "there is no such thing as society" — and left hundreds of thousands of former and potential inmates of residential institutions to 'manage' in a world that had become used to living without them. The potential for scientific studies subsequently diminished, since the closure of institutions made it impossible for doctors to control their patients' conditions and observe them on a daily basis, both of which were necessary to meet the standards for scientific studies.

Attention instead became more focused on acute medicine, whereby doctors could influence life-and-death and quality-of-life issues most effectively. Research was also easier in this setting, particularly with the introduction of computers to process data, and a growing interest in clinical quality. (The recent use of statistics to halt surgeries and intervene early when problems arise with care quality, rather than waiting years before daring to challenge 'experts', shows the direct benefits that data can provide in acute settings once we can accept human limitations.)

As disabled adults moved out of institutions, they also began to make their voices heard about their experiences of segregation, not least the abuse that many of them had experienced in institutions, but also the effects of being excluded from mainstream education. Despite a lifetime of being told otherwise, they asserted their right to be considered normal. This fuelled families' attempts to have their children educated alongside their non-disabled peers, and led, at the end of the 20th century, to the founding of organisations such as Parents for Inclusion and the Alliance for Inclusive Education. Whereas some parents understandably wanted to see their children 'protected' in a segregated education system, many others wanted their children to be recognised as being 'normal' rather than 'sick', and to have provision made for their needs within the mainstream (including providing any treatment and therapy out of school hours).

Today, disabled children are still denied the right to a mainstream education — at the end of the noughties, the British Government opted out of the relevant clause of the UN Convention on the Rights of Persons with

Disabilities, having signed up to the majority of the rest. However, 'inclusive' education is the preferred policy, not least because of cost savings. Campaigners point out, though, that we have yet to see 'real' inclusive educational practice, as disabled children are often left to sit in mainstream classrooms with only the support of an unqualified assistant. As a result, seven out of ten children who are permanently excluded from school have some form of 'special educational need'. This means that many disabled children are still disadvantaged whatever setting they receive their education in.

Classification as a state of mind

Overall, the effects of medicalisation cannot be overstated. Medicalisation is the means by which humans are officially divided into the 'normal' and the 'abnormal', with abnormality being defined as pathological, i.e. as disease. People who are diseased are clearly not 'right', and are also potentially infectious and so to be avoided. At the same time, when something is classified as a disease, then we look to medicine rather than to ourselves for solutions, including solutions to a wide range of health problems that are actually related to our lifestyle. And once we regard people as being diseased, the possibility of a cure is always on the table, making us also regard disability or 'abnormality' as being a transitory state. How, after all, can progress fail to provide what it appears to have done for centuries: a continuing succession of medical miracles?

Our demand that doctors control life and death, and provide a cure for all ills, helps to explain our contradictory attitude to 'abnormality' in infants. On the one hand, we now make sure that pregnant women are encouraged to have every available test for foetal abnormality, and receive abortion counselling when results are 'positive'. On the other hand, we enable far more disabled children to live than we terminate by working as hard as possible to ensure that premature babies are given every chance of survival, usually with the full support of their parents.

Of course, in reality there will be little or nothing to choose between the child whose impairment was detected in the womb and the child whose impairment came about as a result of their birth. The fact that parents are so keen to save their premature children's lives at any cost also shows that disabled children are as lovable as any others. However, the birth of 'incurable' children underlines to us that we have relatively little power over nature at all, while aborting potentially disabled foetuses saves us from having to face this unpleasant fact — as, of course, does segregating and thus hiding away disabled children and adults. In contrast, saving children's lives shows humans controlling nature in a suitably godlike fashion, however impaired the children turn out to be. We continue to demand that medicine works miracles in every case, and would rather obscure the reality than accept that this is unachievable.

In particular, we would like to ignore the fact that millions of people live with unglamorous, non-life-threatening but limiting, apparently simple conditions that doctors are unable to cure, either through medicine or — in the case of amputees and people with spinal injuries — technology. It is far easier to blame disabled people for not trying hard enough to be 'normal', or to believe that they are pretending to be impaired, than it is to accept that doctors' powers are limited. It suits us just as much as, and probably more than, it suits the medical profession to blame the patient for their failure to be cured. And it is far easier to be angry with disabled people for embodying the reality than it is to accept that we could be in the very same situation ourselves tomorrow. Unfortunately, in the process we make life much more difficult for all of us.

8. THE COST OF LIVING or, The survival of the richest

As we have seen, for millennia society has gone to great lengths to control people who have been regarded as being disabled, and to attempt to separate the 'deserving' from the 'undeserving' in the process. The fact that control has been possible has been linked to the economic status of the 'abnormal'. The widespread exclusion of disabled people from the workplace — whether or not they have been fit to work — has enforced dependency on the rest of the community; dependency that has come at a high price for all concerned. As a result, people who have been regarded as being 'abnormal' have almost inevitably lived in poverty, dependent on the rest of society for support and commonly regarded as being a 'burden'. Families have been left as the primary source of support throughout this period; but with the gradual disappearance of extended family units, this has become increasingly difficult for both disabled people and their relatives.

Today, it is widely accepted that disabled people are themselves to blame for not being economically independent and able to fund the support that they need. It is generally believed that society cannot and should not have to meet the costs of people with 'abnormal' bodies, despite the fact that the majority of people needing support simply have impairments related to age. Successive waves of politicians promise to become 'tougher' on disabled people, and to revise state support systems to relieve the 'burden' on society. In reality, however, we are simply perpetuating the systems (and beliefs) that have existed for more than 400 years. If we continue to do so rather than genuinely devising a new way of supporting and including everyone within society, then the people who will bear the brunt of the impact are in fact ourselves. It is therefore worth taking another look at the past in order to see how we reached this point, and how very little has actually changed to date.

Exclusion from the workplace

As we have already seen, the Industrial Revolution meant that there were fewer opportunities for disabled and older workers than previously. Disabled people were less likely to be offered employment than people who were regarded as being 'normal', even when they were just as capable of carrying out work to the same standard and at the same pace. Stereotypical beliefs meant that disabled workers' personalities and characters were thought to be affected by their impairments, along with their bodies, and that they were generally untrustworthy. In addition to this, of course, a minority of disabled people would have been incapable of working in any case.

Today, the majority of employers are still prepared to state quite openly that they would not employ a disabled person, particularly someone with a history of mental health problems — even after they have fully recovered. Other workers find that once they acquire an impairment their employer makes every effort to get rid of them, whether or not their impairment has any impact at all on their ability to do their job. According to Government figures, 80% of British adults who became disabled in the mid-noughties were in work at the time; however, only 60% were in work a year later, and only 36% were in work the year after that. Once they were unemployed, disabled people were then four times less likely than non-disabled people to be able to obtain work. And when disabled people did get jobs, one in three was out of work again by the following year, compared with only one in five of non-disabled people.

The scientific reality of disabled people's ability to work is irrelevant compared to continuing prejudice and discrimination. As a result, more than half of all disabled people of working age in Britain remain out of the workforce compared to a fifth of non-disabled people. Some groups of disabled people are disproportionately affected, but unemployment remains extremely high across all impairment groups. Many disabled people have never worked, despite wishing to do so, and despite the impact of new technologies making this possible as never before.

All of the scientific evidence shows that it is employers' attitudes and the way in which work is organised — and not disabled workers — that are to blame for the current 'burden' that disabled people pose for society. Punishing disabled workers by withdrawing or reducing state benefits is hardly likely to make them more rather than less able to enter the workplace again. Nor is forcing them to attend repeated 'work-focused' interviews and training courses likely to do anything other than damage their mental health and create further expense for the state.

Ironically, work itself is a major cause of disability in the first place. Industrial accidents are far less frequent than in the past, but are still a significant cause of ill health and impairment. Equally, although there is now a much greater awareness of the dangers inherent in certain employment practices, work-related lung problems, hearing impairments and joint problems in particular are still common. Pollution is also most likely to be a by-product of the workplace, and while pollution plays a much more significant role in causing disability in developing countries, where regulation is far less effective, it remains a cause of impairment in the UK too, contributing in particular to asthma and pneumonia rates as well as cancers, thyroid problems, infertility and birth conditions, among others.

Back problems — a major cause of disability — are often related to inadequate seating or lack of training in lifting techniques, together with long working hours and inadequate breaks. Stress — another major cause of disability and ill health — is also related to the 'long hours, short breaks' contemporary working culture, and can be a result of workplace bullying. A long-term study found that one in twenty young workers can expect to experience serious depression and anxiety each year as a result of their job, and the risk doubles in stressful workplaces. Unemployment itself then causes further impairments related to stress and poverty.

Inevitably, the vast majority of unemployed disabled workers have no choice but to apply for state or charitable support, leaving them open to accusations of laziness and criminality and facing the punishing regime of public provision. Being defined as 'abnormal' results in many of these people changing (almost overnight) their social class to end up at the bottom of the social heap regardless of their educational achievements, employment experience and previous social status. Others change class slowly but surely, since they are not entitled to claim state support so long as they have any financial resources, while the cost of social care support has always been high. It is unsurprising that, wherever possible, workers avoid being classified by their employers and the authorities as disabled — disability is still something to be ashamed of and hidden from sight, having dire consequences for the 'sufferer' if revealed.

'Outdoor relief'

State assessment of and provision for the 'deserving' disabled has taken one of several forms, all of which have been more or less popular over the past four centuries. First, there has been support for disabled people living in poverty to remain in their own homes: 'outdoor relief'. Outdoor relief was first introduced in England and Wales in the Poor Law Act of 1601, when each parish was required to appoint an Overseer of the Poor. Overseers were tasked with putting the 'undeserving' poor to work; with providing support for 'deserving' people who were too ill, disabled or elderly to work; and with levying a property-based local rate to pay for the costs of this, including covering the costs of their own wages. Later it became law that parishes were only responsible for people who had either been born there or who had lived there for three years prior to claiming. This created a link between geographical location and entitlement that still exists today in terms of social housing provision, and which often prevents people in need of housing from moving closer to family, friends and/or employment.

By the 19th century, the spiralling cost of outdoor relief meant that disabled people were increasingly institutionalised — of which more below — or left to manage without support. Institutionalisation of younger disabled people continued in the 20th century, particularly after 1906, when 'deserving' people over the age of 70 began to receive a small pension, making it easier for older people to remain living in the community and thus freeing up space in the workhouses. Some disabled people, particularly ex-servicemen, also qualified for state pensions, enabling them to remain independent. Others received accident or illness benefits from insurance policies, often obtained through workers organising themselves into friendly societies. However, benefits were often time-limited, and, as is still the case today, people who were already disabled were usually prevented from joining insurance schemes. This left the majority dependent on some form of state or charitable support and therefore, as is also the case today, dependent on officialdom to decide whether they could continue to live within the community or not.

Although a gradual expansion of pension schemes took place, it was only after the Second World War that the introduction of the Welfare State meant that disabled people found it much easier to obtain outdoor relief. This was because they were officially regarded as being unlikely to work, as well as having, for the first time, legal rights to state benefits. Whereas older people had previously had to work to support themselves if at all possible, it was now assumed that they should retire at a relatively early age however fit and healthy they were, and however much they wished to continue in employment. Soon this became supported by legislation: women over the age of 60 and men over the age of 65 were expected to leave their jobs whether they wanted to or not. This inevitably caused and continues to cause widespread poverty among older people, whether or not they are also disabled.

Despite the establishment of the Welfare State, attempts were initially made post-war to promote the employment of disabled people, particularly those with types of impairment such as amputations that were associated with war injuries. During the war years, over 300,000 'cripples' had been put into training and employment in order to swell the workforce, and, along with women, they had proved themselves to be capable workers. In recognition of the large number of war-wounded — both civilians and members of the armed services — the Disabled Persons' (Employment) Act of 1944 required all employers with a workforce of 20 or more to employ a minimum quota of disabled people, usually 3%, or to pay a levy instead that would create a fund to provide sheltered employment.

However, in practice this law was never implemented or enforced, and soon it was assumed that most disabled people were unfit for the modern workplace. Although all workers were needed during and immediately after the Second World War, immigration and the Baby Boom soon meant that they could be replaced. It therefore suited employers to remove older and disabled people from the workforce, keeping them in reserve as cheap labour for times of need (including times of industrial unrest, where disabled and older people could be put to work to break strikes). In employers' eyes, disabled and older people were likely to be slower, take more time off sick, and have higher welfare needs than younger, fitter workers. Often it suited employers simply to pay the levy instead — if anyone asked them to do so.

As a result, disabled workers were increasingly segregated when they had jobs. New 'sheltered' workshops and 'training centres' were established, by local authorities and the Government-funded company Remploy as well as by charities, and workers with learning difficulties in particular were likely to end up there if they had access to employment at all. Until the end of the 20th century, when the 1995 Disability Discrimination Act was implemented, it continued to be perfectly legal to discriminate against individual disabled workers, even when an employer was subject to the quota. Today, although employers are legally prohibited from discriminating against disabled workers when recruiting and retaining staff, there is no legal imperative for them to employ any disabled workers whatsoever.

Fraudsters, benefits and traps

As a result of their removal from the workforce, benefits for older and disabled people became distinct from those for 'normal' people. A higher rate was generally paid in recognition of the fact that disabled and older people were claiming for the long term. First, however, it became necessary to prove the possession of an older or 'abnormal' body, rather than simply proving economic status or need, as other claimants were required to do. As the 20th century 'progressed' towards the 21st, tests became ever more stringent, while benefit levels continued to decrease in relation to earnings.

Outdoor relief has long since been renamed 'care in the community', but the principle remains unchanged. Disabled people who apply for financial support and social care services are subjected to a battery of tests and interviews in order to establish who 'deserves' help, and who is dishonestly attempting to claim what is not theirs. The assumption is always that, since disabled people are 'known' to be untrustworthy and dishonest, there will be many criminals among the apparently impaired, along with many people who are capable of work but who are simply lazy or have personality problems. (In reality, many long-term unemployed who are denied disability benefits or who later have them withdrawn on the grounds that they do not have significant impairments are people who nonetheless fail to meet the demand for a healthy, fit, 'standard' body.)

Media images of benefit claimants propagate the belief that fraud is overwhelmingly common, demonising disability benefits claimants in particular. The fact that being defined as disabled means that a worker is unlikely to obtain or keep a job does not prevent the rest of society from assuming that being categorised as disabled is highly desirable. The assumption is — now, and for the past three centuries — that poor people are physically capable of earning enough to support themselves, but are feckless, work-shy and have deficient personalities that make them prefer to live off others.

These stereotype-fuelled beliefs result in a huge administrative industry that creates jobs for hundreds of thousands of mainly non-disabled people to assess the merits of disabled people's claims for benefits and services. Although one in ten people of working age is disabled, fewer than 2% of all local authority employees are categorised as such, as are less than 7% of civil servants. Where disabled people are employed in the civil service, they earn up to a third less than their non-disabled colleagues, and it is likely that this is also true of the rest of the public sector. It is notable that the vast majority of state spending on disability — billions of pounds a year —

actually goes on the employment of non-disabled people to administer benefit and care services rather than on the services themselves.

Far more administrators are employed than social care workers, since most care at home is still provided by unpaid family members, and the majority of disabled people are left without significant outside help of any kind. Often the assessment process does not result in any support at all being given to a disabled person. Local authorities are required to assess disabled people and to keep statistics about them, but not to assist them unless they are in 'critical' need. Likewise, much of the contact that disabled people have with the medical system after their initial classification is simply to provide up-to-date paperwork for these same administrators, and thus resources are prevented from going towards treatments. Only a fraction of the money spent on disabled people goes to disabled people themselves in the form of benefits, yet ironically it is benefits that are always cut first.

Ironically, too, it is far easier for a fraudster to get through the assessment process than it is for a 'genuinely' disabled person. The amount of stress and physical and mental energy involved in claiming means that many disabled people decide that it is too difficult to try to access the benefits and services to which they are entitled. It would be more cost-effective to increase funding for fraud detection than to make the claiming process so difficult and demeaning; this would also be more effective in ensuring that funds are received by those who 'deserve' them. Employing disabled people to administer the systems that regulate them would also ensure that fraud was spotted more easily.

The nature of the administrative system set up to identify — though not necessarily to help — 'the deserving' means that once an unemployed disabled person *has* successfully claimed benefits, they are unlikely to seek work again. Apart from the low chance of them obtaining work, there is the fear that if they lose their job they will have to start applying for benefits again from scratch. This is likely to leave them existing for months without an income, as well as risking their not qualifying again without undergoing a further appeal process. As we have seen, with one in three disabled workers losing their job within a year of obtaining it, this fear is very realistic.

With half of all disabled adults in the UK having no recognised qualifications, disabled workers are far more likely than non-disabled workers to be receiving low wages; this means that even when they do find a job, they need to apply for further benefits. This process is just as difficult and demanding as the application process for benefits when out of work, and can leave workers facing impossible levels of poverty while they wait for claims to be processed. Lack of education also makes the form-filling required much more difficult than it would be for the average worker. No wonder that many disabled people believe it best to stay at home — if they have a home, that is. It is this, not being 'work-shy', that creates a barrier to re-employment.

Today, whether or not unemployed disabled people are eligible for disability benefits, they are blamed by the Government for the fact that the overwhelming majority of jobs created over the past 15 years have been taken by immigrants. This is despite the fact that migrant workers tend to fall into one of two groups: either they are highly qualified; or they are fit enough to be able to work long hours in physically demanding jobs within a small range of service and agricultural industries. The new focus is on reducing immigration by forcing benefit claimants to fill the gap. However, with half of all disabled people having no qualifications whatsoever, and with many of the so-called non-disabled benefit claimants still not being young, healthy and fit, this is simply not a viable prospect. Rather, one group of non-standard bodies is simply being played off against the other as scapegoats for economic problems in which they've played no part.

Recent changes to the benefit system to make it even more punitive are likely to increase hardship, but are unlikely to make any fundamental difference to employment rates. Only through tackling the attitude of employers is that likely to happen — and it is hard to see why any employer would take on workers who have been stigmatised as lazy and dishonest by successive governments for claiming disability benefits in the past. Indeed, if the vast industry 'supporting' disabled people includes only a tiny number of disabled workers, it is difficult to see that significant employment options exist elsewhere. If anything, cuts to public sector jobs are likely to result in even higher unemployment rates among disabled people in the future. The fact that this is unpalatable does not make it untrue.

'Indoor relief'

The second form that public support for disabled and older people living in poverty has taken is that of 'indoor relief' — provision for disabled people within special institutions. This has been popular for several reasons. Segregating disabled people from the rest of society meant that family members were 'freed' from the 'burden' of looking after them, thus 'freeing' them to take on paid work instead. Segregation also meant that disabled people were unable to beg or otherwise indulge in criminal behaviours, thus reducing the 'burden' on the rest of society. It also prevented disabled people from having children, as the sexes were separated within institutions, responding to eugenicists' fears. And institutionalisation was generally seen to be less attractive than receiving help at home, thus reducing 'fraudulent' claims.

As time went on, segregation had the added effect of removing disabled and older people from public view and 'normal' life, thus making them invisible; this, coupled with the lack of images of disabled and older people within 20th-century culture and media, has resulted in today's continuing lack of awareness of just how large a proportion of the population is disabled. This invisibility occurred despite the fact that even when institutionalisation was at its peak, the majority of disabled people continued to live in the community. Many remained indoors, of course, or were able to pass for 'normal'; others went unnoticed because they were not 'supposed' to be living outside an institution.

Indoor relief was first introduced at the turn of the 18th century, when Acts of Parliament established workhouses in 14 towns between 1696 and 1712. By the middle of the 18th century this number had grown to more than 600, and by 1834 there were 4800 workhouses in existence. As the name suggests, along with accommodation, workhouses provided employment for their inmates — generally repetitive manual tasks such as picking oakum (a tarry rope), chopping wood, grinding corn, breaking stones or making sacks. The Poor Law Amendment Act of 1834 then brought into law the principle that conditions in the workhouse should be worse than those of "the independent labourer of the lowest class". As with today's Government policy, they believed "It should always pay to work."

Workhouses were explicitly intended to put people off applying for help unless they had literally no other option. (Again, this is echoed today in the experience of applying for both state and charitable support, a process that is deliberately made unpleasant and humiliating in an effort to deter applicants, and which continues to be made more rather than less so.) It was recognised from the beginning that institutionalisation of whatever kind was undesirable, and was in itself a form of punishment. Workhouse inmates were normally segregated according to sex and were made to wear uniform; generally they had no freedom of movement. While outdoor relief continued for some, people who were not deemed to be disabled or elderly could only receive support once they entered the workhouse. As with today, many of these supposedly non-disabled people had significant impairments too, but were not categorised as such by the authorities.

Workhouse occupants were also denied the vote and therefore the right to take part in the democratic process, and this bar was only lifted in 1918 when many ex-servicemen were living in institutions. However, people in asylums — people with mental health diagnoses, along with many people with learning difficulties — were still disenfranchised as late as 1979. Today, large numbers of polling stations remain inaccessible to disabled people, perhaps reflecting the continuing belief that disabled people should be ineligible to vote. Prisoners, many of whom are locked up only because of mental health problems, continued to lack the vote at the end of the noughties, despite legal rulings to the contrary.

Initially, disabled people shared space in workhouses with other groups of 'deserving' paupers, particularly older people, although they were often segregated from non-disabled inmates. However, by the end of the 19th century separate provision was being developed for each group, initially on the same sites and later in separate institutions. Disabled people proceeded to be divided into 'idiots' (people with learning difficulties) — the 1886 Idiots Act had enabled local authorities to build separate institutions for them if they desired; 'lunatics' (people with mental health problems); 'the infirm' (people with physical and mobility impairments); blind people; and Deaf people — each group being assigned to different institutions. Older people were put into different institutions again, regardless of any impairments they might have. By the turn of the 20th century, 28% of the 'adult non-able-bodied' population were institutionalised, and most were divided according to their medical category.

'Mental deficients'

In 1913, the Mental Deficiency Act replaced the Idiots Act with the aim of registering and if necessary compulsorily detaining people with learning difficulties and other 'deficiencies'. In particular, institutionalisation was seen as a way of preventing 'mental deficients' from having children who would be similarly 'abnormal'. Perhaps inevitably, given the eugenicists' beliefs about the nature of poverty as being biologically determined, poor people of working age were often reclassified as being 'deficient' before they were institutionalised, particularly after the beginning of the 20th century.

'Morality' was also regarded as being linked to biology, so prostitutes, girls who became pregnant out of wedlock — including rape victims — and criminals were all seen as being biologically defective, and no real distinction was made between them. People who had committed a criminal offence or had been to an approved school, people with alcohol problems, and people deemed to be ineducable or to require supervision could all be institutionalised under the terms of the 1913 Mental Deficiency Act, since 'deficiency' was intended to mean far more than being intellectually impaired. Many of these victims of eugenics spent the rest of their lives inside an institution, or were only released in old age, when their institutions closed.

The old workhouse work ethic continued to be important, with many institutions offering training programmes and later developing segregated workshops for their inmates. This work was of a low level, often not much different from the oakum picking of the workhouses, and if inmates received a wage at all, it was very low. When inmates were trained for jobs in the community, these were also of low status, such as domestic work. Overall, jobs and training were restricted to what the 'normal' people who controlled the institutions could imagine being suited to their inmates, in moral terms as well as in terms of actual ability.

Workhouses themselves were renamed Poor Law Institutions in 1913, but increasingly these also became institutions that catered solely for disabled or older people. While the establishment of the Welfare State at the end of the Second World War made provision for poor people to claim an income from the state and therefore to remain living at home, disabled and older people continued to be segregated and institutionalised in large numbers, often as a result of inadequate housing. Local authorities were now required to provide accommodation for disabled and older people who had no other means of support, but in reality they often simply took over workhouse premises — in 1960, Peter Townsend found that 35,000 older people were still living in Poor Law premises. Although, of course, many disabled people remained living with their families or independently, a significant minority of the population were incarcerated for most of the 20th century.

Lunatics and asylums

This was particularly true of people with mental health problems. The original 'lunatic asylum', the monastic Bethlem Hospital in London (known also as Bedlam), was joined from the mid-17th century by a number of private madhouses. Although people funded by their parishes were admitted for a while at the beginning of the 19th century, the majority of residents were funded by their families. By the mid-19th century, there were around 100 private asylums, catering for about half of all the 'lunatics' in Britain. Charitable asylums were founded alongside the private madhouses in the 18th century; they also charged for their services, but attempted to compete for state-funded residents by charging less than the commercial asylums. Local authorities were only obliged to provide for people with mental health problems after the 1845 Lunacy Act, which compelled them to build institutions; by 1900, 77 publicly run asylums housed 74,000 people, some of whom were privately paid for.

From the beginning, women formed the majority of asylum patients. The impact of their classification as being 'naturally inferior' to men; the denial of their rights to hold property or be the legal guardians of their own children; the designation of conditions associated with fertility as illnesses; and the wish to control and contain women all contributed to this. However, ultimately, as we have seen, all women were seen as being mentally deficient in comparison to men anyway, making it extremely easy to have them declared insane.

Although from the 19th century onwards asylums were supposed to be providing treatment rather than simply containment, at least half of the residents were never discharged back into the community. The number of people incarcerated in asylums continued to grow in the first half of the 20th century, and institutions were soon being built or extended to accommodate thousands of residents — rather than the hundreds that they had been originally intended for. By 1934, over 100,000 people were detained in asylums in England and Wales — more than today's prison population. Many of these people had learning difficulties rather than mental health problems, despite the former group supposedly being housed separately in the 'mental deficiency institutions' (later renamed mental handicap hospitals), of which there were 150 in 1939.

From the outset, conditions in all types of institutions for disabled people were appalling. Victorian asylums were conceived — and for a long time portrayed — as models of humane care and treatment, but in reality they quickly deteriorated and became over-crowded. As in the workhouses, the regimes punished inmates for their poverty, as well as for their failure to adhere to social norms and behaviour and for their 'abnormality'. In addition, inmates were commonly referred to as 'animal-like' and 'brutish' and in general were considered to be less than human, thus meriting inhumane treatment.

At best, people living in institutions lost control over who provided their care and how; what time they got up and went to bed; what they ate and when; what they wore; who they socialised with (the separation of friends was a common punishment); what work they did (often people with learning difficulties were used to provide support for people with physical impairments); how they spent their leisure time; and when (if at all) they saw their families. Many were forced to take drugs daily to control their behaviour, particularly after the Second World War. From the start they were also subjected to a wide variety of experimental treatments, including the hated electro-convulsive 'therapy', which had a lasting impact on cognitive function. Over the centuries successive enquiries sparked a number of reform movements; however, conditions still remained poor at the end of the 20th century. It is also disturbing to note that many people who now receive 'care in the community' lack as much autonomy as (and in the same ways as) the institutional inmates described above.

Only in the 1960s did the British Government begin a policy of closing down state-funded institutions. This was driven by the 1959 Mental Health Act, which specifically preferred community care for those who could benefit from it. The motivation for this preference was two-fold. First, it was clear that it would be much cheaper for disabled people to live in the community, particularly as many could more or less be left to get on with it without any form of support beyond benefit income. Second, the post-war development and marketing of psychiatric medications had added to the belief that people could 'manage' with the help of medicine. As we have seen, doctors had always sought physical causes for mental health problems and learning difficulties; the availability of drug 'treatments' fulfilled a long-standing demand from the medical profession.

The result of all this was that many people were returned from institutions to the community between the 1960s and the 1980s, often after a lifetime of segregation. Many had lost contact with their families decades beforehand, since families were encouraged to sever contact and to avoid visiting, and institutions were in any case often located many miles from inmates' family homes. Far from welcoming them, communities reacted with suspicion and hostility, particularly when people had come out of the mental health system, and this hostility has contributed to the growing level of disability hate crime in the 21st century. 'Care in the community' has often proved to be anything but.

Meanwhile, other disabled and older people who have been living quite happily in the community have been forced into institutions when it has been deemed to be cheaper than their continuing to live at home. Often, of course, older disabled people have had homes that could then be sold to fund their care, reducing the cost to the state still further. Institutions need not be local to disabled people's home communities, and so much of their contact with families, neighbours and friends is removed. Institutions need not even be age-appropriate; young people are commonly housed in 'homes' where they are the only inhabitant under the age of 70. Cost, in fact, is the only consideration at all. And moves are being made to withdraw the mobility component of Disability Living Allowance — only paid in the first place to people who were younger than 65 when they first received it — from state-funded residents in institutions, preventing them from enjoying any independent activity in the outside world at all. Truly, nothing has really changed.

The role of charities

The third way in which 'abnormal' people have been supported during the last few centuries is through charitable means. As we have already seen, assisting disabled people by relieving their poverty has been recommended by most religions throughout the centuries as a way of helping the benefactor to become closer to God, or otherwise to improve their spiritual status. In more recent years, charitable giving has been a means of improving tax status as well. At no time has this meant that disabled people were equal to their benefactors, nor has it meant that they should be regarded without suspicion. Inevitably, this imbalance has affected the way in which charitable support has been delivered to disabled people, and continues to affect it today.

Initially, charitable support was delivered through the monasteries, alongside health care. Later, from the 18th century onwards, a wave of new charitable foundations were established to help poor people to 'help themselves' through a range of measures. These charities developed their own institutions, as well as operating their own forms of outdoor relief by making grants to the 'deserving' poor. As with all forms of 'relief' from poverty, strenuous efforts were made by charities to distinguish between 'deserving' and 'undeserving' disabled people.

Diagnoses were used to help to determine who was 'deserving' — for example, people with cerebral palsy could have no blame attached to their condition, whereas people who had become injured in accidents were by default already stigmatised as being careless. The undeserving might be at least as severely impaired as the deserving, but be regarded as being morally deficient. Addiction, which owes as much to genetic factors as to the widespread and legal availability of intoxicants such as alcohol and tobacco, was usually viewed as marking someone out as being undeserving, whatever their other impairments might be.

Charities aimed wherever possible to provide work-based training, and to encourage employment among the disabled people they deemed to be capable of it. This often took the form of home-based work, in addition to setting up sheltered workshops for people living within the community as well as in institutions. Home-based work was particularly poorly paid, but sheltered employment was also low status and paid less than a 'market' rate in recognition of workers' 'impaired' abilities. Only ex-servicemen received significant amounts of retraining for new careers, particularly following the First World War, as well as better pay rates within sheltered workshops, but even this was seldom enough to take them out of poverty.

Many of the state-funded institutions of the mid-20th century began life as charitable institutions, and it is therefore difficult to find significant differences between them. As in the state institutions, the sexes were separated in an effort to ensure that disabled people could not reproduce; those who were considered to be capable were given training and/or segregated employment; and family contact was discouraged. Similarly, from the onset, charities operated many of the institutions for children, and continue to retain control of many today, although the number has reduced as parents have preferred to keep their children with them at home.

Perhaps the main distinction is that charitable institutions were more likely to cater for a sub-group of disabled people. Charities were often founded to support people with a particular medical diagnosis, for example to support people classified as having cerebral palsy, rather than supporting all people with mobility and speech impairments. As we have seen, people with the same diagnosis were thought to have the same needs and abilities, as well as to require the same treatment. The same charities also funded medical research into the conditions, with the inhabitants of the institutions providing ready-made research subjects.

Today, the big charities 'for' disabled people continue to operate a certain, much reduced number of institutions, with the vast majority of residents receiving at least some funding from the state to support them there. The state in fact subsidises charities to continue to provide a cheap means of support for disabled people without any means of their own. Children's facilities also often provide a cheaper means of catering for disabled children and their educational needs than the state providing support within the community.

The same charities often continue to operate grant funds to provide essential items to disabled people when they are living in the community, again using the concept of the 'deserving' as compared to the 'non-deserving' and potentially criminal poor. Moral judgements are still paramount, and the cause of the impairment is also still judged to be more important than the impact when deciding who qualifies for funds. As well as medical classifications, charities may use the circumstances in which an impairment was acquired when deciding who to support. For example, some charities cater for ex-service personnel who have received injuries during their time in the armed forces, rather than for all amputees or visually impaired people. The availability of this support enables the state to avoid providing essential equipment such as powered wheelchairs to disabled people as a right.

The main difference today between charitable and state-funded forms of 'outdoor relief' is that the state looks more closely at the impact of impairment, rather than the cause, when judging whether a disabled person qualifies for support and what form that might take. Also, charities are more able to respond to individual circumstances, since their actions are not dictated by legislation. Both state funders and charitable funders take domestic circumstances into account, though: most benefits and services provided to disabled people are means-tested whatever their source; and the decision as to whether to provide support is equally affected by whether or not family members, relatives or friends are otherwise able to provide it. The level of someone's impairment, and their resulting access needs, are always secondary to moral, financial and other judgements when deciding who to support and how.

Forced dependency

Inevitably, this leaves people who are classified as being abnormal or disabled in a very weak economic position indeed. Even within a Welfare State, people's 'right' to support is subject to a complex array of moral and physical judgements about their impairments, abilities and character. In the vast majority of cases, these judgements will be made by people who have no personal experience of impairment, and no idea of how it is to live in a disabling world. This forced dependency on others is a major cause of distress and anxiety among disabled people. It is unsurprising that the treatment they receive often causes mental illness in recipients of state and charitable 'help', even when no mental health difficulties existed originally. It is also unsurprising that disabled (and older) people fail to claim all of the benefits they are entitled to if they can possibly manage without (and not always even then).

It is easy to see why so many disabled people describe their dependency on the state as being far more difficult to live with than their impairments, particularly when harassment and abuse towards them are driven by beliefs that they are being given 'money for nothing', often fraudulently. Other benefit claimants resent the fact that disabled and older people receive higher amounts than they do, as well as believing that disabled people are less likely than other unemployed people to have paid national insurance and income tax in the past. This means that abuse towards disabled people is most common in poorer areas. But even those disabled people who escape poverty are affected by the widespread belief that all disabled people are unemployed recipients of benefits and charity.

Stereotypes of disabled people, and the way in which disabled people are treated within wider society also have an impact on the economic status of people caring for them, and the manner in which that work is carried out. As we have seen, the Industrial Revolution created a separation between paid work, which took place outside the home, and unpaid work that took place inside the home. At that point, caring for children and elderly and disabled people within the home began to be regarded as integral to women's family duties, rather than as being 'real' work that should be paid for. This is why family members are expected to provide support for disabled and older people wherever possible. Since this often prevents them from working themselves, the poverty associated with disability also affects non-disabled people.

As 'women's work', caring is also regarded as being unskilled work that anyone can carry out, rather than work that requires a wide range of skills to do properly. This in turn forces down the wages and working conditions of social care workers. It is unsurprising in the circumstances that social care work currently attracts a large number of people with personal problems, who believe that caring for and controlling someone 'less fortunate' will make them feel better, as well as attracting workers who are consciously sadistic and abusive. Other social care workers are forced to quit when disablist harassment by neighbours is extended to them.

In our capitalist economy, the value placed on people is determined by economic activity — which of course takes place outside the home. (This value system of course affects children, and mothers caring for infants, as well as disabled and older people and the non-disabled people providing support for them.) However much disabled and older people are contributing to the community or have done in the past, they are widely regarded as being a burden on the rest of society whatever their actual circumstances. As children in the 18th century learnt, along with their alphabet: "I is an ill man and hated by all."

The source of the drive to present our bodies as being young and non-disabled, and the search for perfection, is therefore obvious. For centuries, being classed as normal has meant being able to afford to be part of society and to be recognised as a legitimate member of it. Being classed as abnormal has meant being isolated and or segregated, and

Abnormal

above all poor — although widely regarded as still being richer than we deserve.

9. WASHING MACHINES GOOD/ WHEELCHAIRS BAD or, Stigmatising technology

Our dysphoric ideas about what is 'normal' are reflected in our differing attitudes to the technology that now surrounds and extends our bodies. As a result of 300 years of 'progress', we live in an age where we are surrounded by equipment and machinery that aids and extends our bodies' abilities and thus makes our lives easier. Our response to this network of support aids, though, depends entirely on whether or not we associate them with 'normal' or 'abnormal' bodies, and this in turn affects their design, cost and function. If they relate to 'normal' bodies, they are regarded to a greater or lesser extent as being objects of desire. If, however, we regard them as being directly related to the 'abnormal' body, we think it natural to shrink away in horror instead at the very thought of them. Again, this in turn creates a situation that will impact negatively on all of us at some point in our lives unless we begin to challenge it now.

Some of the equipment that we now take for granted helps to support our most basic bodily functions, including utensils for cooking and eating, clothing, seating and bedding; and its form has not changed significantly over millennia. Other technologies, however, have been developed within the last 50–200 years. Washing machines, dishwashers and vacuum cleaners extend our physical capabilities and conserve our time; personal computers, electronic organisers and calculators extend our mental abilities; televisions and radios, the internet and mobile phones extend our ability to communicate; cameras, telescopes and microscopes extend our vision; bicycles, motor cycles, cars, boats and aeroplanes all extend our mobility. And so on and so forth.

We think of it as being perfectly 'natural' to use all this — despite the fact that many people in the world are without some or all of it, and that we can all (just about) survive without it. We also think it is natural for this equipment to be designed well — although only to meet the needs of 'normal' bodies

— and to be aesthetically pleasing. And we think it is natural to have a choice of designs available to us, because we all have different needs and tastes. But when it comes to equipment that is specifically designed for 'abnormal' bodies — often only necessary because standardised design is not inclusive — we also think it natural that this is uniform, unadorned, ugly, medicalised and unfashionable.

Dehumanising disability aids

Even though we know we will join them one day, we seem to take it for granted that disabled and older people do not have the same range of tastes and desires as everybody else. Further, we treat those with the least-uniform bodies as having the most uniform needs. We accept that sub-standard products are 'good enough' and believe that offering choice is 'a waste of money' — again, despite the fact that we know we will probably need them ourselves one day. After all, rather than being objects of desire, we regard disability-related equipment as being a badge of abnormality, and as such as being highly undesirable, however necessary it might be.

One obvious reason for providing disabled people with such inferior products, and for stigmatising them in the process, is punishment — including self-punishment for having become disabled. As we have seen, disabled people embody truths that we find unpalatable in today's society: we are all mortal; and science's ability to 'cure' — to triumph over nature — is limited. Disabled people are also commonly believed to have failed to try hard enough to get 'better', to be lazy and to have defective personalities. As a result we use the language of punishment when describing disabled people's relationship to their equipment: we talk about being 'bound' to a wheelchair, or 'forced' to use a walking stick or spinal brace. Yet, as with mobile phones and bicycles, this equipment is actually extending human abilities, and thus is liberating rather than confining.

The language that we use to refer to the people who use this equipment is equally negative, and often paints a picture of disabled people's lives that is highly unreal. The media frequently describes someone as 'being in a wheelchair for x number of years' — as if wheelchair users do not leave their chairs every day to sleep, bathe, use the toilet, drive, or just to join the rest of their family on the settee in front of the television in the evening. Full-time wheelchair users (only one in twenty of all wheelchair users) are usually described as being 'confined' to their wheelchairs, as if their chair is an object of imprisonment. Other people are described as being 'dependent' on a brace, calliper or walking stick — which is inevitably regarded as being negative — rather than simply as 'using' one.

Often the people who use disability aids and equipment are wholly identified by it (just as they are by medical diagnoses), and they themselves appear to be invisible. For example, a common experience for me on entering a theatre is to see a security guard get on their radio to a colleague and warn them that "a wheelchair has just come in". As with the description of wheelchair users being in their chairs for years instead of just hours at a time, we are regarded as being inextricably bonded to our technology.

The 'tragedy' of wheelchair use

While everything from washing machines to mobile phones is viewed as enhancing human existence and as being part of 'progress', disability aids are viewed as being dehumanising and left over from the past. (Only orthopaedic fetishists take a different view, and again it is the equipment, not the user, which is of importance to them.) Progress is expected to eliminate the need for wheelchairs, braces and so on sooner rather than later, so we see no point in putting any effort into improving them now. Ironically, progress is also expected to make us all superhuman soon, combining organic bodies that will be perfect with technology that will extend our abilities still further. Repeated media stories promise that one day soon we will all become 'cyborgs'. Despite this, though, the use of technology by disabled people to extend their abilities is still frowned upon.

Wheelchairs in particular are regarded as being highly undesirable, despite the liberation and independence that they actually convey on their users. As a result, wheelchair users are expected to loathe their chairs, and having a condition that necessitates wheelchair use is commonly regarded as being a legitimate reason to commit suicide. However much a person would benefit from using a wheelchair, they are expected to resist doing so unless they have absolutely no alternative, when they are expected to be embarrassed to display such a public sign of their abnormality. Often, disabled people are denied access to a wheelchair by professionals in any case, since their goal is for their patients to appear 'normal', i.e. without impairments. Thus millions of people who have severely limited mobility and conditions that cause fatigue 'manage' without wheelchairs, and have far narrower, harder, more painful lives as a result.

This belief that wheelchair use is highly undesirable has been propagated at the highest levels of our modern society. In the first half of the 20th century, President Roosevelt, who was paralysed below the waist following an illness more than a decade before he was voted into presidential office, went to enormous efforts to avoid being seen in public using a wheelchair. Roosevelt was normally pictured standing, using leg irons under his clothes and at least one person next to him for support; and of all the photographs that are in existence of him, just two show him in his wheelchair. In all, Roosevelt was careful to suggest that he had been largely 'cured' of his condition (once thought to have been caused by polio, but now believed to have been Guillain-Barré syndrome), although in reality he remained disabled until the end. Likewise, at the end of the 20th century the last Pope and the late Queen Mother refused to be seen in public using wheelchairs, preferring to be viewed as immobile and dependent even though they presumably used wheelchairs in private.

Perhaps it is unsurprising, then, that so many other older people within our society are leading restricted and difficult lives rather than using a wheelchair. And it is certainly easy to see why people who have suddenly acquired an impairment regard wheelchair use as ending their opportunities in life, rather than as opening up possibilities for them again. However, this attitude has a massive impact on the same people's ability to live independently, as well as to work. In reality, many people now deemed to be unfit to work could be employed, but only if they were prepared to use wheelchairs. Wheelchairs make it possible for people with back problems to sit comfortably, and enable people with restricted energy to make the most of it. However, neither professionals nor disabled people themselves see wheelchair use as being legitimate if it is 'only' to allow them to work — or indeed if it is only to allow them to enjoy themselves. Wheelchair use is only seen as being legitimate for someone who is unable to walk at all, although only 5% of wheelchair users actually fall into this category.

Bizarrely, this obsession with walking ability is highly contradictory, and betrays our body dysphoria. In reality, it is walking that is associated with low social status. The higher someone's status, the more sedentary they are, and the more they depend on wheels. To generalise wildly (and perhaps more than a little unfairly), middle-class men in particular sit down to drive to work, then sit down at their desks in front of their computers all day, before sitting down to drive home again, and then sitting down in front of the television for the evening. If they see someone waiting for a bus, they feel superior to them; if they see someone who can't even afford the bus, they feel pity for them; but if they see someone happily bowling along in their wheelchair, they regard it as being a tragedy. Only dysphoria can explain this.

The long history of the wheelchair

It is equally bizarre that we regard the wheel as being the single most important invention in the history of the world, and hold in high esteem every invention that has resulted from it — except for the wheelchair. Yet wheeled chairs — for infants as well as for people with restricted mobility — have had huge benefits ever since they first became widely available. It is not easy to trace their history, but it is possible that they date back as far as 6000 years. Again, it is useful to pause briefly and look back into the past for the lessons that all this teaches us about the here and now.

Handcarts probably accounted for the earliest forms of wheelchair, with people often reclining or lying down to be pushed. Both the ancient Greeks and the Egyptians are known to have had this form of transport, and the Romans used similar ones to ensure that disabled people could get to work in the fields. Handcarts are echoed in the invalid carriages of the past few centuries, which enable people who need to lie flat to be pushed around outside their homes; however, relatively few people use this type of 'wheelchair' today.

The first lesson to learn from history is that wheelchairs in the early days were not just for 'imperfect' people and people with low social status. The earliest known image of a wheelchair user shows someone sitting in a three-wheeled chair and is inscribed on a slate that was found in China, dating to the sixth century. The Chinese used wheeled chairs to assist people to get around whether or not they were disabled or elderly, pulling rather than pushing them; their use denoted social importance. Likewise the first modern wheelchair can be traced to 1595, when a highly elaborate one with leg rests as well as arm rests was made for King Philip II of Spain to use in later life. This was probably regarded as being extremely cutting edge and as an object of desire by other rulers, albeit of a similar age, as well as being admired by the king's subjects. In all, it is probable that a range of wheelchair designs existed around this time and were used for a variety of reasons, by non-disabled as well as disabled people.

The first known self-propelled wheelchair was actually invented by a Briton: a young disabled watchmaker called Stephen Farfler, who built a three-wheeled chair for himself in 1655. However, self-propelled chairs were slow to catch on, perhaps because being pushed denoted a higher social status than propelling yourself. By the middle of the 18th century, though, the forerunners of the modern wheelchair were being developed, generally with two large wheels at the front and one smaller one at the back. Most were far too heavy for users to propel themselves, whether they wanted to or not, although some were designed so that users could move themselves short distances by pushing on their wheel rims.

Most significantly, the Bath Chair was developed by James Heath around 1750 to transport people who had come to take the waters between their hotels and the Pump Room and Spa in Bath. Again, it is important to note here that, far from simply being there to serve the 'invalids', Bath Chairs were also used by the rich and famous to go about their business, and by 1830 had replaced the sedan chair as a mode of transport. Before the invention of cars, non-disabled people were happy to use wheelchairs; as we have seen, walking has always been viewed as denoting lower status than wheeling. Bath Chairs had two large wheels at the back and a smaller one at the front, and had a pram-like hood and covered front that could be used to protect the user from the weather. Originally they were steered by someone walking beside them using a lever attached to the front wheel, and functioned very much like a sedan chair. Later a number of variations were built, which could be pushed as well as pulled and which could also be drawn by a donkey.

By the 19th century, wheelchairs were commonly made from wood and wicker. Self-propulsion outside was inevitably a dirty business, particularly in the winter, but in 1881 'push rims' were developed, and these continue to feature on wheelchairs today. (Push rims are smaller, lighter rims that are attached to the wheel rims and don't touch the ground themselves.) As time went on, chairs became lighter and more adjustable, and in 1900 wheels gained wire spokes that made them more effective. Designs were also invented that allowed people to propel themselves with one hand, with the axles of both wheels linked together.

Tricycles were actually invented as an offshoot of wheelchairs and were used by both disabled and non-disabled people: in fact, the first powered chair was developed when an engine was fitted to one of these tricycles in 1912. In the early years of the 20th century a number of inventors experimented with more conventional powered chairs, but it was 1916 before the first commercially produced one became available. However, powered chairs did not become widespread until much later in the 20th century, when designs were developed further in post-war Canada.

Modern developments

In the mean time, the modern steel folding manual wheelchair was developed by US engineers Harry Jennings and Herbert Everest in 1933, after Everest, who was paralysed, became increasingly frustrated with the options then available. Everest and Jennings went on to become the first mass manufacturer of wheelchairs, and their design still forms the basis for many of today's folding wheelchairs. In the 1950s they became the first mass supplier of powered chairs, and later developed modern electric mobility scooters. Based in the USA, they soon had a worldwide market. The Everest and Jennings brand remains today, and now covers a wide range of 'medical' equipment. Unfortunately, however, the combination of the brand's popularity and the 1930s aesthetic which associated metal with glamour meant that the wide variety of chairs that had previously been available began to disappear, and with them wheelchair users' individuality began to disappear, too.

In Britain, this process was hastened when the establishment of the National Health Service meant that, following the Second World War, wheelchairs became available on prescription. This was obviously of enormous benefit to people who had previously been unable to afford them. However, the introduction of the National Health Service alongside state socialism set a norm of standardisation, greatly narrowing the range of mobility equipment that was available throughout the country. Classifications of medical conditions were accompanied by classification of the aids and equipments required by someone possessing that diagnosis. As with so many issues when the medical model of disability dominates, the individual was irrelevant, since their needs were expected to be dictated solely by their diagnosis and so to be shared by everyone else with the same classification.

Standardisation meant that the Ministry Model 8 manual wheelchair, introduced in 1951, quickly became dominant in the UK. By the 1960s, it accounted for 95% of all prescription wheelchairs. Needless to say, price took priority over aesthetics and function. The model failed to meet the needs of many of its users, but the belief in standardisation resulted in the belief that only one design could be 'perfect'. For nearly half a century, one model of wheelchair then dominated British streets, and made it uneconomic for other manufacturers to enter the market.

It was only in 1987 that wheelchair supply was devolved to individual regional NHS trusts, who were then able to contract a much wider range of suppliers and designs. Even then, the old 'ministry' wheelchair is often pictured in images of wheelchair users today. However liberating it was for people who would otherwise have been left completely immobile, it was the Ministry chair, more than any other factor, that created the invisibility of individual wheelchair users that continues today.

The ending of the Ministry monopoly meant that towards the end of the 20th century a range of smaller companies began to experiment with lightweight alloys and other new technologies to make the high-tech wheelchairs that are available today. These models enabled many people who had previously had to rely on other people to push them to self-propel. (Although, since ultra-lightweight models are seldom available on the NHS, many people who are unable to afford them remain needlessly dependent on other people's help.) Meanwhile, at the other end of the market, cheap basic chairs began to be imported en masse from China, further undermining the dominance of the post-war brands and designs. All of these developments began to empower wheelchair users, and to allow them to express their individuality through their choice of models as well as to find chairs that could — if they could afford them — meet their individual needs.

Along with improvements in manual chair design, other contemporary wheelchair developments include powered chairs that can stand their users up. This raises the user to the same eye level as people who are standing, as well as bringing counters and shelves into reach. Standing has the added advantage of being highly beneficial for people's kidneys and other internal organs if they are unable to use their legs to stand at all (95% of wheelchair users can stand alone in some circumstances). Other new powered chairs have seats that can be raised by hydraulics to bring the user up to standing height while remaining seated.

More sophisticated still are powered chairs that can be controlled by breath: sip/puff technology allows someone with no independent movement whatsoever to operate switches by breathing or blowing into a small tube. And although they are unlikely ever to enjoy mass popularity in the wheelchair market, controls are now being developed by games manufacturers whereby users can operate switch systems by thought alone. Impairment really never has been less relevant; a fact that I will return to and discuss further in Section IV.

Customisation and decoration

Returning to other disability aids now, it was not the case that this equipment was always so unattractive and poorly designed either. Prior to the era of standardisation, equipment was often custom-made for individuals to use. Provided that a customer could pay for them (and the bulk, of course, could not and had to do without), there was a wide range of not only wheelchairs and walking sticks, but also prosthetics, braces, sticks

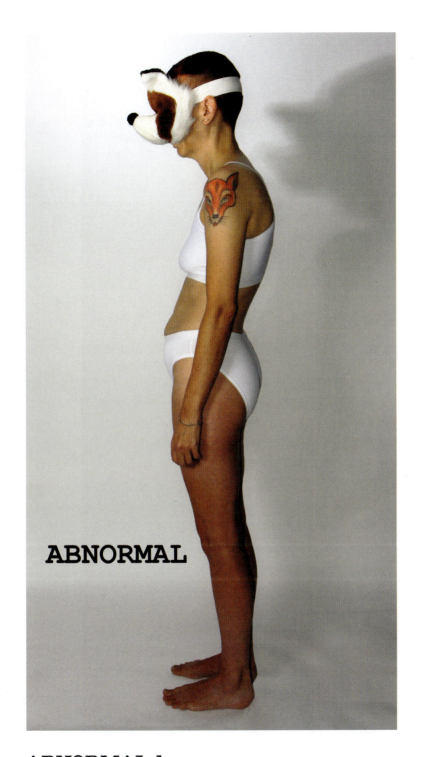

ABNORMAL 1
Lambda print on aluminium, 40" by 22"
© Ju Gosling[ju90] 2008.

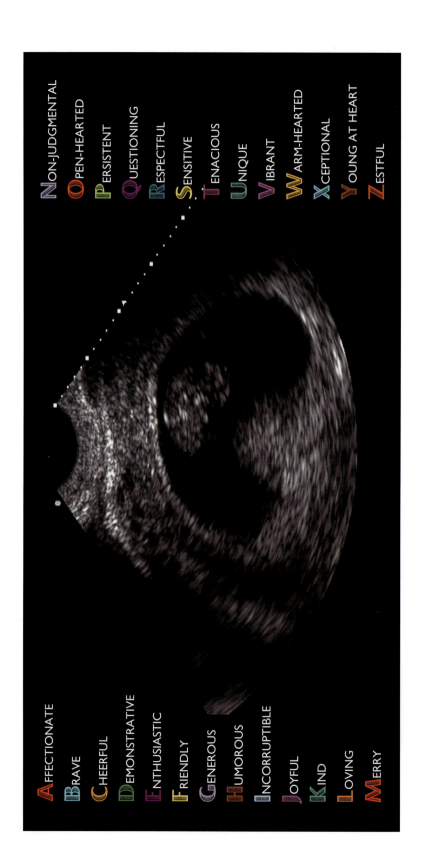

AFFECTIONATE **B**RAVE **C**HEERFUL **D**EMONSTRATIVE **E**NTHUSIASTIC **F**RIENDLY **G**ENEROUS **H**UMOROUS **I**NCORRUPTIBLE **J**OYFUL **K**IND **L**OVING **M**ERRY **N**ON-JUDGMENTAL **O**PEN-HEARTED **P**ERSISTENT **Q**UESTIONING **R**ESPECTFUL **S**ENSITIVE **T**ENACIOUS **U**NIQUE **V**IBRANT **W**ARM-HEARTED **X**CEPTIONAL **Y**OUNG AT HEART **Z**ESTFUL

DESIGN4LIFE
Lambda print on aluminium, 40" by 20" © Ju Gosling[ju90] 2008.

ABNORMAL 2
Lambda print on aluminium, 40" by 23" © Ju Gosling aka ju90 2008.

ROOM 14'7
Lambda print on foamex, 2m x 1m © Ju Gosling ju90 2008.

OUT OF THE FLESH
Lambda print on aluminium, 40" by 18" © Ju Gosling[ju90] 2008.

I want to help the handicapped!
...according to the Charity Model of Disability

I organise social events for non-disabled people. This raises money to create jobs for non-disabled people. Then we provide the disabled people whom we think are deserving with the things that we think they need.

I want to help the handicapped!
... according to the Medical Model of Disability

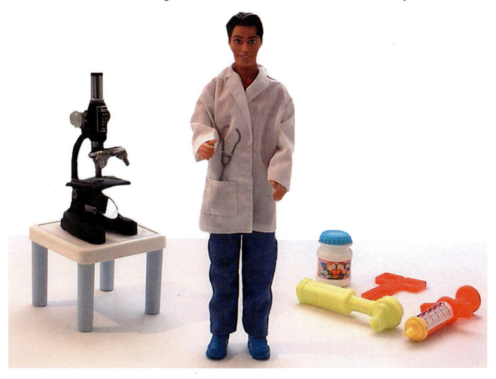

I invent and administer tests to classify disabled people according to what I think are their impairments. Then I carry out experiments to try to make them more like me. If I fail, I try to identify and kill them before they are born.

HELPING THE HANDICAPPED
Digital C print on foamex, 101mm x 33mm © Ju Gosling[ju90] 2003.

I want to help the handicapped!
...according to the Administrative Model of Disability

I invent and administer tests to classify disabled people by what I think are their inabilities. Then I judge the minimum level of benefits and services that I think they need to survive.

I want to help the handicapped!
. . . according to the Social Model of Disability

I fight against prejudice, discrimination and disabling environments.
I fight for equal rights legislation and better health and social care provision. I also fight to eliminate the poverty, abuse, violence and war that cause the majority of impairments.

HELPING THE HANDICAPPED
Digital C print on foamex, 101mm x 33mm © Ju Gosling[ju90] 2003.

LAMED by your language
CRIPPLED by your charity
INVALIDATED by our doctors
VICTIMS of your systems
HANDICAPPED by society

HELPING THE HANDICAPPED

Digital C print on foamex, 101mm x 33mm © Ju Gosling[ju90] 2003.

From the website commissioned by the City of Graz's Sinnlos Festival when Graz was European Capital of Culture. The print version was produced for the Humans Being exhibition at the Chicago Cultural Center in 2006.

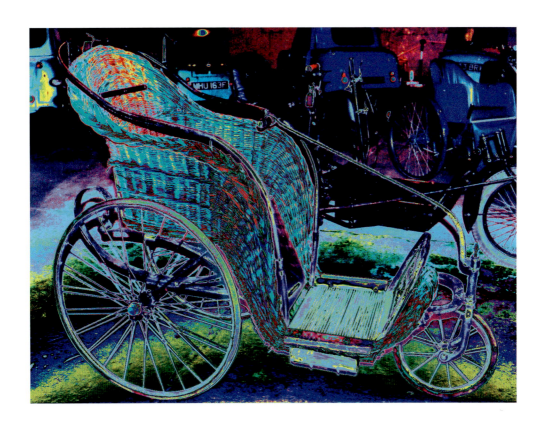

WHEELS ON FIRE 1
Digital C print on foamex, 67cm by 50cm © Ju Gosling[ju90] 2003.

WHEELS ON FIRE 2
Digital C print on foamex, 67cm by 50cm © Ju Gosling[ju90] 2003.

WHEELS ON FIRE 3
Digital C print on foamex, 67cm by 50cm © Ju Gosling[ju90] 2003.

WHEELS ON FIRE 4

Digital C print on foamex, 67cm by 50cm © Ju Gosling[ju90] 2003.

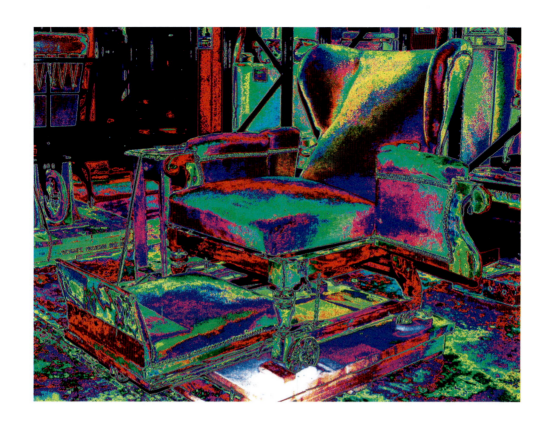

WHEELS ON FIRE 5

Digital C print on foamex, 67cm by 50cm © Ju Gosling[ju90] 2003.

WHEELS ON FIRE 6

Digital C print on foamex, 67cm by 50cm © Ju Gosling[ju90] 2003.

Wheels on Fire features wheelchairs from the Wellcome Collection, photographed in the Science Museum stores at Wroughton. The images were first used as projections to accompany a performance commissioned in 2003 by the Science Museum and Apples and Snakes as part of the Naked Science series.

and so on carefully crafted and built with due regard to aesthetic as well as practical considerations. It helped that, for a brief while, middle and upper-class disabled people were reclassified as 'invalids', a highly romanticised classification that was often linked to having TB and which helped to distinguish them from the common cripple. However, overall, bespoke aids always overlapped with fashionable concerns.

Sticks in particular were regarded for millennia as fashion items, and were used by many people who had no need of them for mobility purposes. 'Canes' — so named because the shafts were originally made out of bamboo or rattan — were widely used in ancient Egypt, and their design was used to denote the user's status and role within society. Canes were buried with the dead, both to help them on their travels and to help to identify them in the afterlife: Tutankhamen was buried with 132. However, it wasn't until the 16th century that sticks became wildly fashionable in Europe. There was then an explosion of literally thousands of different designs, including sticks made from ebony, ivory, porcelain, jade or Venetian glass; sticks that incorporated hidden weapons — or, more prosaically, drinks; sticks decorated with carvings, jewels or precious metals; and so on and so forth. Rather than being a symbol of 'abnormality', these sticks denoted the high social status of their users, reflected in the expense with which they had been crafted. King Louis XIV of France even banned all but the aristocracy from using them, guaranteeing them their desirability in post-revolutionary France.

Stick use as a badge of status reached its peak in the 19th century, with no Victorian gentleman's dress being complete without a cane, and most gentlemen owning as many canes as they did outfits. In London alone, there were 60 specialist cane shops, whereas today there is just one. Stick use quickly spread from Europe to North America, and they continued to be highly fashionable — for men, anyway — into the 1920s and 30s. After that, though, they became increasingly undesirable, although the reasons for this are unclear. The rapid abandonment of canes does not appear to be linked to the coming of war, since officers had had canes as part of their uniforms, and other wars had come and gone without the prevalence of stick use being affected. Fashions had also come and gone while continuing to incorporate canes within different trends. However, it is clear that the increasing need to present the body as 'perfect', and to distinguish oneself from the 'imperfect', played at least some part.

Medicalisation and standardisation

It is probable that the medicalisation of disability aids in the second half of the 20th century had a major impact on the disappearance of sticks as fashion accessories, never mind as badges of social status. As we have seen, beliefs in the benefits of standardisation, and the legislation that enforced these beliefs, made it hard for variations to exist, particularly since the state was usually the customer. In addition to the standardisation of the wheelchair, the infinite variety of canes was replaced for NHS patients by an ugly, metal, adjustable (one size fits all) orthopaedic walking stick, which instantly marked out the user as being 'abnormal' and so as having very *low* social status. No one would want to risk being mistaken for one of *them*.

In all, the 19th-century producers of bespoke equipment for disabled people largely disappeared with the medicalisation of disability equipment, which took place across the world and not just in countries with state medical systems. Medical equipment was serious, scientific; it was important to distinguish it from the frivolity of fashion. Medical equipment was made from scientific materials such as steel and aluminium, not from materials that might well carry disease and be hard to keep sterile. Medical equipment did not require the input of designers; rather, it was the province of engineers and clinicians. Medical equipment was meant to 'normalise' the defective and hide their deficiencies; it should therefore be 'flesh coloured' wherever possible. Medical equipment complied with a scientific standard, and therefore needed to be infinitely reproducible. Medical equipment was there to meet the needs of someone with a medical diagnosis, and everyone with the same diagnosis would by default have the same needs. This attitude extended to many items that would not normally considered to have anything to do with medicine, such as kitchen equipment and furniture, since, within a medicalised approach, these were seen as being therapeutic as well as functional.

The fact that standardised equipment became dominant so quickly was, of course, linked to the economic status of the people who needed it the most. In Britain prior to the coming of the National Health Service, some poorer disabled people had made their own equipment, including on some occasions their own prosthetic limbs. The majority of disabled people, though, had had to rely on equipment that could be bought as cheaply as possible, or, more often, that was lent to them via charities and insurance schemes. With the coming of the NHS, most had no option but to take what they were given and be grateful for it. Overall, the majority of disabled people have never had any choice about what aids they have used or what these have looked like.

The fact that disabled people, with their low economic power, have rarely been the customers is another reason why aids and equipment remain so poorly designed and ugly today. Manufacturers have no need to convince the users of their products to buy them; they only need to persuade the medical and social care professionals who sign the (bulk) purchase orders. Since the vast majority of these professionals are non-disabled, they have little or no personal experience of how the products function in daily use. Matters are made worse by the fact that the recipients of equipment are often afraid to complain about it, in case they are seen as being 'difficult' or, worse, as being unable to manage and therefore in need of institutionalisation.

And since the bulk of disability aids and equipment are provided by the state, the state normally retains ownership and can remove it again if it wants to, which is always an additional fear. The retention of state ownership further reinforces the standardised appearance of aids and equipment, since disabled and older people are prevented from painting, decorating or otherwise customising it, which in turn helps to obscure the users' individuality.

Stigma versus reality

As we can see, the history of our relationship with disability aids and equipment has been extremely varied. There is nothing innately negative about any of the items used specifically by disabled people — rather, all but the worst-designed have at least some potential to improve life, even if a better design would have more impact. And individual items only became stigmatised once they became associated solely with medicalisation and 'abnormality'; canes and wheelchairs were, once, seen as signs of high social status, and canes in particular were deeply fashionable. (Many other items that are of particular benefit to disabled people escaped stigmatisation only because they were not regarded in this light.) This stigma was then reinforced as medicalisation and standardisation meant that aids and equipment were increasingly ugly and poorly designed.

Poor design and lack of aesthetic appeal have not, though, been the overwhelming reason why disability aids continue to have such negative associations today. The new types of wheelchair, for example, are colourful, well designed and, to a wheelchair user at least, extremely desirable, but this has not changed the association of wheelchair use with tragedy one iota. I remember my first public outing in my new powered chair: excitedly I rolled in with a chair resplendent with purple frame, puncture-proof wheels, and adjustable back and leg rests. "How tragic to see you like this," was the first comment that was made. This was despite the fact that I was actually far more comfortable, more able and more mobile as a result of the chair than I had been for years beforehand. Our dysphoria is now so serious that anything even remotely regarded as being linked to an 'abnormal' body is to be reviled.

Mobility scooters have had a similarly problematic reception. Electric scooters were first developed in the 1960s, and by the 1970s these had become extremely popular with older people in particular. Many saw scooter use as being preferable to using a wheelchair, since it did not carry the same stigma. Wheelchair use was associated with people who were quite definitely 'abnormal', whereas mobility scooters were there simply to aid mobility. However, stigma soon became attached to scooter use, too, and mobility scooters now mark their owners out for similar levels of abuse by the general public. They do, however, remain cheaper than powered chairs, which are only very seldom provided by the state.

Public disapproval of mobility scooters is not restricted to youths setting fire to those parked outside homes on outlying housing estates. Every year in the press, more and more column inches are devoted to denouncing scooter users as being a menace to pedestrians, and as people who should be controlled and regulated. Articles calling for cyclists to be compelled to have insurance, or for stricter measures to be taken against the one in four car drivers who lack insurance, appear far less frequently. Indeed, there are at least as many articles challenging any moves to regulate cyclists as there are stories in favour of this. Yet mobility scooters travel at a maximum of two miles an hour on pavements (eight on the road), far slower than many pedestrians — and one never sees stories about pedestrians colliding with each other and causing accidents, let alone demands for pedestrians to carry insurance.

The power of fashion

The example of spectacles shows, however, that it is possible for change to happen, virtually overnight. By the late 20th century, improvements in eye testing and the increasing need for all workers to do close work made it obvious that huge numbers of the population who were currently without spectacles actually needed to wear them. At this point spectacles ceased to be a badge of 'abnormality', and became something that anyone might use.

Suddenly, spectacles were something that you 'wore', like clothes, creating an association with fashion. The number of frame designs available exploded, and people were encouraged to have several different pairs — function was now only part of the picture. (The only drawback was that most of these were unavailable on the NHS, and so were unaffordable by those who needed them most.) The fashion conscious even started to buy spectacles with plain glass lenses, so that they could adopt them as part of their 'look' even when they had no medical need for them.

Canes have also enjoyed brief bursts of popularity in recent years, admittedly among very small sub-cultures. However, the medical profession in particular seems keen to ensure that people who use sticks because of their 'abnormality' can be identified by them, and to ensure that fashion is rejected in favour of functionality. When I used a cane as my main form of mobility support, I used a beautiful hazel stick with the handle carved into the shape of a seal's head. Made by one of the few remaining 'stick dressers' in Britain, Rick Leech, it would not have been out of place in an art gallery, and it was also the perfect height, weight and shape for me. On my first visit to a new hospital, the physiotherapist viewed me with alarm. "We must get rid of *that*", she said firmly, "and get you a *proper* stick." Today, a number of mobility specialists have begun to produce sticks that combine medicalised designs with more fashionable decorations, but these remain unavailable on the NHS despite being no more expensive, and there is still a long way to go.

It is not, however, impossible to imagine a day coming when the stigma of medicalisation and abnormality recedes, allowing powered scooters, canes and the like also to become 'normalised' and fashionable again. I remember becoming increasingly conscious of a young girl's eyes on me when I was using my mini-scooter in a surf fashion shop, and increasingly concerned about what she was about to say. I needn't have worried. Eventually, with a sigh, she looked at me and breathed: "Ooh, I've wanted one of those for *ages*!" I've since had similar experiences with dozens of little boys. There is nothing innately undesirable about disability aids and equipment; the stigma arises simply from the 'abnormal' people that they are associated with. Meanwhile, to include disabled and older people in target markets for 'normal' products, and to have their input into designs would minimise the need for specialist equipment and improve the design of just about everything in the process.

A large number of people with restricted mobility who currently 'prefer' to walk or drive would clearly benefit from a widespread change in attitude towards scooters and their like (as has already occurred in the case of spectacles). And, after all, there would be considerable profit to be made by producers, and money saved by consumers, if use of such items became more 'normalised'. Scooters offer a cheap, eco-friendly alternative for many short journeys currently undertaken by car, as well as offering a more accessible alternative to cycling or using a manual wheelchair.

Maybe one day, fun, funky personal electrical vehicles will be common on our pavements, while pedestrians strut past with their ultra-fashionable canes. And perhaps the 'need' to use them might be defined by the imperative to get to the shops before they close or to impress a girlfriend, whether or not the user also has an impairment. First, though, we would have to tackle our body dysphoria.

10. DYSPHORIC DESIGNS or, Making the world over in a distorted image

As we have seen, the results of our attitudes towards 'abnormal' bodies have had two overarching effects. First, we have learnt to regard the body as being in a state of flux, moving slowly but surely towards a point whereby progress and evolution — science working with nature — will combine to create physical perfection. Second, we have learnt to regard people with 'abnormal' bodies as being outside of 'normal' society, rather than as being an integral part of it. Along the way, we have recast the 'normal', 'standard' body as being young, well and fit. Inevitably, these beliefs and approaches to life have had a huge impact on the man-made environment around us. This will not simply affect every one of us at some point in the future, it already affects us every day of our lives. And every day that we fail to recognise the continuing impact of our dysphoria on our built environment is a day when we are creating yet more long-lasting problems for us all.

Standardisation and segregation

As we have already seen, in the past 200 years standardisation has been regarded as being highly desirable, leaving everyone with a 'non-standard' body to struggle. Before standardisation, though, it was still the case that no one was going to design a world to meet the needs of people who were considered at best to be better off dead, and at worst as being hardened sinners who might well be consorting with the Devil. Rather, the environment was designed to meet the needs of the perceived workforce — young, well and fit 'normal' adults. This has left us with a historic legacy, as well as a modern one, of an environment that fails to meet the needs of the majority, and with which we will all struggle at some point in our lives.

It is worth pausing for a moment here to take a closer look at the equally negative impact of a more sympathetic approach to disabled people, still dominant in much of western and central Europe today. Within a 'caring model of disability' perspective, disabled people are seen as being in need of care and protection. This might be because they are regarded as being innocent and naïve, frail and fragile, or because they are regarded as needing protection from their own criminal tendencies and needing direction towards other, more worthwhile activities instead. Regarding disabled people as being in need of care also resonates with many religious texts: looking after the vulnerable can be a means of becoming closer to God. (Although, as we have seen, this does not make the vulnerable the equal of the people who are 'helping' them.) However, 'caring' for disabled and older people has also been equated with removing them from society, particularly over the past few centuries.

We have already looked at the increasing institutionalisation of disabled and older people in Britain during the 19th and first half of the 20th century. In fact, many disabled and older people remained outside these institutions, but — as I have discussed — most of them were still invisible to the rest of society. Meanwhile, many of the people being 'cared' for suffered horrendous levels of degrading and dehumanising treatment, including serious abuse: the 'caring model' was never particularly caring. Charitable patrons preferred to raise funds to provide care rather than providing the care directly themselves, while local authorities and health authorities simply wanted to provide services as cheaply as possible. And with many disabled and older people institutionalised away from their home areas, and with family involvement discouraged in any case (many people were advised to abandon their children to institutions and 'forget' them), abuse of all types only occasionally came to light at the time.

However, institutionalisation had the added 'benefit' of removing the need to create a wider environment that included people with 'abnormalities' (of whatever kind). As we have seen, institutions provided work-related activities, and in any case disabled people were largely excluded from the workforce, so there was no economic imperative to make standardised facilities accessible to all. If someone was incapable of 'managing' in a 'normal' environment, then the answer was simple: put them into a 'home'. It was, in any case, regarded as being much 'kinder' to institutionalise, since someone who was struggling in the outside world was seen as being in obvious need of care and thus incapable of living independently. "Why", a doctor asked a colleague of mine when she returned to her native Austria recently, "don't you give up work and move into a home instead?" This is despite her having an international career and a thriving relationship.

Removing people from the community rather than changing the built environment to include them has had the added impact of reducing complaints, since the vast majority of people have always struggled as hard as possible to avoid being institutionalised. It is still preferable to accept that you are excluded from accessing the vast majority of facilities that other people use daily than to risk being removed from the community altogether. In any case, though, disabled people did not have any specific rights to enter buildings or to use services until the very end of the 20th century; but even then, rights were still strictly limited (as I will discuss further below). Complaining was never an effective means of achieving change.

The problem with steps

Whether we see disabled people as being sinners, in need of care and protection within institutions or about to disappear altogether, the result has been that the features common to our built environment have remained unchanged since the Romans first introduced modern building techniques to Europe. Critically, entrances have always been raised from the ground, even though the majority of buildings have not required the protection from flooding that this conveys. And despite the invention of the wheel at least 5000 years before the Roman Empire came into existence, steps have been preferred to ramps for reaching said entrances. This is despite the fact that it is far easier to carry items up gentle slopes, while steps make it impossible to use wheeled trolleys or carts to move items in and out of buildings. Slopes, too, exist in nature: steps are an entirely man-made concept; and thus it is actually ramps that are 'normal'.

As for the insides of buildings, the vast majority of domestic properties as well as many commercial ones have only stairs as the means of accessing upper floors. New homes today are built with at least two bathrooms — even tiny houses now commonly have three lavatories; but lifts, popular for a brief period in the 19th and 20th centuries, have all but disappeared in buildings of three storeys or less. This is despite the fact that whenever a lift is available in even a very small building, domestic workers will always prefer to use it to move vacuum cleaners, waste bins and so on between floors; lifts do not just benefit people with limited mobility.

Most people, though, spend a lifetime moving often very heavy domestic weights from floor to floor, with the majority sustaining at least one injury in the process. It is not uncommon for parents as well as children to fall down stairs, particularly when children are young or parents are trying to carry infants between floors. In general stairs pose hazards for all of us at some point in our lives, as well as continual difficulties that we have somehow learnt to take for granted. But although legislation has been introduced to make new homes more accessible (of which more below), nowhere is there mention of constructing floors in such a way as to allow a through-floor lift to be fitted later. Consequently, three-quarters of the cost of retrofitting domestic lifts relates to creating ceiling apertures, which in turn prices them out of most people's reach.

Steps and stairs have also been incorporated into public transport, despite the growing ease of fitting ramps into new vehicles. Some buses now have ramps as an alternative to steps — in the last years of the 20th century, bus operators found the growing number of protests by wheelchair users, when they chained themselves to buses and stopped the traffic, highly embarrassing — but new trains are still being built without ramps in the 21st century. This is despite the resulting facts that many older people find themselves excluded from rail travel because they can't manage the steps; that rail employees risk hurting themselves every time they lift heavy temporary ramps up and down to enable wheelchair users to get in and out of carriages; and that many travellers have to heave heavy luggage — in addition to themselves — up and down steps, and so prefer to drive or fly whenever possible.

Everywhere that a wheelchair user is unable to go is a place where heavy objects will have to be lifted rather than wheeled. This can at best be a nuisance for even the young, well and fit, and at worst can result in their changing status overnight. In all, steps and stairs are responsible for causing or contributing to the cause of the majority of back injuries, which in their turn are one of the leading causes of impairment and time off work. Spines normally sustain cumulative damage, so every time that someone is forced to lift a pushchair containing a heavy toddler, a hefty case or a full shopping trolley up steps into a bus or a building, they risk hurting themselves a little more. Add to this the number of times that someone carries a child or heavy luggage — or both at the same time — up and down a whole staircase, and it is easy to see why back problems are so common, particularly among women.

Back problems are associated with depression and incontinence as well as with pain and restricted mobility — which is why they create so much unemployment; but as a society we never even discuss the possible benefits for the wider population of replacing steps with ramps and lifts wherever possible. Rather, ramps are seen as only being there for the use of wheelchair users (although, of course, a wide range of other people with impaired mobility need to use them, too), so are rarely put into place unless someone is legally obliged to do so. Even where ramps exist, they are expected to be there for the sole use of disabled people. Parents with pushchairs are regarded as being illegitimate ramp users (the invisibility of parents with infants is discussed further below), and parents continue to be expected to lift children up and down steps whatever the impact on their spines. Delivery people are also expected to use steps whenever possible, increasing the number of work-related back injuries still further.

As a result of ramps being associated only with wheelchair use, they are also regarded as being necessary only on a temporary basis — since we believe that in the near future people won't need to use wheelchairs. Therefore, we continue to build a wide range of public and domestic buildings where the entrance is raised and the 'normal' entry is via steps, while the 'special' entrance is around the side or the back, often through a door that is generally kept locked and whose key takes some time to find. It is not necessary to be a regular user of back entrances to be reminded of the days when both women and Black people were required to use separate entrances, in the days when these groups were also considered to be 'abnormal'. In addition, it is ironic that the people who have the most limited energy and mobility are expected to take the most lengthy and complex routes in and out of buildings. However, the real point is that, as we have just seen, we are condemning ourselves, not just other people, to a whole host of problems in the process.

Exclusive designs

Even buildings where everyone uses the same entrance can cause serious problems for people with restricted mobility, and in particular for non-wheelchair users. Indeed, some of these buildings are worse than the old buildings with their 'special entrances'. It is common in large new developments to create a pedestrianised area outside entrances, with massive foyers or atria inside that also require crossing before people reach reception areas and lifts. This means that the distance between the taxi drop-off point or the parking facilities reserved especially for disabled people and their destination is greater than the maximum that people can manage to walk in order to qualify for specialist parking in the first place. Walking across expanses of shiny concrete flooring, though, is not much fun for anyone.

As we have seen, few people who would benefit from wheelchair use actually possess wheelchairs, so many people with restricted mobility effectively use their cars instead. In the past, it was relatively easy for this group to drive to the building where they worked or were attending an event, park outside and walk a short distance to a lift or to where they needed to be. Now, with parking only available further away from buildings, and with lifts often being situated away from entrances, many of the same people are effectively barred from entering whether or not there is step-free access. It is worth noting here that, at the end of the noughties, the Equality and Human Rights Commission and the 2012 Olympics organisers, both organisations that were intended to promote equality and diversity, were situated in complexes with these design features: the 'iconic' More London and Canary Wharf. It is unclear how many people were barred from working for them as a result.

A wide range of other problems with the built environment are also caused as a result of our dysphoric expectations of our future — both our own and other people's. Pedestrianised areas outside, and the need to cross large foyers inside, also make environments much more difficult to access for people with visual impairments. Within buildings, signage is designed for people with 20/20 vision and often lacks any symbols for non-English readers, and contrasting colours are seldom used to draw attention to doorways, switches and other essential features for people with impaired sight. Instead, any features designed for people with less than 'perfect' vision are regarded as extras, such as Braille signage — which of course is not understood by the majority of visually impaired people. It is worth remembering here that visual acuity begins to decline significantly for everyone at the age of 40; it is not simply a condition that affects a tiny minority of us. We all suffer stress, too, when we are in unfamiliar buildings and cannot easily identify where we need to go.

Windows are commonly installed at a height at which it is difficult or impossible to see out of them while sitting down, even though this is the only occasion when most people have time to look. This lack of visibility of the outside environment impacts particularly on older people and people with restricted mobility (who spend more of their lives seated), although of course it affects children too. However, all of us suffer from not being able to see the outside world, and for some people it creates claustrophobia or an atmosphere in which they cannot do the creative thinking that their job requires.

Meanwhile, doors and ceiling heights have been raised over the centuries as average human heights have increased, but room sizes have shrunk, despite the fact that average human weights, and therefore girths, have increased even further. (Small room sizes, of course, also make it more difficult for wheelchair users to move around, and increase the likelihood of older and frailer people falling over.) Overall, a wide range of problems are caused simply because the 'standard' body is still expected to be thin as well as fit, even though statistics show that the average body is now anything but. It is not only domestic furniture that causes difficulties for larger people, but also seats on public transport, office furniture, turnstiles and many other things that are inadequate to meet their needs. And yet more than half of all British adults are now overweight, and a quarter are defined as being obese; again, this is not simply a problem for a small minority.

Failing families

Smaller people have similar problems. As we have seen, with standardisation came the definition of the normal body as being white, non-disabled, heterosexual and male; critically, it was also adult. Children, being outside the labour market, were not considered when standards were being developed. (For the same reason, neither were mothers with infants, which is why they face so many problems with steps.) Small adults — and wheelchair users, who also have many issues with the height of various facilities — may make up a relatively small proportion of the population, but we are all of us small humans for a significant proportion of our lives, and many of us go on to have small humans of our own, too. Again, the problem is not a minority one.

Approaching height issues scientifically, we might consider that it is easy for the majority of tall people to bend down, but impossible for children, short people and wheelchair users to make themselves taller (with the exception, of course, of wheelchair users with expensive specialist chairs). However, we still consider it normal to design our environment for adult men — overall, the tallest members of society. As a result, it is difficult or impossible for a large proportion of the population to reach door knobs, letterboxes, lift buttons and counters; to read posters and signs and so on and so forth.

I often see groups of school pupils being led out of an exhibition by a teacher and gallery education officer who are both congratulating themselves on the educational experience that the children have 'enjoyed'. But as I haven't been able to see more than half the exhibits myself, I know that the children haven't either. No one else, though, seems to notice. It is unsurprising that children are often regarded as being in opposition to the rest of society, since their participation within it is made so problematic for them. How 'included' can children and young people possibly feel when it is patently obvious to them that the world is designed only for adults? No wonder they often feel angry and resentful.

At least disabled people now have some rights to have adjustments made to enable their participation in society. Neither children nor parents have any legal rights to enter buildings or to use services, and the great majority of discrimination against them is entirely legal. Indeed, many groups have to rely on anti-discrimination legislation intended to benefit disabled people before they can access facilities themselves. The fact that all families face a period of years when they are almost as limited as disabled people in terms of which parts of the built environment they can access seems to go unnoticed by legislators. The difficulty is that, with medicalisation, adjustments can only be made for people with 'problems'. And since women spent decades arguing that they were *not* disabled compared with men, and that pregnancy was *not* a disease, families are not regarded as falling into this category. At the same time, their normality is *not* the normality that the environment was designed for, and this is the case for the majority of the population.

Unfortunately, our failure to include the majority — children, parents, and older and disabled people — when designing our environment is creating problems for decades, and probably centuries, to come. At least we can blame history for the wide range of problems caused by design features in older buildings. It is dispiriting to note that it is considered to be more important to preserve buildings' 'historic integrity' than it is to make them more widely accessible by implementing a few structural changes now, but that simply reflects our body dysphoria. With new buildings, though, we are creating our own legacy of inaccessibility for our children and grandchildren — as well as, of course, ourselves at some point sooner rather than later in our lives.

The weakness of legislation

What is most depressing is that, as far as public structures are concerned, we believe that we are already building a truly accessible environment for the first time. In many parts of the world, including the United Kingdom, legislation now provides for construction to take place in a way that enables disabled and older people — but not children — to access the resulting buildings and environment. Crucially, the 1970 Chronically Sick and Disabled Persons Act first introduced some rights to enter public buildings in Britain, along with other rights. Over the four decades since then, a huge amount of expertise has been gathered — partly but not only by disabled people themselves — on how a wide variety of bodies interact with the environment. Access auditing — looking in detail at what environmental barriers exist and how to overcome these — has become a profession in its own right, and many public organisations also gather groups of disabled people to advise them further on the construction of new buildings.

However, there are various shortcomings even with the legislation. For a start, there is nothing within it that requires disabled and older people to be given equality with non-disabled people. As we have seen, inequality has been enshrined in religious and political thinking for millennia. And although race and gender discrimination were outlawed in Britain in the 1970s, it was only in the mid-1990s that disability discrimination began to be tackled with the 1995 Disability Discrimination Act. But rather than providing for equality, this Act said only that disabled people should not be 'substantially disadvantaged' compared with other people; some level of disadvantage was enshrined in law. At the same time the legislation provided for 'legal' discrimination, outlining all of the ways in which disability discrimination could be legally 'justified'.

In the noughties, British public authorities were required to 'promote' equality for disabled people, but this was always a woolly requirement and was subsequently watered down in the Equality Act in 2010. In any case, it is hard to see how public authorities can promote equality effectively when the rest of the legislation does not provide for it. Before the Disability Discrimination Act was implemented in 1999, 'abnormal' people were commonly barred from using pubs, restaurants, clubs, holiday camps and other facilities because it was felt that their presence might put other customers off, while 'special' facilities continued the segregation of disabled people. Unsurprisingly, the same providers feel under no obligation today to ensure that disabled and older people can benefit equally from their services and facilities. They see no reason why they should treat 'abnormal' people differently from 'normal' ones, even when their needs may be entirely different, and see no reason why they should respond to complaints by people who are 'invalid' anyway. It is therefore unsurprising that many people believe they have complied with the law by 'allowing' disabled people to enter a building or to access a service at all, however disadvantaged they might be in the process. Inevitably, this attitude is often echoed in the courts.

Designing future difficulties

It is also inevitable, given the overall shortcomings of the legislation, that laws covering the construction and fitting out of new buildings has only provided for a minimum level of access. Perhaps it is inevitable too, given the previous lack of awareness of disabled and older people's needs, that the majority of people involved in commissioning, constructing and inspecting new buildings continue to believe that this is a 'best practice' standard, a 'politically correct' aim to be fulfilled if at all possible, rather than a legal requirement. Unfortunately, though, this often means that plans drawn up by architects — who do understand the importance of legal compliance — are subtly changed during construction. Beliefs that disability is a transitory condition, while new construction is designed for the long-term future, mean that accessible features are the first to be cut when costs run over budget.

The lack of visibility of disabled and older people also leads everyone concerned with new buildings to underestimate the numbers of these people within the population, and thus the numbers who could potentially use their buildings. As we have seen, disabled and older people are all but invisible within media imagery and popular culture. Where environments are semi-accessible — such as shopping centres with level access — older and disabled people are visible in large numbers, but this visibility is rare. Even where access is possible, disabled and older people are excluded from the workforce, and they also lack the economic power to enable them to participate in many cultural activities. In addition to this, many built environments are inaccessible anyway, at least on a practical basis, so the bulk of disabled and older people remain largely unseen today.

The underestimation of the numbers of people affected by the design of the built environment further increases the likelihood that access will be far more problematic than anticipated when new buildings are completed. As the example of the Tate Modern shows, lifts that are suitable for a certain number of people prove entirely inadequate when the visitor numbers are double or even triple the estimates. This does not just make life difficult for disabled and older visitors and parents with pushchairs, but also the many young people who feel that using the stairs or escalators is a step too far. Then there are the lifts that are too small for a double-buggy or an adult's wheelchair to fit into, even though there was enough room to install lifts that were double the size — not to mention the lift doors that close on the people who are entering them, and the gaps by the door that act as traps for wheelchairs and pushchairs.

Dysphoric Designs

Lack of awareness of disabled and older people's needs by builders is another major issue — particularly as user groups mostly participate only at the design stage. Features that looked good on paper may have changed out of all recognition by the time that the builders have finished with them. Add to this the fact that many people do not believe that disability will ever affect them personally, and it is easy to see why the law is so ineffective. The people who fit out buildings usually have no idea why a particular feature exists and how a particular item is used, and cannot put themselves in the place of the people using them to work it out for themselves. So, for example, toilets designed for disabled people become impassable because basins, radiators and grab rails have all been installed in the wrong places, preventing entry in a wheelchair at all.

This lack of awareness and imagination further problematises access into and out of the environment around buildings. Cobbles are commonly used around new buildings, although they cause major problems for wheelchair users, people who are visually impaired, and people with a wide range of other mobility problems. Gravel — virtually impossible to negotiate in a wheelchair or scooter — is ubiquitous as a 'security feature'. 'Accessible' entrances are often reached across cobbles, or potholes, or grassy — for which read muddy — expanses. None of these are any easier for parents with pushchairs to use, or indeed for women wearing heels. Again, only the 'standard' fit young (male) body has been catered for.

Inside buildings, 'accessible' toilets are commonly used as broom cupboards, because of the lack of belief of the existence of disabled people who would want to use them. Disabled people and parents of infants, both of whom are likely to require longer in the lavatory than other users, are made to use combined facilities for the same reason. Then there are the 'accessible' toilet doors that open the wrong way, trapping users inside or making it impossible for anyone to wait outside them.

Neither emergency alarms nor hearing aid loops are regularly tested. Portable ramps and loops are often locked away with no one being aware of where the key is. Stairlifts are usually switched off: keys then take a long while to find; and even once keys are found, the stairlift's operation is often faulty.

Meanwhile, doors are often too heavy for disabled or older people to open, leaving everyone to struggle. Seating in public areas may be limited or non-existent, or uncomfortable for people with back problems and impossible for people with limited mobility to get out of again. Fold-down seating is now rare in lifts, although this is essential for people with balance problems. Hard, shiny walls, ceilings and floors make acoustics a nightmare for anyone with even slightly limited hearing: reception areas where it is impossible for anyone to hear what is being said are all too common. Carpets are difficult for wheelchair users to propel themselves across, while their patterns may set off migraines or seizures in those who are susceptible. Other floors are so slippery that falls are common among people with even the slightest difficulty in walking — including women wearing heels. All of this makes a potentially accessible building a nightmare of barriers and difficulties — even though it is entirely possible to make buildings truly inclusive.

Dysphoric choices

In the outdoor world, the way in which we have naturalised car use — and before that, use of the horse and carriage — has led us to change the natural environment considerably. Mountains and valleys, hills and plains, coastlines and countryside have all been irrevocably transformed by our desire to make it possible to drive through them. We could have created pathways to walk or ride on that would not have affected the landscape a fraction as dramatically; we could have relied much more heavily on railways, which have much less environmental impact; we could have continued to use water as a means of transporting goods to a much greater extent. Instead, we have not hesitated to create roads, even in areas of great natural beauty or historic value.

For more than 2000 years it has seemed entirely natural to us to change our landscape, largely to ensure that people who are able to walk do not need to do so — not even the short distances required to use public transport. But it has not seemed natural to us to drop kerbs or to build ramps, so that those who have difficulty in walking can access the environment along with the rest of us. Yet when an environment becomes even partially accessible, the number of disabled and older people within the community instantly becomes more visible. This makes it even more damaging that so little of our environment is without barriers — ironically, the natural environment is often more accessible than the built one. While we believe that disabled and older people are a tiny minority of the population, it is much easier for us to believe that impairment and ageing will never happen to us — and the people most harmed by this attitude are ourselves.

A truly inclusive environment is more comfortable and enjoyable for all of us. When access is impossibly difficult for some, it is accompanied by an environment in which we all struggle. Where steps are the only means of accessing a building, all of us will have days when we are too tired or are carrying too much to get in easily. Rooms that are too crowded with furniture for wheelchair users to get round make us all twist and turn and feel claustrophobic. Acoustics that are impossibly difficult for people with hearing impairments mean that we all strain to hear. Lighting that is too low for people with visual impairments to see makes us all strain our eyes. Chairs that are impossibly painful for people with spinal problems to sit on are uncomfortable for the rest of us. Buildings that make people with fragile mental health feel unsafe, or are impossible for people with cognitive difficulties to navigate easily, are stressful for us all to be in. Inclusive design is simply good design.

It is hardly surprising that the disability rights movement points not only to social attitudes but also to the built environment as being a major disabling factor within our society. If we change our attitudes, then change to the environment will follow, and technology can supply the remaining means of providing equal access for everyone. In contrast, and as we will see in the next sections, science and medicine have little, if anything, left to offer when it comes to transforming the lives of disabled and older people. If we continue to ignore this unpalatable truth, then we will only have ourselves to blame when we become the victims of our own dysphoria.

SECTION III

FACING FACTS or, Why the human race will never be 'perfect'

All of us are capable of recognising our body dysphoria and of making changes to our lifestyle and approach to life. Most people, though, are content to wait, secure in the belief that sooner rather than later science and technology will make personal change unnecessary. For reasons that we have already explored, consciously or unconsciously, many of us believe that science and technology will soon alter our bodies in such a way as to make us, quite literally, immortal.

The belief that our bodies will soon be 'upgraded' by these means is fuelled by media reporting. Almost every week we are told about the development of drugs and technological processes that promise, some day soon, to cure terminal illnesses, improve our quality of life, make lifestyle changes unnecessary, and, ultimately, reverse the ageing process. It is because of this that we happily trust that disability will soon be a thing of the past: after all, if scientists can prolong all our lives, then surely they can effect a few cures first?

This belief plays a part in the development of our modern body-dysphoric environment. If we will soon be able to take a pill to make us thin, why should we design seats and doorways for larger people? If we will soon be able to cure all illnesses and reverse the ageing process, why should we design buildings and transport systems that are accessible to people with mobility problems? Equally, why should we prioritise financing social care over funding the armed forces or new road building?

To what extent, though, should we take media claims seriously? Do these stories really promise us enough to prevent us from making the lifestyle choices that we might otherwise consider necessary? It is to science itself that we must look for a clearer picture.

11. SCIENCE FICTIONS or, Ten reasons why science teaches us that it doesn't have all the answers

i) Yesterday's miracle cure is today's dead end

We are all used to seeing media stories about the development of new miracle cures — for cancer, for HIV, and for ageing itself. If there is one thing that encourages us to believe that science is all-powerful, it is our constant exposure to these utopian visions of a future where everything can be cured. Yet the vast majority of these stories turn out to be misleading, and very often the research goes nowhere at all.

In the 1980s, scientists were confident that a vaccine against HIV would be found within two years. Even in the noughties, media claims that a trial vaccine was about to prove effective proved to be untrue time and time again. Today, it is uncertain whether a vaccine can ever be developed, due to the changing nature of the HIV retrovirus. Rather, drug treatments have been developed that, for as long as they continue to work, have rendered HIV into a chronic rather than fatal condition; but a cure, let alone a vaccine, is as far off as ever. Even then, HIV continues to mutate within the body, meaning that people living with HIV require different and more expensive drugs as time goes on.

In the 1990s the focus switched to genetic engineering. As a result a whole new industry was developed, funded by investors who believed that they had discovered the Holy Grail of medicine. However, while a minority of biotech industries have delivered — and continue to deliver — important new treatments, the majority have collapsed, with nothing to show for their investment. All of them, though, originally believed that their research would produce a new generation of treatments that by now would have been firmly on the market.

Undaunted, in the 21st century we have turned to stem cell research for the answers. In doing so, a wide range of ethical questions have been discussed: for example, to what extent is it permissible to use aborted foetal tissue to develop stem cells? But what we have failed to question is the extent to which stem cell treatments are likely to succeed — and when this is likely to happen. In the teens, while stem cell research is teaching us important lessons about human biology, the promised results are as far off as they ever were.

Apart from in a tiny minority of conditions, doctors' claims to be able to treat patients successfully with stem cell therapies have turned out to be either fraudulent or hopelessly over-optimistic. Doctors are not, after all, scientists, but are as susceptible to media stories as the rest of us. In the future, stem cells still hold out the promise of useful treatments, but these therapies are likely to be far removed from the initial media hype, and will also be far more expensive to administer than the breakthrough drug treatments of the 20th century.

Somewhere along the line, we have learnt to conflate the following two concepts: 'It's possible to imagine, one day, this development being the first small stage on the road to achieving X' and 'As a result of this development, we will soon be able to *do* X'. This in itself is further evidence of our body dysphoria, as well as our dysfunctional attitude to scientific research. We know better than to believe these utopian myths, but it suits us to accept them as being true anyway.

Of course, there are many reasons why scientific research is presented in the rosiest possible light. We seem to forget that drugs companies are not in themselves scientific institutions, but exist primarily to make a profit through selling their products. They *employ* scientists to develop their products, but they are not *controlled* by scientists. Drugs companies have a mixed heritage: along with the pharmacists who used to make their own medicines and scientists themselves, their ancestors include the travelling salespeople of recent history who sold everything from coloured water to snake oil while claiming that it cured all ailments.

According to a 2006 report by Consumers International (a federation of more than 230 organisations from 113 countries), the 20 biggest drugs companies were then estimated to spend around £33 billion a year on promoting their products. Between them, they were found guilty of breaching rules on publishing misleading drug information around a hundred times a year, and this did not include the activities of their media officers. When the media misreports stories with the encouragement of drugs companies, the latter cannot be held as breaching any regulations at all.

Science Fictions

To give just one example of media misrepresentation, in March 2006 every British newspaper front page and television news programme was dominated by the 'news' that a new drug could reverse the effects of heart disease by clearing clogged arteries if taken daily. Front-page headlines included: "One pill a day to beat heart disease" (*The Times*), "Pill to beat heart disease" (*Daily Mail*) and "Drug that reverses heart disease" (*Daily Express*). Commentators suggested that the drug would also enable people to continue with the same unhealthy lifestyle that can cause heart disease, so long as they continued to take the drug.

However, the drug in question was a statin — a drug to control cholesterol — that had actually been launched three years before the story was published. Evidence had soon emerged that it could cause a serious muscle-wasting illness, greatly limiting its use and availability. The manufacturers then carried out a two-year trial, involving a statistically small group of 349 patients. Despite the patients being given the maximum daily dose of the drug, the effect on their arteries after two years was miniscule: a 6.8% reduction by one measure, but only a 0.9% reduction by another. Crucially, the trial did not run long enough to find out whether the drug had any impact whatsoever in reducing the rate of heart attacks among these people.

Yet only one journalist picked up the fact that: "This was a victory for marketing, rather than for the research department." Jeremy Laurance, health editor of the *Independent on Sunday*, had his article published in the Business and Media section of the paper, the readership of which was miniscule compared to that of the original story. The *raison d'être* of the media is to tell us what we want to hear, not what we need to know. Bad news sells when it affects other people, but is less popular when it affects us all. Likewise, scientists are under pressure to attract funding in order to continue their work, making it tempting for them to paint a picture of their research that's as optimistic as possible.

Another drug that was expected to make a significant contribution to fighting heart disease was a drug aimed at reducing cardiac inflammation. Inflammation is as significant as cholesterol as a cause of heart attacks, but there had previously been no drugs available to treat it. The new drug, called simply AGI-1067 by its UK manufacturers, AstraZeneca, was therefore expected to represent the first new approach to treating heart disease for 20 years. However, trials eventually showed that it was no better than a placebo in reducing the number of heart attacks, strokes and deaths. For the US biotechnology company that developed AGI-1067, this was the fourth drug that they had abandoned at a late stage, after drugs for stroke, diabetes and blood-clot prevention had all failed, too. Shortly afterwards, they also abandoned the development of a drug to tackle the RSV virus in infants after finding it was no more effective than an existing drug, but with additional side-effects.

The closest that we have to a wonder drug is still aspirin. Apart from tackling pain, it has been shown to lower blood pressure, to reduce the risk of heart attacks and strokes; and to reduce the risk of developing certain cancers; new uses are still being explored. Rather than initially being created in a laboratory, its active ingredient was originally derived from willow bark and has been used by humans for millennia.

No one can doubt the contribution that medical research scientists have made to improving the world's health. Research scientists must continue to be supported to explore all possible means of combating disease — and, as importantly, to continue to extend the bounds of human knowledge. But we must remember that all too often yesterday's miracle cure turns out to be today's dead end. And there are far, far more dead ends in medical research than anything else. We need to be very careful indeed to distinguish between science fact and science fiction when assuming that, given enough time, medicine will be able to cure everything.

ii) Some illnesses that have killed humans for millennia may never be permanently defeated

In the mid-20th century, the use of penicillin led us to believe that eventually we would be able to defeat every organism capable of causing disease, either by killing it or by vaccinating ourselves against it. This belief was later encouraged by the discovery of a range of other antibiotics, along with the development of chloroquine to treat malaria. These discoveries were hugely significant. They allowed doctors to cure tuberculosis (TB) and malaria, two of the biggest causes of disease worldwide until then, as well as vastly improving survival rates following infections and surgery. Doctors were also able to eradicate the smallpox virus through the widespread use of vaccination.

However, we now know to our cost that bacteria can adapt and become resistant to antibiotics. It is entirely possible that by the end of the 21st century antibiotics as we now know them will be entirely useless at treating infection. And so may a range of other treatments that we once thought had provided us with permanent weapons against disease. Meanwhile, other diseases are becoming more widespread, for no apparent reason.

In fact, antibiotic-resistant bacteria started to emerge only four years after mass production of penicillin began in 1943. Resistance initially develops from spontaneous mutations in bacteria's genetic code as they reproduce, which quickly become the norm as the stronger strains survive and become increasingly more common. This process is speeded up when people fail to complete a course of antibiotics, allowing the bacteria to fight back and gain resistance to the antibiotic being used to treat them. Scientists have also now discovered that genes that convey resistance can be passed between bacteria. For example, the NDM 1 gene can be passed between different strains of E. coli, thus making 'last line of defence' antibiotics powerless; already widespread in India, NDM 1 has now arrived in the UK as a result of 'medical tourism'.

In 1993, half a century after the mass production of antibiotics began, the World Health Organisation (WHO) declared TB to be a global emergency again. According to the WHO, there are now almost 400,000 new cases of drug-resistant TB worldwide each year, and in 20 years' time the majority of the world's TB cases could be antibiotic-resistant. Drug-resistant TB is now found in 104 countries, and is soon likely to spread to every country in the world. Whereas multi-drug-resistant TB (or MDR-TB) was resistant to two or three drugs in the past, today's strains are resistant to an average of between 6 and 11 drugs. Most recently, a strain of TB has developed that has been named extensively drug-resistant TB (or XDR-TB): this is virtually untreatable with existing antibiotics.

While TB used to take six months to treat with drugs costing around $2000 for each patient, cases of MDR-TB can take any time from 18 months to three years to treat, and can cost between $28,000 and $1.2 million per patient (US figures). In the developing world, treatment costs between $300 to $4000 per patient, which puts an unbearable economic strain on health care systems. As a result, the majority of people living with TB have not been treated, speeding up the spread of the disease. Scientists warn that as many as 249 million new cases of antibiotic-resistant TB may occur worldwide by 2030, causing 90 million deaths. As in the past, TB continues to threaten the health of the worldwide community.

Similarly, before the discovery of penicillin, infections in hospital patients following surgery were a major cause of death. With the introduction of antibiotics this seemed to be a thing of the past, but in the noughties an increasing number of hospital patients in the United Kingdom started to catch MRSA. The abbreviation MRSA stands for Methicillin-resistant *Staphylococcus aureus*, but is commonly used to describe any strain of staphylococcus bacteria that is resistant to one or more conventional antibiotics. Staphylococcus is a family of common bacteria which many people carry naturally in their throats, and which will cause only a mild infection in a healthy person. However, in someone with a compromised immune system it can be lethal if not detected and treated quickly. MRSA is not resistant to all antibiotics, but can take much longer to treat than normal infections. However, worryingly, there are now strains of staphylococcus that have developed resistance to all antibiotics. Infection is fast becoming a serious threat within our hospitals again.

Even bubonic plague, which decimated the populations of Europe and Asia in the Middle Ages, has developed resistance to antibiotics. Scientists in Madagascar recently discovered a strain of the plague bacterium that was resistant to no fewer than eight antibiotics that were previously used to treat it. It had achieved this by swapping genes with common food bacteria such as salmonella, probably while being carried in the guts of fleas: bacteria are becoming increasingly efficient at appropriating genes that give them resistance.

In the past few decades, the WHO recorded outbreaks of plague in 125 countries, and in 2005 the Democratic Republic of Congo reported 1174 suspected cases and 50 deaths. If an antibiotic-resistant strain of the plague should spread, either naturally or at the hands of terrorists, it would be very dangerous. If left untreated, bubonic plague kills between 40% and 70% of those infected, usually within a week, while untreated pneumonic plague has a fatality rate of almost 100%. As in the past, infections are a leading cause of death in hospital, and an increasing cause of disease outside it.

Malaria, caused by a parasitic micro-organism, has similarly adapted to become resistant to chloroquine, which was developed by British and US scientists in 1946 after its initial discovery by a German scientist in the 1930s. This process of developing resistance had begun by the late 1950s, but accelerated towards the end of the 20th century. Newer drugs have been developed in an effort to replace chloroquine, but because of their cost and stronger side-effects they have not been so widely used. In the mean time, malaria parasites have started showing resistance to these drugs, too, including sulfadoxine/pyrimethamine, mefloquine, halofantrine and quinine. More than 60 years after we believed that malaria could be defeated, it continues to be the number one killer of children under the age of five worldwide, and the problem is continuing to grow.

Scientists are now concentrating on developing a vaccine that will provide children with some protection against the most lethal side-effects of the parasite. It is no longer thought to be possible to develop a vaccine that will be effective against infection by the parasite in the first place. Neither is it thought to be possible to develop an anti-malarial treatment that is guaranteed to work in the long term. Meanwhile, global warming is expected to result in malaria-bearing mosquitoes spreading into areas that have previously been exempt, such as western Europe. As in the past, malaria continues to threaten the health of the worldwide community, and only low-tech resistance such as the distribution and use of mosquito nets is likely to make any real impact.

Influenza, meanwhile, was a leading cause of sudden mass death in the first half of the 20th century; most famously after the First World War, when it killed more people than the war itself. In the second half of the 20th century, influenza vaccines and anti-viral treatments were developed and made widely available, while the virus itself became less threatening to human life. But it is now expected that, sooner rather than later, the human influenza virus will combine with bird flu to produce a new type of influenza that will kill on a scale never seen before. It is not thought to be possible to develop an effective vaccine before the virus develops into a pandemic, because our modern travelling habits mean that the disease will spread far more quickly than it did in the early 20th century. As in the past, influenza also continues to threaten the health of the worldwide community.

Conditions that we take for granted as affecting only a small percentage of the population can also become more widespread even when there is no infectious agent involved. For example, there is no apparent explanation for the rise in short-sightedness, which around the world now affects between 30% and 80% of all young adults. All we do know is that our previous belief that our eyesight is entirely dictated by our genes is wrong.

Likewise, Type 1 diabetes develops in childhood. There is no known cure for it, and people who have it must inject insulin daily for the rest of their lives in order to stay alive. Unlike Type 2 diabetes, it is not caused by poor diet, lack of exercise or obesity, and there are no known means of preventing it from developing. Until recently, it was believed that people were born with a genetic susceptibility to Type 1 diabetes, which meant that the proportion of the population affected would remain stable, but we now know we were wrong about this, too. In 2007, researchers in the UK found that over a period of 20 years the percentage of under-fives with Type 1 diabetes had increased by 500%, while the percentage of under-15s with it had doubled. Researchers in Europe had already made similar findings. However, the reason for the rise remains unknown.

Similarly, childhood asthma is now twice as prevalent as it was in the 1960s, but no one knows why this is the case, either. It might be that exposure to infection, or protection from infection, or diet, or environmental factors are responsible for the increase in both Type 1 diabetes and asthma, but unless and until the cause is established, the rise may continue. Even then, we may be powerless to do anything about it. In the mean time, childhood admissions to hospital for both conditions increased throughout the noughties, and some of those children died.

Medical research scientists have been extremely creative and resourceful in finding ways of overcoming diseases that have affected the world's health for millennia. However, we now know that victories over disease-causing organisms may only be temporary, rather than being permanent as we had previously believed, and that new solutions may be harder to come by than the old ones. And we cannot assume that serious illnesses that have affected only a small percentage of the population in the past will continue to do so in the future: all sorts of changes in our environment may cause a much larger group to be susceptible, and most of the time we cannot predict this. We have to accept that scientists may continue to be occupied with finding ways of overcoming ancient threats to human health for the foreseeable future.

iii) New illnesses develop constantly to take the place of old ones

It is of course true that, in some cases, illnesses can be defeated completely. Most famously, smallpox was eradicated during the 20th century, and it is hoped that polio will go the same way during the 21st. In both cases an effective vaccine has been developed, followed by a programme of universal vaccination. However, since bacteria and viruses are continually changing in nature and mutating to create new types, we are constantly facing the prospect of new threats to human health replacing the old ones.

In 1980, there were no known cases of Aids (acquired immune deficiency syndrome) worldwide. Today, in some countries between a quarter and a third of the entire population is believed to be infected with HIV (human immunodeficiency virus), which causes Aids. According to the WHO, an estimated 2.3 million children were living with HIV/Aids at the end of 2006, 2 million of them in sub-Saharan Africa; and Unicef (United Nations International Children's Emergency Fund) estimates that around 15 million children have now been orphaned as a result of HIV.

More money has been spent on researching into cures for Aids than for any other disease. Despite this, and despite more than a quarter of a century of dedicated research, no cure has been found. The best that we have been able to achieve is a treatment that is expensive, toxic, does not work for everyone who is infected, and is unproven to be successful in the long term. Unlike smallpox, HIV has the ability to mutate constantly. It is therefore unlikely that we will ever be able to develop a vaccine against it. Rather, it will only be defeated by halting its spread; something that is unlikely to be achievable during this century. The more that we learn about viruses, the more we understand what a powerful force they represent, and how resistant they are to our best efforts to defeat them.

And, of course, it is not only viruses that cause disease. In the mid-1990s, British people who eat beef — i.e. the vast majority — learnt that we may have been exposed to the agents that cause variant Creutzfeldt–Jakob disease (vCJD). This is a human form of bovine spongiform encephalopathy (BSE), a disease that had spread through British cattle herds from the 1980s onwards. In turn, BSE was thought to have developed in cattle because they had been exposed to 'scrapie', a disease in sheep, through being fed feed containing animal products (cows, of course, are normally vegetarian).

Rather than being caused by a virus or bacteria, scrapie and cVJD are caused by 'prions', which are proteins. Prions normally play an integral part in the body's functioning, but the prions that cause scrapie and vCJD are 'rogues' that can cause healthy prions to mutate to become like them and spread the disease. As prions do not trigger an immune reaction or contain any genetic material, there is no means of testing blood to see if someone has been infected. vCJD is therefore notoriously difficult to diagnose and there is still no known treatment for it, let alone a cure. In the past two decades, more than 160 people are known to have died from vCJD in the United Kingdom, but because the presence of the disease can only be confirmed by autopsying the brain, the exact number may be much higher.

It is also possible that most people who have been exposed to BSE-infected meat will take much longer to develop the disease because they are not so genetically susceptible — all of those who have died so far have fallen into the 40% of the population whose own prions are most susceptible to attack. It is also not known whether vCJD can be transmitted by contact with surgical instruments (since prions are not destroyed by heat, sterilising has no effect on them). However, in the late noughties the first death was announced as a result of someone contracting vCJD from an infected blood product; something that scientists had previously hoped was impossible. The action taken to remove BSE-infected meat from the food chain may have prevented vCJD from becoming a widespread illness despite its potential to be so — or that action may not have been taken quickly enough; the jury is still out.

vCJD reminds us that new illnesses can develop which our normal medical defences are powerless against, while the rapid growth of HIV worldwide during the late 20th century has reminded us that there is no such thing as the status quo of a micro-organism. The defeat of smallpox during the last century was a huge victory for medical science; however, its successor, Aids, has proved to be even more lethal. Meanwhile, TB and malaria continue to make a comeback. Even as we think that they have been defeated, viruses, bacteria and parasites all develop to form new threats to the world's health. Our scientists are challenged enough just maintaining the status quo.

iv) Cures that work in the laboratory cannot necessarily be mass-produced

We take mass production so much for granted now that we assume that everything we can do in a laboratory can be recreated on as large a scale as we desire. However, this may not be true of biotechnology, since its very nature limits its possibilities.

For example, one of the most well-known developments of the last decade has been the ability to grow skin cells in the laboratory. Skin cells can now be taken from patients and grown in the laboratory, before being replaced over damaged areas. In particular, this has been of the most enormous benefit to people who have suffered severe burns; but it has also made a wide range of reconstructive surgeries more effective.

Alongside this, scientists in the USA developed artificial skin patches that could be used to treat deep vein ulcers. These ulcers, which most commonly are a side-effect of diabetes or circulatory illnesses, can be life-threatening, particularly in elderly people. Conventional treatments are lengthy, and are often unsuccessful in achieving a complete healing of the wound. Meanwhile, if their own skin is removed in order to be grown for grafting, patients like these are likely to develop more problems as a result. The artificial skin patches, though, quickly proved to be effective. Equally importantly, they could be administered quickly and easily on an outpatient basis using only local anaesthesia. However, the company manufacturing the skin could not meet demand, and eventually went into liquidation. No matter how hard they tried, they could not find a way of 'scaling up' the laboratory process.

This may sound like a simple problem just waiting to be overcome in the near future; but despite the use of robotics, biotechnology is dependent on a great deal of human input, which in turn brings in the ever-present danger of bacterial contamination. Once a production process is contaminated, all production must be closed down and the contaminated products scrapped. It may take months to reopen a production line, and it would cost vast amounts of money to achieve decontamination. Potentially, perhaps, these problems can be overcome by the development of more sophisticated (and expensive) robotics systems. After all, we have substantial experience of using these in vehicle manufacture. But this still leaves us with the difficulty that biotechnology takes place in 'real time'.

As computer-processing power has become ever faster over the last decade, we have come to believe that technological development will keep pace with this. However, increasing processing power has a limited impact on biotechnology compared with other industries. This is because a biological process takes a fixed amount of time to complete, regardless of how fast the observed results of this process can now be analysed. A cell will take x amount of time to divide in a laboratory regardless of how powerful the laboratory's computers might be, and there is only limited potential for increasing the speed of that division. Faster and faster data analysis has and continues to offer much to bio-science, not least in sequencing the human genome, but has far less impact when it comes to producing products.

Biotechnology has been one of the most exciting technological developments of the late 20th century. Research scientists have enhanced our understanding of the human condition, and continue to do so. However, we need to accept that as far as treatments derived from biotechnology are concerned, mass production — the 'scaling up' of treatment that works in the laboratory to make it widely available — may never be possible in many cases. We also need to be aware that the likely costs of producing these treatments will, more often than not, place them out of the reach of the majority in any case (as I discuss further in ix below).

v) The body has an innate resistance to being 'enhanced'

In the 1990s, developments in technology led us to believe that eventually the human body would be routinely enhanced by technological implants, combining bio-engineered components with machine parts. Many people today believe that, in their lifetime, they will receive implants that will increase their natural abilities. These implants, they believe, will turn them into 'post-humans', 'trans-humans' or 'cyborgs'. However, if the experience of the past is taken into account these developments seem rather less likely, and it is clear why the vast majority of believers are non-scientists themselves.

In 1967, the South African doctor Christiaan Barnard performed the first successful heart transplant surgery. Today, major organ transplants involving the heart, lungs, liver and kidneys have become routine. However, organ rejection is common, both immediately after surgery and in the months and years ahead. For example, although between 80% and 90% of transplanted kidneys are functioning one year after surgery; only four out of ten kidneys are still working five years on; and ten years after having a kidney transplant, only half of transplanted kidneys are still functioning. Similarly, although between 85% and 90% of heart transplant patients survive their surgery and live for at least a year after the transplant; and 75% are alive after five years; only between 50% and 60% are alive after ten years. Yet the vast majority of these organs would have continued to function for some decades to come if their original owner had lived. And this is despite the fact that organ donors and recipients must be carefully 'matched' in terms of tissue type before a transplant takes place in order for it to have any chance of succeeding. Overall, organ rejection rates after five years have not improved since the 1980s.

In order to combat rejection, organ recipients must take daily doses of steroids to suppress their immune systems and prevent them from reacting against these 'foreign' bodies. The drugs have a range of toxic side-effects, some of which are life-threatening, as well as making transplant patients more susceptible to disease. Side-effects of drugs taken by kidney transplant patients, for example, range from excessive growth of the gums, swelling of the face, high blood pressure, high cholesterol levels and thinning of the skin to osteoporosis, diabetes and liver damage. Despite this, about 40% of kidney transplant patients will still experience acute rejection of their donated organ within the first three months, and although most can be treated successfully, this involves the use of even higher doses of even more toxic drugs.

The reason why organs are rejected, and why organ recipients must take immunosuppressive drugs, is because the immune system's function in life is to fight anything that invades the body. This would normally include viruses and bacteria, as well as objects such as splinters. Our blood streams carry two types of natural defenders: white blood cells, which stick to invaders and try to kill them; and antibodies (smaller than white blood cells), which stick to invading germs and either make them burst apart, or help white blood cells stick to them. The immune system is very powerful, and, apart from where transplants of the same blood type are involved, is very good at recognising anything that is not part of its own body.

The development of organ transplants is yet another example of the achievements of medical research scientists during the second half of the 20th century. Transplants have increased the lifespan of and improved the quality of life for many people. If more people could be persuaded to sign up to the donor register and to donate the organs of deceased relatives, then the number of lives saved could be increased still further. And, of course, scientists are continually working on ways to combat organ rejection; stem cell research seems to offer real possibilities in this field. For example, in the future it may be possible to remove all but the underlying structure from a donated organ and then regrow it by introducing stem cells from the intended recipient in the laboratory.

However, the experience of decades of transplant surgery has also underlined its limitations and taught us a valuable lesson. The body, it seems, has an innate resistance to being modified. And while it may be financially viable to use stem cells to minimise the risk of organ rejection in the future, will it really make economic or any other sort of sense to use them to 'upgrade' the human body with computer and robotics technology?

vi) The best engineering solutions cannot match the body's own designs

Of course, most of the 'upgrades' that are envisaged for the human body are technological, not organic. However, the experience of the past shows that implanting technology into the body is, at best, problematic.

Perhaps the most successful implant technology to date has been the heart pacemaker, which is able to regulate the heart beat by detecting irregularities of rhythm and then firing electrical impulses to regulate them. However, despite more than half a century of research, scientists have failed to create an artificial heart capable of keeping a recipient alive beyond, to date, a year. The first patented artificial heart was invented by Paul Winchell in 1963, and the US government believed that artificial hearts would become routine by 1970. However, in the years that followed, patients could not be kept alive for more than six months. Today, artificial hearts are still only used as a stopgap for patients waiting for a transplant, or to support the recipient's own heart.

Abnormal

Yet the heart is basically a pump, and human-made pumps have been in existence for millennia. (The earliest known type of pump, the Archimedes screw, may in fact have been in use as early as the seventh century BC.) Creating an artificial pump that works within the human body has always been seen as a relatively easy challenge. However, it now seems less and less likely that we will ever be able to produce an artificial heart that will provide an effective long-term substitute for the real thing. We have grown to understand that the heart is a far more complex organ than we originally believed, and is subject to sophisticated chemical controls.

Similarly, humans have been making artificial human joints since the 1960s, and ball-and-socket joints are widely used in manufacturing, particularly within motor vehicles. Yet in the teens it is still impossible to produce an artificial hip or knee joint that will reliably last beyond a decade. This is why older people in need of joint replacements are encouraged to wait until their seventies, in order to avoid undergoing the surgery twice. Replacing the hip the second and third time is less likely to succeed because of the bone loss involved in each surgery, and is twice as costly as the first operation.

Another common surgery involves inserting a rod alongside the spine to straighten and support it, following the development of a spinal curvature in adolescence or an accident affecting the spine. Again, these rods commonly break and need to be replaced: the best technologies are less effective than our own organic bodies.

In the 1960s and 1970s, engineers turned their attention to developing prosthetics that would meet the needs of children born without limbs. Many of these children had been damaged in the womb, after their mothers were prescribed the 'wonder drug' thalidomide to prevent nausea during pregnancy. At the time, there was a great deal of confidence in engineers' ability to develop prosthetic solutions that would rival or even surpass the body's own powers. So great was this confidence that some children had non-standard but functioning limbs removed in order to fit their prosthetics more easily. Overall, children damaged by thalidomide were subjected to a wide range of experimental solutions. Some still feel scarred by the experience today, while others admire the engineers' dedication to improving their lives. Ultimately, though, all of the solutions failed in their aim of creating substitute working limbs. Children were left to wear prosthetics that ultimately had no function other than to 'normalise' their appearance.

The best prosthetics available today are simply high-tech versions of the artificial limbs available to wealthy Victorians. There is some limited progress being made in creating prosthetic arms and hands that are controlled by brain activity, driven by the growth in amputees arising from the war in Iraq. But, at best, these will provide a partial solution for a small number of amputees in the future: a solution that will never function as well as a human limb. (A small number owing to both the high costs of the technology and the fact that specialist medical practitioners — orthotists — will always be needed to fit them. Many amputees around the world are unable to walk today only because of a shortage of orthotists and funds to fit them with much lower-tech prosthetic feet and legs in a process that takes hours instead of weeks.) These developments will certainly not result in routine and unproblematic body extensions for non-disabled people.

In the 1980s, engineers turned to spinal injuries, believing that they would be more likely to succeed in this area. The most obvious engineering solution to paralysis appeared to be to control the body below the spinal cord break from outside the body itself. British woman Julie Hill participated in research for more than five years: it involved implanting electrodes into her spine which connected directly to the nerves that control the leg muscles, with the aim of helping her to walk again. However, despite some limited success, the researchers discovered that the way in which the brain controls the lower limbs is so much more complex than was previously realised that conventional computerised engineering techniques were unusable.

Despite these limitations, the development of artificial joints by research scientists has made a huge impact on the quality of life for many older people in particular. Lower limb prosthetics have also been enormously successful in improving independence and mobility for amputees. Meanwhile, cochlear implants have enabled Deaf people with a particular type of hearing impairment to gain some level of hearing, and in the future it seems increasingly probable that some basic degree of vision may be provided for blind people via implants. Likewise, implanted electrodes are proving successful in the treatment of neurological symptoms such as tremors from Parkinson's disease and cluster headaches.

However, even the most carefully researched and developed engineering solutions do not appear to be a match for the body's own designs. And if 'upgrades' should ever be successfully developed, then, as with artificial joints and transplants, they would be unlikely to function without creating other difficulties. Medical engineering has much to offer disabled people with sensory and mobility impairments in particular, but is highly problematic when it comes to 'enhancing' the rest of us.

What if we were to develop technologies that were cleverer than humans: artificial intelligences (AIs) that could solve the problems that confound us? This is one possible solution that has been suggested to overcome the limitations of our humanity. However, one symptom of our body dysphoria is the continual undervaluing of our existing abilities. The brain is actually extremely complex and extremely powerful, involving around a hundred billion neurons with possibly a hundred trillion connections (synapses) between them; it is hard to imagine that an all-round artificial intelligence could be developed that is superior to this.

For example, humans have little difficulty in understanding a wide variety of handwriting that we have never seen before; we are very good at 'pattern recognition'. We are also very good at understanding unfamiliar voices. Computers, though, still need 'training' before they can recognise even one individual's script or voice; it has still not proved possible to programme a computer to recognise patterns.

Even the humble mouse has a brain that is far superior to any existing computer. In 2007 it was deemed worthy of reporting that researchers at IBM and the University of Nevada had succeeded in simulating a small fraction of the power of just half a mouse brain using IBM's BlueGene L supercomputer — which contains 4096 processors, each using 256MB of RAM. It is possible, then, that we may never be able to create an AI that has superior brain-power to our own.

But if we do manage to create an AI that is more powerful than human intelligence (probably by creating an AI that is able to improve itself beyond human capabilities), what then? An AI could potentially analyse existing medical knowledge and data, draw conclusions and make recommendations for future research directions. However, it could only carry out those tasks on the basis of the information that we already have, and help us to gather further information. The phrase 'garbage in, garbage out' has become common in the computing world for just this reason.

We also need to think about whether intelligence is the same as creativity and imagination. Do androids dream of electric sheep? Or is AI limited in the problems that it could solve? Humans problem-solve by imagining solutions, and then by working to create these. Science and technology depend on imaginative creativity to at least the same extent as the world of arts and literature. To what extent, then, is the development of artificial imagination possible?

If the possibilities of AI are realised, they might have far more to contribute away from the world of medical science. If AI can be developed successfully, it is more likely to result in an army of robotic machine-slaves, reinventing themselves as being ever more efficient at our request. They should be able to manufacture and service themselves, and be able to replace humans in some parts of the manufacturing and service industries if this proves to be cost-effective. More worryingly, they may be able to fight wars on our behalf. The imagined future of robots replacing humans may yet come true, whether this is seen as liberating us from labour or as a tool of oppression.

However, AI is still unlikely to result in robotic body parts that can be successfully combined with human flesh to 'upgrade' the body. The best that we can hope for is the development of better prosthetics for people with impaired bodies, and improved implants to help with control of neurological symptoms and to transmit sensory information such as sound and vision. We should certainly not rely on AI, then, to provide us with the secret of eternal life.

vii) Drugs may have side-effects that are not apparent until it is too late

A debate that emerged in the 1990s about the 'post-human' concerned the body that is upgraded by drug therapy. Since then, there has been a growing interest in 'smart' drugs to enhance our intellectual and cognitive abilities. Drugs developed for people with diseases such as Alzheimer's are believed to offer us all the potential to become 'smarter'. Increasingly, there is also an interest in the potential effects of giving 'smart' drugs to children, so that their brain structure is permanently altered as it develops. Some people even believe that in the near future children will routinely be given smart drugs in order to create more intelligent human beings. However, all drugs have a range of effects on the body apart from the desired one, and these are not always easily apparent.

Unwanted drug effects are described as 'side-effects', but are often nothing of the sort. Instead, they are simply the other normal effects of the drug acting on the body. For example, thousands of people who take prescription drugs such as beta-blockers, corticosteroids and psychiatric medications experience rapid and significant weight gain leading to obesity. A further 'side-effect' can be addiction — addiction to prescription drugs is an increasing problem worldwide — which brings with it a range of unwanted impacts on the addict's quality of life. This is as much an effect of these drugs as is the effect intended by the doctor who prescribed them. Individuals differ in the extent to which their bodies can cope with these effects — and when the effects other than the desired ones become problematic, we call them 'side-effects'.

Whatever benefits drugs may offer in the short term, long-term use increases the effects of and the risks from side-effects. Even drugs that are commonplace today, such as non-steroidal anti-inflammatories or NSAIs, have potentially lethal side-effects. Over 7000 people are estimated to die each year in the USA from stomach ulcers caused by the NSAIs that they take for conditions like arthritis. Those who take them may make an informed choice on the basis that the relief offered outweighs the risk; others are unaware of the dangers. Overall, estimates at the end of the noughties put the cost to the NHS of treating unwanted prescription drug side-effects at nearly £2 billion. At best, we can conclude from this that a particular drug will never be suitable for all members of the population. At worst, we can conclude that many drugs will only be shown to be widely unsuitable after a relatively long period of time has elapsed.

Often, of course, side-effects cannot be predicted. An obesity drug that was commonly prescribed in Britain in the noughties, Reductil, was withdrawn from sale in Europe in 2010 after it was associated with an increased risk of heart attack or stroke — reducing the risk of these by losing weight was, of course, a major reason for taking it in the first place. In France, the weight-loss pill Mediator, prescribed there for over 30 years, was blamed for causing more than 500 deaths and 3500 hospital admissions by the time that it was withdrawn in 2009. Other drugs for which pharmaceutical companies had high hopes had to be withdrawn for similar reasons. Then anti-depressants from the SSRI group (selective serotonin re-uptake inhibitors) had to be restricted to adult patients when it was discovered that some younger people actually became suicidal after taking them. SSRIs were also associated with damage to foetuses — thalidomide may be the best-known example, but other drugs have also unexpectedly caused damage when taken in pregnancy.

Meanwhile, scientists spent many years developing a new generation of NSAI drugs such as Vioxx, which would not have the harmful side-effects of traditional NSAIs. Vioxx was eventually released to great acclaim, but it was later withdrawn when it was found to increase the risk of heart attacks and strokes by around 400%. Then, in London in March 2006, six young men who were taking part in a drug trial for a new anti-inflammatory drug were rushed to intensive care when they became seriously ill. Their skin had turned purple, and their heads had swollen to three times the normal size. Calls for doctors who could help find a way of saving their lives went out internationally. The search for a successful, side-effect-free anti-inflammatory continues.

Science Fictions

In 2010, the diabetes drug Avandia was withdrawn from use in Europe after the European Medicines Agency (EMA) ruled that its potential dangers outweighed the benefits. Avandia had been hailed as the first of a new generation of drugs for diabetes, helping the body make better use of insulin and therefore reducing dependency on insulin treatments and minimising the impact of diabetes on the rest of the body. Two million people were taking it worldwide by the end of the noughties. But as evidence mounted that the risk of having a heart attack or stroke was significantly increased when taking the drug, the regulators concluded that it could not be guaranteed as being safe to use.

Whatever anyone's moral position on animal testing, the reality is that drugs that are found to be safe for animals are not always safe for humans. As with Vioxx, the anti-inflammatory drugs that had such appalling side-effects on their human guinea pigs had already passed animal testing. Thalidomide, responsible for killing an estimated 100,000 foetuses and 5000 babies in the first year of their lives and leaving another 5000 babies with serious impairments, was also passed as being safe after animal testing. It may also be true that drugs which are scrapped after being found to be unsafe for animals would actually be beneficial for humans. But the main point here is that there is no means of guaranteeing the safety of any drug we take, other than taking it and seeing what later comes to pass.

It should also be pointed out here that the majority of drugs that have passed human testing will still only have been tested on men. The example of thalidomide showed that the effects of drugs on human pregnancies could never be learnt from animals. Drugs companies therefore moved away from testing drugs on women, believing that all women could theoretically be pregnant. They felt that however small the actual risk, it was still not worth taking. The effect of any drug on women, therefore, is only known once the drug is released for clinical trials, or even for general use.

Children, too, are rarely included in drug testing — for obvious reasons, including their lack of ability to consent and the fact that their bodies are still developing. In 2006, a House of Lords enquiry found that 90% of drugs aimed at newborns and 50% of those aimed at children had not been included in any clinical trials involving children, and so were technically unlicensed for this purpose. Where children were involved in drug trials, 98% took place without an independent safety monitoring committee. It is hard to predict the long-term effects of any new prescription drug on children.

Of course, many people already take drugs that they don't require, using them recreationally instead of medically. Recreational drugs such as Ecstasy provide us with a great deal of information on the likely effects of smart drugs on a healthy population. Most people suffer no short-term ill-effects, but a minority suffer severe side-effects including death. It may be that in the future we will be able to predict who is physically or genetically unsuitable for particular drugs, and will be able reduce the side-effects in this way. However, the long-term effects of any drug will still only become known after years of drug-taking.

It is therefore inevitable that the only way to test a drug's long-term safety is to take it in large numbers, and then to hope for the best. For people with chronic illnesses, the long-term risks of taking a drug may well be balanced out by the benefits of it. Many disabled people (including me) make an informed choice to take drugs that may shorten their lives. Similarly, parents take decisions on behalf of their children when they feel that the benefits outweigh the disadvantages. Recreational drug users, meanwhile, are prepared to put up with a certain amount of risk in return for the instant gratification that the drug provides.

People may well be prepared to take smart drugs in the short term, to improve exam performance, for example; but will people be prepared to take long-term risks when the drugs at issue are both entirely unnecessary and offer no immediate pleasures? It seems highly unlikely that more than a small group would be willing to try, particularly as there is no research to show that intelligent people are necessarily any happier than those who are less intelligent.

And what of parents? Will parents really be willing to expose their children to drugs that are entirely unnecessary, and which have unknown long-term effects? The experience of the MMR vaccine in Great Britain suggests not. The MMR (measles, mumps and rubella combined) vaccine has been shown in countless trials to be effective and safe, while the diseases that it prevents can be lethal or leave victims with severe impairments. Despite this, many parents have not been prepared to take the risk of administering it to their children, concerned that — despite the evidence to the contrary — in a small number of cases it might cause autism and bowel disease in previously healthy children. It seems highly unlikely, therefore, that parents would flock to give their children smart drugs, whatever the promises made for them.

The language of smart drugs is certainly seductive. Who would turn down the chance to pop a pill and immediately become brighter and more intelligent? If only it were that simple. Education combined with good nutrition is the only method that has been proven beyond all doubt to maximise the mental functioning of both children and adults. Meanwhile, it would be unwise in the extreme to risk developing an illness that is preventable by, for example, eating sensibly, in the assumption that a drug treatment for it will be easily available, completely effective and totally unproblematic. Research scientists have improved and/or saved the lives of countless numbers of people with the development of ever more powerful drugs; but all of these drugs should be taken with caution — or, if possible, never taken at all.

viii) Genes are for ever

It took nearly a century of work after Darwin developed his theory of evolution and biological inheritance, but in the mid-20th century scientists finally discovered the double-helix structure of DNA. At last, scientists could study the 'building blocks of life'. As research continued, though, this turned out to be a much more difficult task than anticipated, and it became evident that DNA was far less malleable than had been hoped.

The roots of the research that led to the discovery of DNA can be traced back to the 19th century, and as with all scientific discoveries, it built on developments by a wide range of other researchers. In 1953, Cambridge scientists James Watson and Francis Crick were the ones who succeeded in publishing the theory that proved to be correct. In this they were assisted particularly by research being carried out at Kings College London by Rosalind Franklin and Maurice Wilkins, which had enabled Franklin to produce an X-ray photograph of the crystalline structure of the DNA molecule. Of the four, only Franklin was excluded from their 1962 Nobel Prize, since she died of cancer in 1958 at the age of 38 and the award cannot be made posthumously.

From the middle of the 20th century onwards, many scientists worked to discover more about DNA, encouraged by popular and (more pertinently) political and commercial interests who believed that at last we were about to be able to understand how life works and then control it. By the turn of the millennium, scientists were finally able to produce a more or less complete sequence of an entire human genome. Funded by the US Government and the Wellcome Trust, the Human Genome Project was initially led by James Watson himself.

Although the success of the project came far more quickly than had been expected (it had taken just a single decade), the overwhelming result of the sequencing was to show how very much more there is still left for us to learn about genetics than we had thought. Critically, it turned out that there are not much more than 25,000 protein-coding genes within DNA, far fewer than had been expected and about 98% of which we share with chimpanzees. However, the way in which these genes work proved to be far more complex than had previously been believed.

Initially, it had been popularly supposed that there would turn out to be individual genes for different illnesses that could be easily identified once the genome had been decoded. For example, it was expected that there might be a 'cancer gene'; or at most that there might be different genes for different types of cancers. It was also thought that there would be genes that could easily be identified as affecting intelligence, sexual orientation, alcoholism and so on and so forth. Although scientists always knew that the truth would be more complicated, people were encouraged in this utopian belief by previous research into inherited illnesses. After all, it had been relatively easy to identify the cause of Down's syndrome (an additional chromosome); and other inherited conditions such as cystic fibrosis, muscular dystrophy and sickle cell anaemia had been identified as being caused by a mutation on a single gene.

As we have already seen, though, the wider picture is far more complicated. There are hundreds of different genes associated with cancer, and with the majority of other health conditions, too. On their own, these genes' presence generally cannot be taken to signify anything at all: whether they 'express' themselves or not, and the impact this has on the body, depends on a number of other, largely unknown, factors including the environment and the presence or absence of other genes. How many copies of each gene are present also affects how they impact on the human body, and so on and so forth. At best, all we can do is to predict the likelihood of a given disease developing. The purpose of this book, though, is not to provide a simple explanation of genetics (even if this writer were capable of it), but simply to point out that the underlying mechanisms of life are much more complicated than we originally supposed.

One thing that the Human Genome Project has proved conclusively is that the body is not a machine — a 'clock'. Rather, it is more like the most complex, most sophisticated, largest orchestra ever imagined. Symphonies of largely unknown chemical reactions are constantly taking place: genes are interacting with each other in millions of different ways that we may never fully understand; and the musicians themselves are continually rewriting the music. The overall part played by the bulk of the human genome — which is not actually formed of genes — still remains a mystery. All we do know is that the bits we used to refer to as 'junk', thought to be 'left over' from evolution, may be far more important to the whole thing than we previously imagined.

As a result of all this, our earlier belief that we would easily be able to manipulate and change our genes at will has had to be rethought. As we have seen, there are a (relatively small) number of conditions where the genetic cause can easily be identified, and there have been a smaller number of cases still where scientists have been able to manipulate a carrier's genetic material by inserting a copy of the non-mutated gene into the relevant cells of the body. However, this work has shown just how difficult it would be ever to make wholesale changes to the human genome. Genetically altering the structure of a bacterium, which is relatively straightforward, is a very different thing to altering a human being.

The most common way in which scientists have attempted to change the genetic structure of a human cell is to use a virus to carry the new genetic material into the relevant part of the body. Viruses are uniquely well equipped to invade cells: however, they can also provoke an immune response from the body; and therefore experimental treatments have previously been blamed for causing leukaemia in their recipients, while other cancers may also result in the long term. Genetically engineered viruses also have the potential to reactivate themselves and attack the body, although this is less of an issue. Critically, though, 'gene therapy' is often only of short-term benefit. As the body's 'normal' cells continue to divide, the cells containing the manipulated DNA may be overwhelmed and cease to be effective at overcoming the particular disorder that is being treated. Lungs, for example, are particularly resistant to gene therapy, yet it is here that treatment must be delivered in order to treat cystic fibrosis.

Nonetheless, researchers have been successful in stimulating the immune systems of children born without a functioning immune system by delivering gene therapy directly to the bone marrow. It is also probable that scientists will ultimately find more effective ways of delivering gene therapy to the small minority of the population who possess a mutated gene that can easily be linked to their medical condition, such as cystic fibrosis. However, it would only be (theoretically) possible to alter the genetic structure of someone's entire body by manipulating it when it is still an embryo, or even by manipulating an egg or a sperm before they have come together to create life. Researchers have already succeeded in manipulating the chromosomes of marmoset embryos to incorporate a glow-in-the-dark gene from jellyfish, but this is a gene that is extraordinarily easy to transfer between species.

The process of replacing a gene responsible for ill health while a human was still in the womb would be so difficult that any ethical considerations would be far outweighed by the unlikelihood of it succeeding. But in any case, in the current political climate at least, ethical considerations would prohibit the attempt from taking place. Although we might sympathise with would-be parents who could only give birth to a child that is biologically their own if a lethal gene was altered first, we could have no idea about the impact on the resulting child, let alone the health of future generations. If we did go ahead, though, we would certainly be restricting foetal treatment to diseases like cystic fibrosis.

The Human Genome Project is likely to be central to the majority of the knowledge that we gain about the human body in the 21st century. But one thing it has already taught us is that the genes you are born with are, more or less, the ones that you die with. It is probable that by identifying gene sequences that are associated with an earlier death, we might be able to target people who would particularly benefit from preventative medicine. However, given that all medication involves risks from side-effects, this would be a risky strategy. The chances are good that any individual possessing a gene sequence that increased their risk of developing a particular disease would not develop it anyway.

Similarly, it may well be that in the future we will be able to manipulate the genes that we do have to help fight disease and therefore prevent premature death. However, on the basis of our current knowledge, it is highly unlikely that we will be able to do this routinely any time this century — if at all. Certainly, even if it existed, the 'immortality gene' is not about to be successfully inserted into our bodies any time soon.

ix) We can't afford or are unwilling to pay for the cures that we have invented already

Scientific research has already given us the potential to extend many lives and improve the quality of others. However, every year millions of people who could benefit from these developments are denied access to them on the grounds of cost. Thousands of other people die unnecessarily because of delays in receiving treatments.

Even in Britain, with its state-funded NHS, there are serious delays in receiving treatment because of lack of funding. Patients may wait months or even years after first approaching a doctor before being diagnosed with life-threatening illnesses such as cancer and heart disease. Once they are diagnosed, patients may wait months more before receiving the treatment that they need. For example, in 2005 more than half of all cancer patients were waiting longer for radiotherapy treatment than the Government's recommended maximum of four weeks, according to a survey carried out by the Royal College of Radiologists (RCR). This was because of a national shortage of radiotherapy machines and of operators trained to use them, fuelled by a shortage of financial resources. All this helps to explain why Britain continues to lag behind the average European cancer survival rate, with a very significant difference indeed in the survival rates of certain cancers.

Similarly, patients in Britain are, on grounds of cost, routinely denied access to drug therapies that may extend or improve the quality of their lives. A new generation of drug treatments, while becoming ever more effective, simultaneously becomes ever more expensive. In 2006, insulin inhalers that would have reduced or removed the need for diabetics to inject themselves daily were rejected by the NHS on the grounds that the benefits were largely psychological, and this decision was made despite the number of children who were affected. In 2007, children with sickle cell anaemia were similarly denied a tablet-based treatment that would replace painful daily injections.

In the early noughties, the British Government also introduced policies that for the first time placed restrictions on the drugs that doctors could make available to patients. Drugs were restricted to particular groups of patients, or to patients in later stages of a disease. In many cases, drugs were banned from use by the NHS completely, because the costs were not deemed to be worth the impact on patients' quality of life and life expectancy, even when the patients themselves disputed this. The sight of patients campaigning for access to the medication that their doctors believed would help them became commonplace in the British media.

In some cases, of course, drug prices are kept artificially high, in order to cover the costs of developing them and to make profits for the companies who have invested in that development. The costs incurred by the company's unsuccessful attempts to develop other drugs along the way are included in this process. Over time, as the costs are recouped, the prices come down. There is some potential here to reduce costs: governments would have to work together to develop drug treatments rather than leaving this to individual companies working in isolation to beat their competitors. However, other drugs will always be prohibitively expensive, because the production processes that are used to manufacture them are so complex and costly.

Apart from restricting access to drug treatments, in 2010, representatives of six surgical disciplines claimed in a letter to the *Guardian* newspaper that patients were routinely being denied surgeries including knee replacements, varicose vein removal, hernia treatments, carpal tunnel releases, tonsil removals and treatments for glue ear in children. This was a cost-cutting exercise, they claimed, rather than being based on clinical need. All of these surgeries, according to the surgeons, could have significant impacts on people's quality of life and independence, and in the case of children and young people, on their development.

In many countries, access to any kind of medical treatment depends more or less completely on an individual's ability to pay. In the USA, the richest country in the world, an estimated 45 million people had no health insurance in the noughties, and most of this group had only limited or no access to health care at all as a result. Legislation introduced by President Barack Obama aimed at tackling these inequities was controversial, and was only intended to reduce the worst suffering. Worldwide, many people with chronic disease are only able to remain healthy until their assets are exhausted. Once their insurance runs out and their savings have gone, they are left to feel the full brunt of their disease again. Others — millions of others — die each year for want of the most basic access to medical care.

In the 21st century, research scientists continue to discover medical treatments that have significant potential benefits for improving and extending the lives of people with life-threatening and chronic conditions. However, the gap between what is available and what we are able to afford to buy is likely to grow ever wider for the vast majority of us. We are unlikely ever to reach a point at which every member of the world's community has access to unlimited resources. Since the population is increasing at the same time as finite resources such as carbon power are being used up, we are more likely to reach a point at which the resources available to each individual shrink year on year. Would governments really prefer to fund genetic manipulation for foetuses with conditions like cystic fibrosis, for example, to abortion?

As a result, it is unrealistic to believe that, in the event of scientists developing treatments that can extend our active lifespan, more than a small minority would have access to them. Indeed, it is hard to see how, in a state-funded system like the NHS, politicians would ever agree to provide treatment that would still, inevitably, increase the financial demands that an individual makes on the state. Inevitably because, in the real world, longer life means more disease and therefore more treatment, and also a longer period of receiving state benefits, without necessarily an increase in our contribution back to the state. We need to remind ourselves that where disease can be prevented by personal lifestyle choices it would be wise of us to take those choices. The cost of doing otherwise may be more than we can afford.

x) Life is what kills us

Research into genetics has already taught us many things about the human body. In particular, it has shown that the body is not 'programmed' to die. Our genes do not contain a self-destruct mechanism; we are not allotted a certain lifespan after which our genes cease to renew our bodies and shut down.

Initially, these research findings were welcomed with enthusiasm. If our bodies are not programmed to die, then surely we all have the potential to live for ever? And even if this turns out to be too expensive for many of us, then surely it will be available to the lucky few? However, a self-destruct mechanism would actually be much easier to overturn. If our bodies had a self-destruct switch, then we might be able to find a way of turning this off. Once that switch had ceased to function, immortality would be in our grasp. The fact that there is no self-destruct mechanism is not really very good news at all.

Geneticists have discovered that we age because our genes as well as our bodies become damaged by the simple act of living. To some extent we can control the speed at which this damage results, by careful diet and exercise, together with avoiding exposure to the sun, tobacco smoke, pollution and so on, and by having access to good medical care. Research scientists have already shown us the way to extend our lifespan, as well as improve our quality of life, by helping us understand how to remain healthy. Ultimately, though, our genes will still sustain some damage for every day that we live, and the cumulative effect of that will eventually kill us. How quickly this occurs depends on the extent to which we possess gene variants that protect us against a range of age-related diseases such as high blood pressure, heart disease and dementia.

In the future, we may well find a way of preventing some of this damage from occurring, and may even be able to reverse it. Research is already taking place into how, for example, to persuade different cells within the body to grow to create new joint tissue or even a new limb. Research is also progressing into how to persuade the stem cells found in our bone marrow to grow into new cells in other parts of the body. One major difficulty, however, is that we also need to find out how to stop the cells growing once they have achieved their intended result. Without the ability to switch cells off as well as to switch them on, the tissue would continue to grow uncontrollably and, like more conventionally caused cancers, might well kill us in the process.

Abnormal

At the same time as facing enormous challenges in how to overcome the genetic damage that we already experience, we are likely to face new causes of damage as environmental changes impact on us. For example, cancer cases are already expected to rise in western Europe because of pollution and climate change, as well as because of increasing obesity rates. Other cancers are rising too: head and neck cancers increased by 50% in men in the past 20 years. Scientists will therefore need to find new means of combating this and of regenerating the body simply in order to maintain the status quo. More likely, cancer will become more and more prevalent, particularly if treatments improve so that it is increasingly a chronic rather than a terminal disease.

As we have seen, Descartes' idea of the body as a machine is still prevalent today. Much of the popular discourse around the prevention of ageing compares the body to a machine, most commonly a car. By repairing and replacing parts of a car, it is argued, vintage vehicles remain driveable and on the road for many decades after they were intended to be scrapped. If we repair and replace parts of the body, then, through surgery and drug treatments, it is argued that we can keep our bodies going, too. In reality, though, far from being comparable to a car, the body is an infinitely complex organism. The language of the garage may be seductive but, as we have seen, unfortunately it is entirely irrelevant.

12. DESIGNER BABIES 1 or, Why redesigning the human race is not an option

Our trusting acceptance that science will soon be able to 'cure' disability and ageing has also led to our belief that science could soon be able to affect evolution itself. Alongside discussions of 'upgrading' the body to increase the length and quality of our own lives have come discussions about improving the length and quality of the lives of the next generations through genetic selection. This can, of course, be regarded as the latest manifestation of the eugenics movement, and it is this that has fuelled our concerns. This in turn has reinforced our belief in the omnipotence of science as well as our feeling that our own bodies and offspring are unworthy, which is why we need to look at the facts before we can resist the temptation to lapse back into our body dysphoria.

By the turn of the millennium, there was a growing belief in the importance of genetic influence on a child's personality, intelligence and behaviour, rather than believing that upbringing was at least equally important (the view that had dominated post-war). This was a result of girls and boys for the first time being offered similar educational and employment opportunities in the second half of the 20th century, and them still continuing to make life choices along traditional gender-stereotyped lines. Parents felt that this showed genetics to be all-important, however 'unscientific' this conclusion might be, given the paucity of the evidence.

In the last decades of the 20th century, Western society therefore began to debate the ethics of having 'designer babies': babies who are conceived in the laboratory and who are then selected for particular genetic characteristics. Although scientists have never claimed that this is achievable, many people now believe it will soon be possible to 'design' babies for intelligence, appearance, physical ability and sexuality through the pre-selection of embryos before implantation in the womb. Since embryos would be selected before implantation, this removes many of the moral objections of a eugenics policy. Despite this, though, the creation of life in the laboratory has become one of the most emotive ethical issues of the 21st century.

However, as with stem cell research, the only question that has been asked is whether or not this is morally acceptable to us, not whether or not it is actually possible to achieve. When we look more closely at the science involved, it becomes apparent that the possibilities for genetic selection are in fact extremely limited. Our concerns owe more to the horror fiction of the 19th-century Romantics than to the scientific reality, and in our paranoia we make life even more difficult than it would be anyway for the small group of people who could actually benefit from the technology.

IVF technologies

The 'designer baby' debate began with the development of in vitro fertilisation, or IVF, technologies in the 1970s by British scientists based at Cambridge and at Oldham General Hospital. Although other scientists were also working in the field, Robert Edwards and Patrick Steptoe were the first to succeed in fertilising a human egg with a sperm in a laboratory, before implanting it into a woman who later gave birth to a healthy child in 1978. IVF has since provided many infertile couples with the opportunity to become parents, and has been widely welcomed by them.

Louise Brown was the world's first 'test-tube baby', and her birth began a debate on reproductive technologies that continues to this day. This debate was later fuelled by developments in genetics in the 1990s. These developments allowed research scientists to identify the genes responsible for several life-limiting genetic diseases. Scientists then discovered that they could remove a cell from an embryo and test it to ensure that it did not carry a particular gene, before implanting the rest of the embryo into the womb. This technique became known as preimplantation genetic diagnosis, or PGD.

PGD has provided some would-be parents with the possibility of having a living child for the first time, after they have experienced repeated miscarriages and stillbirths of foetuses carrying a defective gene. It has also been welcomed by parents who already have one or more living children with a genetic illness, and who want more children while at the same time feeling unable to cope with another child with a similar level of impairment. Other people have felt able to attempt reproduction for the first time, since they were previously unwilling to take the risk of having a child affected by a particular defective gene that they themselves carry, and do not believe in abortion. Still others have been able to conceive a child whose tissues were genetically suitable for donation to a sibling, thus gaining two live children. For these people, as for infertile couples, the development of reproductive technologies has been enormously beneficial.

However, since PGD is based on IVF, it is an expensive and difficult process and has a low success rate. The process is not without its risks either — one in ten IVF cycles trigger ovarian hyperstimulation syndrome, and in half of all affected women this is deemed to be 'moderate' or 'severe', accompanied by the risk of stroke or even death. For every 100,000 women undergoing IVF, six will actually die as a result. Aside from when PGD is being used, the trend now is therefore to administer fewer drugs, and be content with just one or more viable eggs.

With IVF, a woman must take drugs for about 21 days to suppress her natural hormone cycle, with the resulting symptoms being similar to the sudden onset of the menopause. Then she must inject herself for 8–12 days to stimulate her ovaries, before having a final late-night injection to mature the eggs. Thirty hours later, egg collection occurs — assuming that any eggs have been produced, that is. Despite the hormones that have been administered, there is no guarantee that any eggs will result at all, and treatment cycles are also aborted if early signs of ovarian hyperstimulation are detected.

This means that women may have to go through the drug-taking process more than once before they have eggs ready for IVF. Egg collection in turn involves surgery, which is inevitably uncomfortable and frequently embarrassing for the woman concerned. It then takes an average of three cycles of fertilisation and implantation treatment to achieve a pregnancy (using stored eggs from earlier cycles if possible), but many women will still not have conceived after this.

Top clinics report overall success rates of around 30%, but the majority of rates are much lower — the majority of couples who attempt IVF do not succeed. Higher rates can currently only be achieved by implanting multiple embryos, with subsequent risks for all involved: women who only receive one embryo are five times more likely to give birth to a healthy child than if they receive two. As it is, research published in the journal *Human Reproduction* found that children conceived by any form of IVF are four times more likely to be stillborn than naturally conceived babies, with a rate of 16.2 deaths per thousand live births rather than 4.3.

The innate limitations of PGD

Doctors hope that IVF success rates may be increased in the future by testing all embryos for genetic damage — around half of all embryos created in the laboratory are now believed to be genetically unsustainable. Unfortunately, this is not likely to increase the success rates of PGD. Would-be parents who are using PGD are doing so because some — perhaps the majority, or all — of their embryos are carrying an unwanted gene, or because only a minority will have the genetic characteristics that they seek to match an existing child's. Once the few 'suitable' embryos are able to be surveyed for genetic damage, it is likely that many PGD treatment cycles will not result in any embryos being placed into the would-be mother at all. As well as the large number of embryos that fail to implant successfully, babies conceived as a result of IVF are currently 30% more likely to have conditions such as cleft palate and problems with their heart or digestive system than children conceived naturally. Although many of these conditions cannot be detected at such an early stage, it is doubtful whether doctors will agree to implant any but completely 'normal' embryos.

Many women find that the hormones they take during IVF have a huge and negative impact on their moods and quality of life, and they suffer this solely because it is the only way for them to have a successful pregnancy or to conceive a child whose umbilical cord tissues could be used to provide a transplant to a sibling. Other women reject PGD when they are able to conceive naturally and there is a good chance of them conceiving a healthy, if possibly disabled, baby, because they are unwilling to suffer the side-effects of IVF when there is no guarantee of a pregnancy resulting.

Of course, further scientific and technological advances are likely to improve the success rate of these techniques. However, the potential to improve may be more limited than we think. Previously, scientists believed that only older people had eggs and sperm that were of 'poor quality', but recent research has shown that the majority of human eggs and sperm have some genetic damage, and that many could never result in a living child. This is why many 'natural' pregnancies end before a woman even realises that she is pregnant, and why the miscarriage rate is so high. It may therefore be that, on average, the 'natural' pregnancy success rate of 25% is unlikely to be significantly improved upon in the laboratory.

The first real question to ask about 'designer babies', then, is whether large numbers of women who are already fertile would really be prepared to put themselves through unnecessary and demanding fertility treatment, particularly when the treatment is more likely than not to be unsuccessful.

To some extent women have always 'designed' their babies, through their selection of sexual partners. Unlike the reproductive technologies, this old-fashioned method of selection is fun, free, unproblematic and under the complete control of women themselves. Conception itself then involves no risk to health, and is more likely to succeed than the alternative laboratory conception.

In addition to this, the majority of women who wish to become mothers simply want to have a baby, rather than wanting to control the characteristics of their child. Anything that makes pregnancy less likely is regarded by them as being highly undesirable. Currently, women seem more concerned with being able to control the age at which they give birth, so that they can delay pregnancy until they feel it is the right time for them in economic and career terms — or simply until they meet the right partner. Improvements in IVF techniques are more likely to be used by women to enable them to store eggs for the future, so that their chances of success are improved if they become infertile before they have an opportunity to get pregnant. IVF is never likely to become anyone's first choice.

The limitations of selection

However, even given the unlikely scenario that IVF was a first choice for women, another question that we need to ask is whether in fact it will ever be possible to select embryos for characteristics such as intelligence or appearance? PGD has been very successful in its current use, because it focuses on diseases caused by one damaged or mutant gene that is relatively easy to identify and test for. But our intelligence, appearance, physical ability and sexuality are affected by multiples of genes working together, as are the majority of genetic diseases. We would have to be able to identify and test all genes that relate to sexuality, for example, before we could attempt to pre-select an embryo for sexual preference; there is no one single 'gay gene'. And it is highly unlikely that we will ever reach an understanding of genetics that is sufficiently sophisticated for us to be able to do this.

However, the overriding issue is that in order to be able to pre-select embryos for intelligence, appearance, sexual orientation, sporting ability and so on, these multiple gene combinations would have to exist within the embryos being selected from in the first place. As we have seen, attempting to manipulate the genetic material itself by 'gene splicing' is unlikely ever to get past the regulators for very good reasons; but if it is made safe, it will be useful in cases where families have a history of illness caused by a single mutated gene that can be easily substituted. 'Splicing in' the multiple genes that affect characteristics like intelligence is the stuff of science fiction.

Meanwhile, it is unlikely that an IVF cycle will produce more than ten eggs, of which around half are likely to be of optimum 'quality' for conception. There may potentially be far more choice among sperm than there is among eggs, but the vast majority will not be viable at all; besides, it is currently impossible to analyse a sperm cell without damaging it. Even then, it could still not be predicted which genes carried by the individual sperm would be passed over to the embryo and which would come from the egg; genetic analysis can only start to take place once an embryo has been formed.

Many IVF cycles only produce two or three embryos that are currently deemed to be fit for implantation into the womb, and once we are able to improve screening techniques, this number will fall further. At best, women receiving IVF treatment produce five or six embryos that appear to be of sufficient 'quality' to have the potential to be implanted into the womb. Of these, around 50% will not be viable (which is why IVF has commonly involved putting back at least two embryos in the past). This means that, at most, women might have 15 embryos to choose from after three cycles of treatment, none of which would be guaranteed to result in a living child.

The likelihood of one of these embryos having, for example, the intelligence or sporting ability found in the top 2% of the population is therefore very small. And if none of the embryos carry gene combinations that show they are likely to be athletic, then it will be impossible to select a potential professional football player from among them. Similarly, if the parents only carry the genes for brown eyes, it will be impossible to select a blue-eyed embryo. If all of the embryos are heterosexual, it will be impossible to select a lesbian. And if all the embryos are of average intelligence, it will be impossible to select a genius.

As we can see, in reality the likelihood of being able to select an embryo for just one characteristic such as sexual orientation, appearance or intelligence resulting from multiple genetic combinations is small enough to be statistically improbable. And besides, it could not then be guaranteed that that particular embryo would implant successfully. The potential for being able to select an embryo on the basis of appearance, AND intelligence, AND sexual orientation, AND resistance to disease is non-existent.

A more appealing — and theoretically more possible — use of PGD would be to select embryos on the basis of their genetic predisposition to illnesses such as heart disease and cancer. We have always been able to observe that some families have a much higher incidence of heart disease and breast cancer than others. Now researchers are beginning to detect the mutated genes that are making some people more prone than others to these diseases. Again, though, scientists could only pre-select from the embryos present: in many cases, every embryo will inherit these mutated genes. Equally, successful embryo selection will not guarantee that the resulting child will be free of the illness. There are many causes of heart disease and cancer, and genetic predisposition is just one of them. And, of course, an embryo that is free of genetic risk of heart disease may be genetically predisposed to cancer, and vice versa.

The more we discover about genes, the more it becomes apparent that the way in which they operate is enormously sophisticated. For example, rather than there being one 'cancer gene', scientists have already identified over 100 genes that, if mutated, can cause cancer. Rather than there being an 'autism gene', every person with autism spectrum disorder may have their own unique variant, with only the way in which each person is affected by it being the same. Scientists also know that we carry multiple copies of genes, and whether or not a gene works in a particular way depends on how many copies of that gene we carry. Genes also work in combination with other genes, so a gene that might cause cancer in the absence of another gene might not cause cancer if this additional gene were present. Instead of being straightforward, testing would be enormously complicated. Only in a tiny number of cases will there be one inheritable gene that is linked with causing a serious illness.

Even then, genetics could only tell us about probabilities. It may be probable that someone will get heart disease or cancer if they carry certain mutated genes, but there is no certainty about this. Many other factors affect susceptibility to disease, particularly lifestyle, environment and upbringing. And, of course, none of this stops someone being treated successfully by the medical profession if they do develop cancer or heart disease — nor does it stop them being run over by a bus before ever becoming ill.

The impact of environment

Supposing for a moment that we could identify, test for and pre-select genetic characteristics and predisposition to illness. Would this be enough to 'design' a baby? No, science has already shown us that it isn't: genes are only part of the story; and environmental factors and upbringing also impact on a child's development. Many studies were carried out in the 20th century to attempt to discover which mattered most in a child's development: 'nature or nurture'; overall, it has been concluded that both play a significant role.

The example of 'identical' twins who have developed from the same embryo also shows us that, while one may develop an illness like childhood diabetes or leukaemia, the other may not; or while one may have severe multiple sclerosis, the other has a much milder form of the condition; or while one may be heterosexual, the other may be homosexual or bisexual. Twins' personalities and intelligence vary widely too. This is because our individual genetic make-up develops within the womb itself, and this is a lengthy process. The genes that exist in an embryo in its early stages are not completely fixed in terms of their outcomes and effects.

To explain this a little further using the example of twins: two out of three sets of 'identical' twins separate between five and nine days after the egg is fertilised, while the remaining third probably do not separate until close to the fifth day after that (i.e. fourteen days after fertilisation). This means that at the point in embryo development when researchers would remove a cell for testing as part of the PGD process, the vast majority of 'identical' twins are still one individual embryo. Given the many differences that they will go on to develop, no one could have predicted their final intelligence levels, sexual orientation, appearance and personalities from analysis at this point, even if we had achieved this highly sophisticated understanding of how genetics operate.

When an embryo does separate to form twins, their DNA is still identical following the separation process; it is not the separation that changes their DNA. Instead, scientists have discovered that, as time goes on, various genes will mutate and others will develop in subtly different ways even when twins share the same placenta, and so the way that their genes are 'expressed' will vary. After birth, minute differences in the way in which they interact with their environment, and the varying infections that they catch, affect the expression of their genes still further. This explains many of the differences in personality, sexual orientation, intelligence and health between 'identical' twins. It also underlines the limitations of the PGD process: the only things that PGD could ever predict are the commonalities between twins. We know that identical twins can have much in common, but since twins can separate as late as day 12 after fertilisation, it is possible that the longer it is before they separate, the more features they share. But either way, it is the subtle differences in their genetic make-up as they develop that will affect twins' lives, and it is the subtle *differences* that would be important in 'designing' a baby.

Exaggerated fears

It is unlikely, then, that a much wider range of families will ever opt for PGD than those who are currently benefiting from it. And, as now, most will continue to be grateful simply for the birth of a live child, since many will try for this and be disappointed. PGD and related technologies offer hope to families who have previously had to remain childless, or who have undergone pregnancy after pregnancy only for this to result in miscarriage or stillbirth. But they cannot and never will be able to deliver babies by design. Concerns about the impact of being able to 'design' our future children through genetic selection are, at best, premature, but more likely are entirely unnecessary. As we have already seen, it is so difficult to alter even one pre-existing gene to avoid disease that we could never 'design' a child through genetic manipulation.

Our continuing belief in the hysteria about designer babies unfortunately has a very negative impact on the families who would benefit most from PGD and related technologies, as well as on the ability of scientists to carry out their work. Exaggerated fears about scientists' powers also help to create a funding situation whereby many thousands of people with fertility problems cannot access the treatment that would benefit them, since such fears make IVF politically unpopular. In the UK, very few women received state-funded IVF in the late noughties, and those who did were limited to one cycle. Meanwhile, it cost an average of £13,000 in treatment and three cycles to achieve a successful pregnancy.

The last lesson that we can learn from this is that even if we could design a baby and it became socially acceptable to do so, the vast majority of people would still conceive naturally on grounds of cost. However, the reality is that — as with so many of our dystopian fantasies about what scientists can achieve — we are unable to do any such thing.

13. DESIGNER BABIES 2 or, Why we could all live to regret a eugenics-based abortion policy

At the same time as worrying about designing future generations to be 'super-normal', we have been quietly attempting to ensure that the birth of 'abnormal' children is prevented wherever possible. From the late 20th century onwards, foetal testing and abortion were increasingly used to prevent the birth of children with potential genetic abnormalities. This followed post-war developments whereby policies to prevent disabled men and women — who were widely believed to be certain to give birth to disabled children — from reproducing had become less acceptable. However, policies presented as being 'good for the whole family' have in fact been drawn up solely with the benefit of the state in mind. In addition to fuelling our body dysphoria by suggesting that our offspring may not measure up to 'the norm', they could have consequences that all of our families will live to regret.

The preference for abortion

As we have seen, eugenic concerns meant that the forced sterilisation of disabled people had been common throughout the world in the first half of the 20th century, together with the segregation of disabled men and women in institutions to prevent them from forming sexual relationships. By the beginning of the 21st century, some countries had abandoned segregation altogether in favour of disabled people living 'normal' lives within the community, and this is a growing trend today, at least in the USA, Scandinavia, the UK and the rest of western Europe. Alongside this, a number of disabled people began to take legal action in the same countries for being sterilised against their will, while the UN Convention on Human Rights conveyed the right to a family life on the citizens of every country who had signed up to it. This did not make it easy for disabled people to parent: children continue to be routinely removed from disabled parents rather than being provided with the necessary support; and pregnant women in institutions continue to be 'persuaded' to have abortions. However, it did refocus attention on alternative means of controlling the birth of 'abnormal' foetuses.

In addition to this, by the late 20th century research had also provided a greater understanding of genetic diseases. Research had shown that only a minority of genetic conditions were passed down the generations, while many people who were carriers of the genes concerned were not disabled themselves. Scientists now understood that genetic illness can be inherited from apparently healthy parents, or can develop spontaneously during conception rather than needing to be inherited. Tests had also been developed to predict the probability of a foetus having a range of genetic diseases, while abortion had become widely acceptable in many developed countries. (Even in countries where religious considerations make abortion illegal or very strictly limited, exceptions are still often made where the abortion of potentially disabled foetuses is concerned.) This made foetal testing and abortion the preferable option for 'eliminating' disability — from both a political and a scientific perspective.

At the turn of the millennium, foetal testing followed by abortion counselling was increasingly adopted as policy by governments. For example, when the 1997 Labour Government came into power in Britain they introduced a policy of providing all pregnant women with the full range of foetal tests that were available, followed by abortion on request after counselling. Parents who decided that they did not want to take the tests because they did not want to abort whatever the result were routinely persuaded that it was the 'right' thing to do. This policy was presented as benefiting parents, but the impetus undoubtedly came from reducing what was perceived as being the financial 'burden' of disabled people on the state.

There is also no doubt that, for some politicians at least, eugenics philosophy played a role as well. Our misunderstanding of Darwinian theories of 'natural selection' means that we have been keen to terminate foetuses that have unusual bodies, despite the fact that these would ordinarily be as 'fit' to survive as any other child. As discussed above, the vast majority of potential human embryos could never survive; all those that *do* survive possess some powerful genetic strengths. Due to the continuation of eugenic beliefs, though, the liberalisation of abortion law in the 1960s and 1970s was linked to the resulting ability to abort potentially disabled foetuses. Feminists also supported their demand for a woman's right to choose whether or not she proceeded with a pregnancy by declaring that no one should have to bear a disabled child. Disabled women were brought onto platforms to declare, "No one should have to be like me." Overall, the availability of foetal testing was critical in the decision to legalise abortion.

The growth and drawbacks of testing

The first test developed by scientists was for Down's syndrome: initially thought to be a sign of regression to an earlier form of human development, it is actually caused by the possession of an 'extra' chromosome which is easily detectable. The 'need' to prevent children with Down's syndrome being born has become a key part of testing philosophy, and in Europe more than 90% of foetuses with Down's syndrome are now aborted. Research has shown that many adults living with Down's syndrome are acutely aware that they would have been aborted if detected in the womb and that many non-disabled people view their existence as a scientific error, and this knowledge must be very hard to live with.

The policy of 'counselling' women to abort Down's foetuses continues today despite considerable evidence that, in the 21st century, the quality of life for people with Down's syndrome can be as good as everyone else's. In particular, doctors can now operate easily and routinely to correct the life-limiting heart problems that are associated with Down's. It has also become apparent that institutional neglect contributed towards the shortened lifespan associated with Down's syndrome in the past, rather than this being wholly due to organic causes. Today, people with Down's can expect a similar lifespan to everyone else, so long as they are not denied medical treatment. More often than not, children with Down's are now also successfully attending mainstream schools, passing exams and growing up to live and work independently, albeit with more support than their peers may require.

Worryingly, the British policy of offering foetal testing and abortion as standard has developed despite the fact that the vast majority of tests are fallible. Testing can predict the *likelihood* of a foetus having a particular impairment, but can rarely predict this with any absolute certainty. But even when tests *can* predict an impairment with certainty, they cannot show the extent to which a child will be affected by it. A child with Down's syndrome, for example, may have significant health problems and learning difficulties, or may lead a similar life to their siblings. Equally, many foetuses who go on to develop significant health problems and learning difficulties in childhood will 'pass' tests in the womb. It is therefore important that prospective parents fully understand the limitations of the testing process when making a decision whether or not to continue with their pregnancy. Parents also need to understand the reality of disabled people's lives today, rather than relying on media and charity stereotypes that bear little resemblance to the truth.

It is particularly important that parents are fully informed because foetal testing takes place at a time when the majority of pregnant women have already made the decision to proceed with their pregnancy. Their pregnancy may, of course, have been planned, perhaps for many years, and abortion would normally be the last option that they would consider. Even if their pregnancy is accidental, though, women will usually have taken a decision on whether or not to seek an abortion by the time that they are eight weeks pregnant. This is because in countries where abortions are legally available, they are normally limited to foetuses with a gestation of 12 weeks or less; abortions have usually taken place before women are eight weeks into a pregnancy.

Most foetal testing, however, cannot take place until after the 12th week of pregnancy, and so the law has sanctioned later abortions in cases where a foetus is at risk of impairment. In general, around 70% of 'serious abnormalities' are not detected until a scan at 20 weeks, just a month or so before a foetus becomes potentially viable outside the womb. The majority of pregnant women have by that time already bonded with their foetus and made plans for its future life. This makes later testing extremely stressful and distressing for them.

Invasive types of testing, such as amniocentesis to confirm Down's, also put a pregnant woman at risk of miscarriage. At the end of the noughties, it was estimated that between 250 and 400 'normal' babies were miscarried each year as a result of invasive testing. This was in order to 'achieve' less than 700 abortions of foetuses with Down's syndrome.

It is hoped that non-invasive tests for Down's may soon become available. However, the stress involved in any foetal testing process is counter-productive to all pregnant women's health, particularly but not only when they have conditions such as high blood pressure or are already at medical risk of miscarriage. Recent research published in the journal *Clinical Endocrinology* shows that maternal stress is passed on to the foetus and can affect the development of its brain; other researchers have found a measurable impact on the development of the foetus's immune system.

Many pregnant women report being given very negative information about disabled children, their life chances and their impact on the rest of the family, in an effort to persuade them to opt for testing and, later, abortion. A great deal of pressure is brought to bear to persuade women that comprehensive testing is the 'right' thing to do. Women are also encouraged to believe that parenting disabled children requires very different skills to 'normal' parenting, and that their own skills will not be sufficient for this. This is despite the fact that the information is being given to them by pregnancy specialists, who may well have had no experience whatsoever of disabled children and adults. Again, all of this increases the stress on them, stress which is passed directly on to the developing foetus.

Crucially, potential parents are taught that disabled children are 'different' from 'normal' children. This is reinforced in the media: an influential Channel 4 series about a group of disabled children in the noughties was entitled *Born to Be Different*. But different from whom? The only thing that was fundamentally different about the children featured was their level of contact with the medical system, which in turn was not, in the majority of cases, necessary in life and death terms. Indeed, much of their contact was simply in order for doctors to 'monitor' (i.e. study) them as they grew up — or, indeed, so that the 'science' behind their abnormality could be explained by the programme makers. Difference from their peers was dictated by their cultural and social backgrounds, not by their genes. However, programmes like the Channel 4 series continue to reinforce the belief that disabled children — and adults — are 'different', all the more so because the channels involved are public broadcasters.

The irrelevance of impairment

It is also important to remember that parents' main motivation for bringing a child into the world may be the pleasure that they receive from the parenting process. This pleasure occurs regardless of whether a child is disabled or not, since the parenting process is exactly the same. Decorating a nursery, choosing baby clothes and toys, bathing, dressing and feeding their baby, the first smile, the first communication, the first day at school — all of these and many more are similar experiences for all parents regardless of whether their child is disabled or not. Similarly all parents suffer as they watch their children face frustration, disappointment, illness and grief: no parent is able to protect their children from these. And all new parents discover that contact with the medical profession is an inescapable part of childhood, too.

While children with Down's syndrome are unlikely to become rocket scientists, they are equally unlikely to become drug dealers or armed robbers, or to fail to appreciate their parents in adult life. (And, as we have seen, no parent can guarantee giving birth to a particularly gifted child in any case.) The difference between parenting disabled and non-disabled children lies largely in the difference in the way that disabled children and their families are treated by society — treatment which we all have the power to change. It is simply illogical to assume that disabled people cannot be enabled to participate on an equal basis in today's society, something that we will discuss further and in more detail in the next section. Even today, it is just plain wrong to suggest that families with disabled members are doomed to be less happy than others.

The impact of disabilism

In November 2006, the Royal College of Obstetricians and Gynaecologists (RCOG) called for the 'active euthanasia' of disabled babies, particularly those born extremely prematurely who would not survive without medical care. This, they argued, was for the overall good of families, to "spare parents the emotional burden and financial hardship of bringing up the sickest babies". "A very disabled child can mean a disabled family," they said. "If life-shortening and deliberate interventions to kill infants were available, they might have an impact on obstetric decision-making, even preventing some late abortions, as some parents would be more confident about continuing a pregnancy and taking a risk on outcome."

It was noticeable that the RCOG ignored the fact that the vast majority of parents wanted their children to be saved at all costs: once their baby enters the world, parents generally want them to live; and every year some go to court to argue for their child's right to life, against the advice of doctors. Likewise the RCOG did not represent paediatricians, who would have had some experience of infants and young children. They also ignored the experiences of disabled people and their families, and in particular the many disabled children and adults who have exceeded all of the predictions made about their lives at birth, including many adults whose parents were told that they would not survive childhood.

In contrast to the professionals, most parents of children with life-limiting conditions talk about the need to 'treasure every day', not to cut their children's lives short, and about having too *much* free time after their children have died. (Those who disagree have normally been ignored when arguing against aggressive medical treatment for their children at an early stage: parents really do know best in the vast majority of cases.) Some parents even find life too unbearable to go on living after their disabled child dies, just as parents of non-disabled children do. What really makes parents' lives difficult is the lack of support services — perhaps society's means of punishing them for having a disabled child in the first place, whether this was by 'refusing' to have an abortion or through being 'careless' enough to let their child become ill or have an accident.

Unfortunately, since many people have grown up in a segregated society, with disabled children educated separately, prospective parents may not have any personal experience of disabled people. Parents of disabled children also report being isolated from the rest of society, leaving prospective parents with no choice but to rely on professional advice. It can understandably be extremely distressing for both men and women who made an agonising 'choice' to abort a potentially disabled but much-wanted foetus in the belief that independent living for disabled people was impossible, when they later come into contact with 'seriously' disabled people and their families who are nonetheless leading fulfilling and happy lives. Facing a future where you have to manage without adequate support is not in itself enough to make most pregnant women want to abort.

Women also report that when they have chosen to proceed with a pregnancy after testing suggests foetal abnormality, they are repeatedly asked to change their minds at subsequent medical appointments. They feel that their choice is not respected, because it is the 'wrong' one — if they have made the 'right' choice, of course, then there is no going back. Women also say that abortions are organised with undue haste — often in less than 48 hours, giving them no time at all to reflect on all of their options. Prospective parents' right to choose, and their right to make an informed choice, seems to be sacrificed to an official desire to limit the number of children with genetic impairments who are being born. Again, all of this further increases the stress that is passed on to the developing foetus, and which is also likely to impact on the health of the pregnant woman herself.

Real and illusory choices

As a result of all this, many disabled feminists now believe that foetal testing should only be available as an option that is specifically requested by a pregnant woman, rather than being offered to every pregnant woman as routine. They also believe that women should receive counselling before they choose to proceed with testing, in order for them to appreciate the limitations of the tests and the realities of having a disabled child. This information then needs to be repeated during further counselling if tests prove 'positive', and women given sufficient time to absorb it before any abortion is proceeded with. Disabled feminists take the view that unless a woman makes an informed choice to have foetal tests, a resulting miscarriage or abortion may leave permanent psychological damage. This is particularly true for women who may never succeed in becoming pregnant again, and for whom the aborted foetus was their only opportunity for motherhood. (There is no guarantee that pregnancy can be repeated simply because it is desired; and this is not helped by the fact that one in seven British couples is now infertile.)

The growth of foetal testing for potential abnormalities, alongside PGD and the wider 'designer baby' debate, has had some other damaging side-effects for families, too. Many prospective parents now believe that they can choose whether or not to have a disabled child, rather than accepting, as previous generations did, that this is a matter of chance. This belief has been supported by the courts in some developed countries including France, with a number of parents successfully suing doctors who have failed to detect foetal abnormalities. Parents have argued that to have a disabled child is a matter of choice, and that they would not have chosen this option had they known that the foetus would be impaired.

However, the majority of children become disabled during the birth process itself, because of prematurity or a problematic labour. Thousands of other children develop impairments following birth, because of accidents or illnesses. In the developed world, the extent to which this can be minimised by high-quality pre-natal and obstetric care and paediatric medicine has largely been achieved already, although there is still a need for a great deal more research into how to prevent prematurity.

We may only really lose interest in designer babies when we realise fully that choosing an embryo for its low risk of developing heart disease or cancer will not prevent the resulting child from having cerebral palsy as a result of a difficult birth. Aborting a foetus with Down's will not prevent the next child who is conceived from developing autism in infancy, nor the following from catching meningitis in childhood. Given the risks involved to women, PGD must not be extended to include non-life-limiting medical conditions without those who then choose it really understanding its limitations.

The most important factor in foetal development will always be the welfare of the pregnant woman. Women who don't smoke, who drink only moderate amounts of alcohol, who exercise adequately, and who have access to good nutrition, health care and sufficient rest, will continue to have babies who are healthier and have fewer impairments than those who do the opposite. Women who are overweight will also continue to have more problems in pregnancy than those who are not. Women who avoid as much stress as possible will be healthier and have healthier babies.

As is so often the case, scientific research has taught us these valuable lessons, but the means of implementing them is low-tech and down to us. Poverty is the biggest factor influencing pregnant women's health, and therefore the health of their unborn children. But women also need access to information, and to be able to value themselves sufficiently to care for themselves as well as others.

Prospective parents who state that they could never cope with a disabled child should be encouraged to think about whether they want to have children at all, not be supported in the illusion that they have a choice. Encouraging parents to believe that they can choose whether or not to have a disabled child results only in heartbreak. Disabled children are commonly abandoned to the care of the state, their parents feeling cheated out of the perfect child that they thought they had been guaranteed, as well as believing — usually mistakenly — that parenting a disabled child will require skills that they do not have. Critically, potential parents have been led to believe that disabled people are 'different' from 'normal' human beings, while parents naturally wish their children to be like themselves.

The same language that is used to persuade pregnant women to have foetal tests tells parents of disabled babies that something enormously negative has happened to them. The latter are encouraged to 'grieve' when their child is born, reinforcing the fears common among all pregnant women that they will not be able to bond with their baby. The level of abandonment of disabled children would therefore be predictable even if many parents were not still being actively encouraged to give the children into the care of the state at birth. At the same time, the vast majority of parents who keep their disabled children would not swap them for the world, but their voices are heard much less often.

The importance of genetic diversity

As we have seen, however popular the rhetoric, babies can't be chosen by design. But suppose for one moment that we could select the genetic characteristics that we consider to be important. Would this really be a good thing? Or would it instead prevent the human race from continuing to evolve? Might it even lead to the end of humanity? Genetic diversity is enormously important in order to resist the spread of disease. It is our genetic diversity — diversity that makes all of us susceptible and resistant to different diseases — which has helped humanity to survive as long as it has.

And we have no way of predicting which genes will be of value in resisting new diseases, including genes that are currently associated with 'abnormality'.

For example, as we have seen earlier, so far all of the people known to have died from vCJD — a disease caused by a protein called a prion — have come from the 40% of the population whose own prions are most susceptible to attack. But until the population was exposed to vCJD through eating beef infected with Bovine Spongiform Encephalopathy (BSE), there was no reason to suppose that anyone at all was vulnerable to illness caused by prions. There was also no reason to suppose that humans could be infected by a cattle disease in the first place; in all, there was no way of predicting the episode and of knowing that particular genes were valuable in preventing infection. Yet 60% of the people exposed to infection by vCJD have remained unaffected, at least in the medium term, only because their diverse genetic make-up has protected them.

Even genetic conditions that are considered to be impairments can protect us against disease. For example, the prevalence of sickle cell anaemia in certain ethnic communities arose because the genetic mutations that cause sickle cell also protect against infection by the malaria parasite, since the shape of the blood cells in people who carry the sickle cell gene is different to those in the rest of the population. People who carry the sickle cell gene have therefore been better able to survive malaria than the rest of us, so their genes have become more dominant.

If everyone carrying the genes for sickle cell and for thalassaemia (a similar illness) was eliminated from the population through the widespread use of PGD, the human race would no longer have any natural defences against malaria. Given that malaria is now becoming resistant to known treatments, this is potentially very serious. Any global disaster that left the population without access to clean drinking water or relatively advanced medical treatment, would also leave large areas of the world where malaria could wipe out every human being living there.

And, of course, genetic diversity is necessary if the human race is to continue to evolve. We have no way of knowing whether a genetic mutation that causes impairment also conveys benefits by making the carrier better able to survive in the conditions that we face in the future. It is clear that some genetic mutations are lethal, and this is where PGD is proving to be so useful. But it is not clear at all which mutations are helpful to us, both in fighting disease and, possibly, in the evolution of the human race. This is where the new eugenics becomes threatening to us all, rather than simply affecting foetuses and their families.

A final word. The latest test under development targets autism, by measuring the amount of testosterone acting on the foetus (scientists have found a correlation between testosterone levels and the risk of the child later developing autism). As in the case of testing for Down's syndrome, the test would not be able to identify the degree to which the foetus would be affected (if at all). However, the example of Down's — and the very negative media coverage that autistic children continue to receive — suggests that many parents would abort a potentially autistic foetus. Yet many of today's best and brightest scientists would be considered to be on the 'milder' end of the autistic spectrum, as would people working in other areas where enormous focus and attention to detail is critical and an obsessive nature is part of the job description. The belief that we can redesign the human race might cost all of our descendants as well as our families today a great deal if we do not begin to challenge it now.

14. MISUNDERSTANDING EVOLUTION or, The importance of the individual to the survival of the human race

We have already seen that it is exceedingly dangerous to apply Darwinian principles of natural selection to create *unnatural* selection in the future — to attempt to remove certain genes and combinations of genes from the human race, and to remove potential humans from the planet, in the guise of 'helping nature to undo its mistakes'. However, in order to secure our future and to tackle our body dysphoria, we also need to improve our understanding of evolutionary theory itself. This is not simply because of the importance of the continuation of genetic diversity or the impact of 'unnatural' selection on ourselves and our immediate families, but because individuals play a uniquely important role within our human species. We need to understand, once and for all, that humans differ in this very important aspect from all other forms of life before we can eliminate our body dysphoria.

As we have seen, Darwinian theories of natural selection, developed through the observation of birds and animals, have been interpreted as meaning that disabled people are not 'naturally fit' to survive. Disabled foetuses have been described as being 'nature's mistakes', while disabled people have been regarded as having been 'naturally destined' to die and existing only because of medical intervention. (This is, of course, in itself a misunderstanding; medical intervention may improve quality of life and reduce the impact of impairment, but only in a minority of cases is it a factor in survival.) The widespread acceptance of eugenic beliefs make us concerned that disabled people's survival and reproduction will render the human race weaker in the future.

These beliefs are allowed to go unchallenged, but they actually affect us all. Since none of us are 'perfect', then at some level we are all made to feel unfit to reproduce, and selfish for doing so: we are too old, or too young, and our families are too fat, too stupid, too short-sighted, too prone to heart disease, cancer, dyslexia or depression for our reproduction to be valid.

For disabled parents and for the parents of disabled children the results of these beliefs are far more wide-reaching. It will be impossible for these families ever to live without facing prejudice and discrimination until we examine and change our misunderstandings about 'natural selection'. And so long as there is a belief that disabled people are contributing to the downfall of the human species, whether their impairments are actually affected by their genetic make-up or not, all disabled people will experience additional prejudice and discrimination. Since disability is a club that any of us can join at any time, this affects us, too.

However, all of this is still to miss an even more important point. With the exception of some religious communities, we have adopted the principles of evolution more or less wholesale, and when we have rejected the idea that humans are simply another form of animal, we have done this principally on the basis that animals don't have souls. What we have generally failed to recognise is that individuals play a very different role in human societies from the role that animals play in their world, and that every human individual, however 'abnormal', may play a role that is critical to our development and very survival. In turn, we have failed to recognise that, disabled or not, it is our individuality that makes us important already, without any need to change.

The fundamental difference between people and animals

Although we have always praised the contribution of individuals to our history, we are only now beginning to recognise quite how profoundly history is affected by the actions of these figures — to realise that individuals can actually affect the future of our species to a greater extent than can economic and social conditions. For example, although most scientific discoveries today are made by teams of people, we remember the names of the team leaders and give them Nobel Prizes as individuals. The reason for this is that without these individuals and the crucial role that they played, the discovery in question would not have been made. Team leaders envisage their goals, shape their teams and determine their workloads; without them, the team would not exist. Similarly, Marie Curie, Einstein, Isaac Newton, Robert Louis Stevenson… they may have had assistants, or partners, or have been otherwise supported by people whose names were lost to history who made huge but invisible contributions, but in the end, their actions as individuals were what counted.

There is no other species on the planet in which the conscious or unconscious actions of one individual can affect its survival in any significant way at all, yet the survival of our species may rest entirely with one single human being. For example, the discovery of a vaccine or treatment for a new and lethal virus, or a way to mitigate the effects of global warming, or a way to avoid some as yet unforeseen threat to our species, will, in all probability, depend on the actions of just one person. Equally, so may whether or not the human race destroys itself by nuclear war, or whether a skilled politician avoids this.

What is certainly true is that the future of the human race has always been, and will continue to be, shaped on an ongoing basis by a *number* of individuals, often acting quite separately from each other. Some of these individuals may become famous scientists and politicians and be remembered by history; others (including the wives of many famous men) may remain in obscurity but still make equally important contributions in defining the way in which we live. All of them, though, will have one thing in common: whether or not they are 'genetically desirable' in a Darwinian sense will be quite irrelevant to their importance in contributing to the survival of our species.

To give an obvious example, Professor Stephen Hawking would under any eugenics system be defined as genetically undesirable. No eugenicist would choose an embryo that was known to carry genes for motor neurone disease: all would opt for an embryo that was free of the condition within the preimplantation genetic diagnosis, or PGD, process; and many would urge abortion of a foetus known to be a carrier. (It should be pointed out here that only a minority of people with motor neurone disease have inherited genes that are linked to this condition; most people develop the condition for reasons that are still unknown, including Stephen Hawking.)

Despite having a life-limiting and ultimately lethal condition, Professor Hawking has added vastly to the body of our human knowledge. This has already had profound effects on the future of our species, and is likely to have as yet unforeseen benefits. The fact that Professor Hawking has motor neurone disease has not affected his ability to add to the body of human knowledge; indeed, it might well have enhanced his ability to do so by, for example, forcing him to develop his problem-solving skills. To remove Professor Hawking from history would be to have impoverished us beyond measure; it might well have affected our future survival as a species.

Preventing him from having children would also have negated the possibility of his brilliance being passed down to future generations.

Even Darwin himself would have been regarded as an unsuitable candidate for life under a 'eugenetics' policy. He experienced periods of profound depression, which prevented him from working for months at a time. Mental illness may often have a genetic component, in that people carrying certain gene combinations may be more likely than others to develop a condition such as depression (though, as we have already seen, there are no certainties here). Conditions such as depression may also be more common in particular families. Depression can be life-limiting, and it can be fatal; it is as genetically 'undesirable' as motor neurone disease. Yet without Darwin, our understanding of human biology and our ability to respond to conditions such as HIV would have been far poorer.

The political philosopher Friedrich Nietzsche (1844–1900) even claimed that impairment was *necessary* for 'progress' to take place, writing:

> Wherever progress is to ensue, deviating natures are of greatest importance. Every progress of the whole must be preceded by a partial weakening. The strongest natures retain the type, the weaker ones help to advance it. Something similar also happens in the individual. There is rarely a degeneration, a truncation, or even a vice or any physical or moral loss without an advantage somewhere else. In a warlike and restless clan, for example, the sicklier man may have occasion to be alone, and may therefore become quieter and wiser; the one-eyed man will have one eye the stronger; the blind man will see deeper inwardly, and certainly hear better. To this extent, the famous theory of the survival of the fittest does not seem to me to be the only viewpoint from which to explain the progress of strengthening of a man or of a race.
> (*Human, All Too Human*, 1878)

The flawed example of Guinea Pig Island

This is not to argue with Darwin. Let us look for a moment at an example from the animal world. A guinea pig carrying a genetic condition that causes it to deteriorate physically in the prime of its life may well be undesirable in a Darwinian sense. It will be particularly undesirable because the said guinea pig is able to reach maturity and breed before dying from the condition, thus passing on its 'faulty' genes to a new generation. And since a guinea pig does not mate for life, and females have multiple births, a male suffering from a condition that will kill it in its prime may still before dying be able to create countless litters that all carry the same lethal gene.

If the same population of guinea pigs is limited to one geographical area, for example a small island, then eventually the majority of them may end up carrying the lethal gene. At this point the survival of their species may well be threatened, for example because the females fail to live for long enough to have the same number of litters as was previously possible. Sick guinea pigs are also likely to be picked off by predators, as are young guinea pigs that no longer have the protection of a large number of mature adults.

If we assume that the remaining guinea pigs are the toughest of their kind, then wouldn't the deaths of the rest be a good thing? Wouldn't they be free to breed and evolve to become super-guinea pigs, unencumbered by the 'weaker' genes in the population. This, after all, is the belief on which eugenics is based. But both Darwin and the history of countless extinct species tell us that this is unlikely. It is far more likely that guinea pigs would completely cease to exist on the island, because there wouldn't be enough of them remaining to create sufficient genetic diversity to sustain a population at all. Without genetic diversity, illness would, sooner rather than later, wipe out the population.

In the case of Guinea Pig Island, by removing the first guinea pig with the faulty gene from the population before it was able to breed, preferably by preventing it from being conceived, or alternatively by simply stopping that guinea pig from reproducing, all of this would have been avoided. The removal of one individual guinea pig would not have had any other importance whatsoever; even the 'positive' genes that it carried would, given guinea pigs' multiple partners, have been passed on in the population anyway. It is theoretically possible that a guinea pig with a lethal condition would also have been carrying a mutated gene that would lead to a species of super-guinea pigs, but the likely benefits of this would still have been far outweighed by the negative impact on the population as a whole. And, of course, a lot of suffering by affected animals would have been prevented along the way.

It is important to note here 'defective' guinea pig that dies *before* it can reproduce is really neither here nor there in the Darwinian scheme of things. It will not divert any significant resources, nor a significant amount of its mother's attention, away from more 'deserving' members of the litter. No other guinea pigs will be affected by its poor health, nor will grief affect its mother's ability to parent the rest of the litter. Preventing a 'faulty' human foetus from being conceived in the first place is the ideal only since it is perceived to have the potential to deprive another, stronger foetus of its mother's resources, although in reality parents are *more* likely to want siblings when they have a disabled child.

So what does the human race have in common with these guinea pigs, and what does our world have in common with our fictitious Guinea Pig Island? Well, we are both mammals, and that is about it. We have only a small number of partners over our lifetimes, and generally bear just one child at a time. We don't have vast numbers of offspring — in fact we have far fewer now than we ever did in the past. We have never been limited by geography, as genetic analysis tells us (and we are far less limited now than we have ever been before). We have the ability to offset the impact of all medical conditions to some extent and to cure or treat an increasing number of them, meaning that our quality of life is not determined by our genetic status. And, as the example of Professor Hawking shows, just one person can make a profound difference to our species, regardless of — or perhaps because of — their 'defective' genetic status.

Survival instincts and facts

We will never, ever, have the ability to determine the survival of the human species by deciding who has the right to live based on their genetic make-up. But we do have the ability to threaten our collective future in a highly dangerous way by making uninformed judgements about whether an individual is genetically 'fit' to survive. There may be all sorts of very good reasons why a pregnant woman does not wish to continue with her pregnancy, including her personal circumstances with regard to impairment and disability. However, misguided advice about Darwinian principles of 'natural' selection and the threat that her foetus poses to the future of the human race can never justify ending a wanted pregnancy.

Rather, instead of regarding disabled children as being weak, we need to recognise their strengths. Disabled children who have survived despite being premature, or despite a difficult birth, or despite having a genetic condition that often kills in the womb or in the first days of life all carry some very strong survival genes indeed. The same is true of those disabled children and adults who have acquired their impairments through surviving serious accidents or illnesses. Who is to say that their genes will not be the very same ones that ensure the survival of our species in a harsher future? Rather than making it as difficult as possible for disabled people to parent, we should be ensuring that they are able to do so.

Similarly, we need to recognise that survival is as much about skill as it is about genetics; that ordinary people are as important to the survival of our species as the extraordinary; and that impairment is irrelevant. The prevalence of genes for diseases such as cancer or stroke within the general population today also shows that being prone to an earlier death did not prevent prehistoric peoples from surviving. Stone Age people did not survive because they were able to run away from predators: survival came from being able to adapt to all of the conditions that people faced.

'Fitness' to survive has little to do with physical strength, or even the ability to resist illness, and everything to do with being able to experiment, to problem-solve, and to do things differently depending on the circumstances of the situation. Far more of us would now be ideally adapted to athletic activity if in the Stone Age the ability to run away from predators had been crucial. Disabled people are problem-solvers par excellence since problem-solving is necessary every day in order to find ways of doing 'normal' things differently, including different ways to learn; and experimentation is integral to this process. People with mental health problems are more likely than others to be creative and imaginative. And although people with learning difficulties may take longer to learn something, their ability to adhere to the 'right' way of doing things once it is learnt is a pre-eminent survival skill.

Creativity, problem-solving and adherence to proven strategies are the essential survival skills, and disabled parents are role models in them, not only for their own children, but also for other people's. Disabled people have had to learn to develop these skills whether they have been born with an impairment or have acquired it in later life. In addition to enabling disabled people to parent, we urgently need to recognise that disabled parents have valuable lessons to teach us all, and to ensure their full participation in society instead of leaving them isolated and disrespected.

Similarly, we need to recognise that humans have not survived by abandoning each other when anyone became sick or disabled. In fact, the other qualities that will enable us to survive the next century are cooperation, compassion, empathy and mutual respect. All of these are, of course, qualities associated with providing care and support in disability and old age. Even at a genetic level, it is the genes that can cooperate with each other to form, eventually, whole organisms that survive. Their very 'selfishness' leads them to work with others in order to ensure that they continue for generations to come. New research shows that the way our genes express themselves in future generations may actually be affected by our life experiences before we conceive. If this is true, enhancing qualities such as problem-solving and empathy today may actually change future generations for the better.

We are most likely to be able to tackle our body dysphoria when we recognise that it is the preservation of the most genetically diverse world population possible that will ensure the future of the human race. Only when we recognise that even the most 'abnormal' of us can make a significant contribution to the wellbeing of our whole society will we be able to view ourselves as being genetically 'perfect' just the way we are — and begin, finally, to relax. Failing to do this will threaten our future far more than any 'faulty' gene can ever do.

SECTION IV

ALTERNATIVE FUTURES or,

Do we really have a choice about changing?

If we understand that we are all 'normal', and that we cannot rely on science to eliminate impairment and old age, then where does that leave us? It is not an exaggeration to say that, today, we are at a point where we have some fundamental choices to make about our use of science and the resulting future of humanity. That is not to say, of course, that we can make choices about scientists' achievements. As we have seen, demanding that their work produces the results that we want is not enough to make this happen. We need to be mature enough to distinguish between science fact and science fiction, however much it hurts us to do this. We can however choose what to prioritise in terms of scientists' work, and what to fund them to do.

We can also make choices about how and whether to implement the knowledge that we have already gained from science. In particular, we can choose whether to implement the very many low-tech, inexpensive ways that science teaches us can make a critical difference to human survival — widening access to clean drinking water and mosquito nets are just two actions that would save the lives of millions of people across the world each year. In making these choices, we can use the knowledge that scientists have given us about humanity: that we are all part of the same human race; and poverty is not biologically determined. Or we can continue in our dysphoria, refusing to accept our mortality and expecting science to meet our demands for eternal youth, doomed instead to eternal disappointment.

15. THE NEW ANCIENTS or, Who wants to live for ever?

Around the world today, there are a growing number of people who believe that their lives can be extended for at least hundreds of years, and who are working actively with researchers to achieve this. They have been supported in this belief, of course, by several decades of media reporting. When deciding if we want to be immortal, it is helpful to speculate on the fate of those who would pioneer attempts to prolong life beyond what is possible to achieve from a combination of a healthy lifestyle, good social and medical care, and luck in the lottery that forms the inheritance of genes and the interplay of genes with the environment.

Those who put themselves forward as candidates for being 'ancients' are likely to have a variety of motives. They may be enormously self-absorbed and egotistic, or be driven by unfulfilled goals, or have families or partners who are significantly younger than themselves, or simply have a desire to prolong what they regard as being a happy and fulfilling life beyond what is normally possible.

The first would-be 'ancients' are also likely to be extremely wealthy, contributing the majority of the necessary research funds themselves. This in itself will make them vulnerable to exaggerated claims for the efficacy of the research, in order that they continue to fund it. After all, scientists will be keen to extend their own knowledge whatever the outcome, as well as to solve the ultimate medical mystery. But governments will not fund research to prolong life until they are sure of the economic impact of longevity. Meanwhile, private pharmaceutical companies are already funding some research, but are unlikely to devote huge amounts of their resources until they are first sure that real progress is being made. Funding from individuals is already key to the 'immortality' research that is taking place now.

The inevitability of impairment and isolation

Of course, it is not completely impossible to suppose that one day scientists may be able to reverse all of the genetic damage caused by the act of living, and may be able to continue to do so on an ongoing basis. Nor is it out of the question to suppose that everyone in the world will have access to so many resources that longevity treatment, however expensive, will be accessible to all. It is simply illogical to suppose that either of these things will happen based on the evidence that is currently available to us. However desirable it may seem for all of us to have unlimited access to unlimited resources, and for scientific achievement to be boundless, there is no 'scientific' basis for this belief.

Despite this, would-be ancients must adopt both possibilities as an act of faith if they want to be assured that their lives, if extended, will bear any similarity to the lives they lead now. After all, unless immortality is available to the majority in the future, ancients will be unwelcome in wider society except perhaps as curiosities. Until then they will face continuing hostility and criticism from those whose moral and religious beliefs are offended by their attempts to attain immortality, or who are simply jealous of their ability to be able to afford to try. Would-be ancients will certainly not be made welcome by the majority of the population while they remain in a minority.

What is certain is that the road to longer life will not be an easy one. It is highly unlikely that scientists will be successful in holding back every effect of ageing at once, even using a combination of surgery and joint replacement technology together with anti-ageing drug therapies to maintain the body in as youthful a condition as possible. (The 'body as classic car' approach that we have inherited from Descartes.) Some would-be ancients will fall at the first hurdle, of course: all surgeries involve risk; and all experimental treatments have their casualties. Since the nature of the research will be so experimental, some would-be ancients will also have to come to terms with the fact that in seeking to prolong their lives, they have instead shortened them, or at least have reduced their quality of life.

The remainder will still witness the change and deterioration of their bodies and minds, albeit at — possibly — a slower pace than others. The hope, presumably, will be that one day they will regain their lost physical and mental abilities, as attempts to achieve longevity become more successful. However, given what we know at present, it is more likely that the majority of would-be ancients will continue to experience a range of permanent physical impairments and cognitive difficulties, however youthful their outward appearance might — or might not — be.

With this slow deterioration of mind and body will inevitably come mental health problems, as would-be ancients attempt to process what is happening to them at the same time as witnessing the continuing deaths of their peers. As the circumstances that they will face will be unique, some may discover that they have a genetic propensity for mental illness for the first time in their lives, and the change in their mental wellbeing is then likely to be permanent. There will be no way of pre-screening would-be ancients for this, because we have no data on which to base any conclusions.

Ancients will not even have the comfort of food to sustain them. Scientists have already established that if someone puts themselves into a permanent state of near-starvation, this will almost certainly prolong their life, and so calorie restriction will be a necessary part of the first ancients' daily regimes. As we can see from the obesity epidemic, most people do not consider a few years' extra life worth denying themselves the many pleasures associated with food. But of those who currently do, more than a few may suffer from eating disorders. Restricting your diet to the degree that your body goes into an otherwise unnatural state of energy conservation can never be healthy in the wider sense. Our bodies are programmed to enjoy food, and to crave it constantly once our intake drops too low. Not too far into the future, life for the would-be ancients really wouldn't be much fun at all.

Rather than becoming the norm, then, 'ancients' are likely to remain a small, self-selected group, increasingly dependent on medical treatments and technologies and disability aids. As their funds run low, they may turn to the media, becoming part of a reality television freak show — although they are more likely to be mocked bitterly than envied. Or, if their wealth continues to support them, they may simply remain behind closed doors, becoming less and less connected to the society in which they live. Or perhaps they may eventually decide to let go, and accept death after all.

Would-be ancients must be prepared to commit years, perhaps centuries, of their lives to being guinea pigs for technologies and treatments that are likely, at best, to offer more to future generations than to themselves. However attractive immortality may seem, in practice only the truly dysphoric will be prepared to have a go at achieving it.

Leaving 'the meat' behind altogether

The alternative, which is also being discussed quite seriously around the world today, is to attempt to upload our intelligence, memories and personalities into a computer. It is the ultimate in body dysphoria: the desire to remove our bodies from the equation altogether, at the same time as gaining immortality. Would-be silicon humans talk about 'leaving the meat behind', believing that the body and mind have very little to do with each other at all. In this they echo centuries of philosophy, and in particular the old belief in the Cartesian mind–body divide, but very little contemporary science. And, of course, there is nothing in our current scientific knowledge that leads us to suppose that this will ever be possible in any case.

Current research into decoding the brain's activities is centred on studies of the brain that illuminate neural connections: studies that make visible the brain's reaction to stress, to different types of information, to different emotions and so on. Most recently, scientists have focused on measuring intention to choose between two different courses of action, thus allowing people connected up to electrodes to operate a simple switch system by thought alone. It is believed by some that this will one day enable us to determine character, personality, honesty and so on by measuring the brain's activity. However, it is hard to take this completely seriously when we remember that the Victorians spent many years believing that skull measurements could tell us the same thing: a 'fact' that we know now to be completely false.

As is so often the case with scientific development, research funding is driven by military requirements. More sophisticated lie detectors are always sought; but the real desire is to be able to access an individual's memories in total rather than simply being able to ascertain whether or not a suspect is telling the truth. It is this research that drives the belief that 'uploading' our minds will one day be possible. However, today we still have no clear understanding of how the memory actually works, let alone any way of accessing and decoding it. It is highly unlikely that we will ever be able to access an individual's memories and replay them on a video screen, as depicted in science fiction. Crude uses for the technology by the military and the police are all that are likely to come of the current research.

The importance of feelings

But even if we could access our memories and load them into a computer, that is still a very long way from being able to upload the mind as a whole:

we are far more than the sum of our memories. What, though, if this was possible too? What if we could upload our personalities as well? 'Virtual' humans would then have two options: to live entirely in cyberspace; or to obtain new, probably artificial bodies to enable them to live within the world.

What would a cyberspace life be like? We could spend an eternity listening to music — or perhaps not, since sensory pleasures would remain physical and therefore confined to the body. At best, we could appreciate music's mathematical splendour — unless we found the mathematical dissonance that most music also entails to be illogical. Pleasure in all of its forms would in fact be entirely absent from our lives, unless we are programmed to simulate the chemical effects on our brains of different experiences.

Otherwise, life without emotion could also affect silicon humans' ability to make decisions. As we have seen, in the not-so-distant past, it was generally accepted that emotions undermined our ability to make rational decisions. Women, and people from the 'lower races', were thought to be more emotional than men, and therefore less suited to roles in life where decision-making was central. However, scientists now know that emotions play a critical role in making fast, good decisions. This follows research carried out on people whose decision-making abilities became impaired after surgery on their brains. Emotions may well be seated in a relatively 'old' part of the brain, but that is because rapid, appropriate decision-making was essential for both animals and humans to survive.

With or without emotions, as silicon humans we could spend an eternity acquiring knowledge — or perhaps not, since as silicon life-forms we would be able to access and understand the world's knowledge almost instantly. We could spend an eternity simply appreciating and enjoying knowledge — but, again, only if we are programmed to simulate pleasure. We could interact with our friends, as well as with any number of strangers. This, too, would require us to be programmed to simulate any emotional response to their company. Otherwise it is doubtful that we would have any interest in interacting, particularly as we would be able to access their entire silicon essence in an instant. What would be the point of asking someone's opinion if we already knew it, or if we already had so much knowledge about them that we would be able to predict it?

It is likely, too, that silicon humans would face controls on them, in order to counteract any possible threat they might pose to the rest of society. Silicon humans could potentially have great power, so they might well be prevented from having free access to the world's computers. For the same reason, they would be much sought-after to carry out acts of espionage and terrorism. Freedom of movement would be impossible, even in the virtual realm.

Controls would also be thought necessary because no one could predict the effects of silicon life on an individual's sanity. The impact of transition would obviously be severe — nothing could prepare the mind for the experience of 'leaving the meat behind'. At the same time, it is unlikely that a silicon human could change their mind and die if they wanted to. The very nature of digital data means that it can be copied endlessly, and any company that has invested the resources necessary to create a silicon human would be unlikely to let it commit suicide, at least in the short term.

Faced with this existence, it is logical to suppose that silicon humans would seek a robotic body, either to reside in or to control remotely. There is nothing to suggest that we will ever be able to replicate the complexity and sophistication of the human body; robotic life could not compete with it. Silicon humans might gain independence of movement by having a robotic body, but pleasure and sensuality — which make up much of our personality — would still be absent or artificial. Again, only the truly dysphoric could find this discourse either believable or attractive.

We as humans are clearly characterised by a refusal to accept our own mortality. Many ancient cultures buried their dead with their possessions, since they believed that the dead would need them in their future lives — for example, Tutankhamen was buried with 132 walking sticks. Today, a number of religions reject cremation because they believe that their members' bodies will be resurrected. Other would-be ancients have been freezing their bodies — or in some cases only their heads — for several decades now in the belief that scientists of the future will be able to revive them.

In the end, though, as we have seen, science has shown us that life is what causes death. Anyone believing that there is an alternative may have read a lot of science fiction, but they will have studied very little science. We need to concentrate on improving the quality of our lives, however we define this, rather than defining our lives as being second-class and second-rate compared to the promise of immortality. We also need to concentrate on improving the quality of our deaths, rather than refusing to accept that this will ever be necessary. Only then can we have a real chance of lasting happiness.

16. MEDICAL MELTDOWN
or, What will happen if we continue in our dysphoria?

As we have seen, there are a growing number of people out there who believe passionately that, if further funding is put into anti-ageing research, those of us who are alive today could reach 500 or even 1000 years of age. And while only a small minority of wealthy would-be ancients are experimenting on themselves to date, our dissatisfaction with our bodies and our desire for eternal youth has already distorted our priorities for medical research. This is despite the fact that the results will ultimately be of little benefit. If we don't tackle our body dysphoria, then sooner rather than later there will be widespread consequences for us all.

Profits and priorities

The finite amount of research funding available will always go to the area with the greatest potential profit, rather than to the area with the greatest potential to do good or the one that is most likely to succeed. Even state-funded medical research now has profitability as one of its primary goals: researchers are expected to improve the wealth, as well as the health, of their nation. The demand that scientists extend our natural lifespan therefore diverts funding away from vital areas such as cancer research, where the state has already made it clear that it won't pay for expensive new treatments.

It is important that we understand how medical research funding works in practice before we can understand the impact of our body dysphoria on the wider picture. With profit as a primary influence on funding priorities, research into HIV/Aids has only progressed as quickly as it has done because the virus has spread from Africa and the Indian sub-continent into the much richer West. Researchers who are trying to combat malaria — one of the world's biggest killers — through developing a vaccine receive no private funding at all. Rather, they are largely dependent on charitable and, to a lesser extent, state funding, because malaria is overwhelmingly a disease of the very poor. (Britons can be proud that we lead the world in state funding for the battle against malaria.) Meanwhile, pharmaceutical companies have virtually halted research into new antibiotics (despite the overwhelming need for these in the West as well as elsewhere) because the speed at which organisms now develop resistance makes that uneconomic, too.

In all, worldwide more than £50 billion is spent each year on medical research, but only 10% of this money goes towards researching treatments for the diseases that cause 90% of the world's health problems. Meanwhile, 90% of medical research funding goes into illnesses that affect only 10% of the population, many of which are linked to lifestyle, because this is where the profit lies. The majority of this research is not even original, but is directed into producing slightly different versions of existing drugs in order that pharmaceutical companies can continue to make profits from them once their original patents expire. Other current research priorities include drugs to tackle obesity, now defined as a medical condition rather than one arising from lifestyle choices, since obesity is by its very nature a disease of the relatively rich.

Inevitably, drug treatments aimed at richer people will always be more profitable than drug treatments aimed at poorer people, while pharmaceutical companies have a legal duty to their shareholders to maximise profits at all costs. It is irrelevant to pharmaceutical companies whether or not the diseases being treated are actually related to people's wealth (such as the growth in diabetes arising from obesity), and are easily preventable by better health education and greater controls on the processed food industry (the impact of which is not covered here for the reason that it would take a book in itself). And, of course, it is not in pharmaceutical companies' interests for people to make the necessary lifestyle changes. State-funded medical researchers are also being placed under ever-increasing pressure to produce profitable drug treatments, not only in order to self-fund their work, but also to boost national incomes. Health education as an alternative — i.e. prevention rather than cure — is not in anyone's commercial interests, and it is as well to remember that.

Meanwhile, drug treatments taken by healthy people — to 'upgrade' their abilities or to ward off ageing — will always be potentially much more profitable than drugs to treat diseases. This is because there are far more healthy people than there are people needing medical treatment. Healthy people are also far more likely to be able to afford to pay for drugs than sick people — as we have seen, illness not only affects people's earning ability, but often results from poverty in the first place. And since many existing illnesses result from poverty, and the related pollution and war, there is enormous potential to reduce the numbers of sick people needing medical treatment by tackling these problems. Continuing to develop treatments for diseases could reduce the numbers even further: a cure for a chronic illness like arthritis would eliminate the need to take daily drug treatments for the rest of someone's life. It is in pharmaceutical companies' overwhelming interest, then, to persuade healthy people to take drugs on a long-term basis.

An ever-increasing proportion of the Western population is over 40, and so is experiencing the effects of ageing. Drugs that hold out the promise of combating the ageing process, and of enhancing intelligence and memory, are therefore inevitably the most attractive drugs of all for marketing to healthy people. It is irrelevant, in the short term, whether or not the drugs work — it will, after all, be impossible to prove this conclusively for decades. Antioxidants, for example, have now been shown to be completely useless in preventing ageing, but have made fortunes for their manufacturers in the interim. In addition, repeated research has shown that many existing drugs licensed for use today either have little benefit, or benefit only a proportion of the people who take them, but they are still widely prescribed nonetheless.

When it comes to the profitability of anti-ageing drugs for healthy people, hormone replacement therapy (HRT) is a case in point. In the mid-1960s the menopause began to be redefined from being a natural stage in a woman's life — a stage that could be celebrated as marking the end of child-bearing and menstruation and the start of greater independence and power — to being an illness that marked the end of a woman's attractiveness and sex life. Oestrogen therapy was then offered as a treatment to combat this part of the ageing process; it was regarded as a treatment that could be taken to keep women youthful and sexually active for the rest of their lives. Later, as oestrogen therapies were found to have a wide range of unwanted side-effects, modern hormone replacement therapies were developed to take their place.

It was only in the mid-1990s that serious doubts emerged over HRT, when a landmark study involving 121,700 women was published in *The New England Journal of Medicine* in 1995. This found that women who used HRT for more than five years increased their risk of developing breast cancer by 30–40%. In women aged between 60 and 64, the increased risk after five years rose to 70%. Other research has questioned these findings, but it is generally accepted that long-term use of HRT can increase a woman's risk of developing cancer and heart disease, although there may be a protective effect in terms of other diseases.

Today, doctors are much more likely than they were previously to offer women drugs to treat specific 'symptoms' of the menopause, such as excessive sweating or loss of calcium from the bones, rather than HRT. Where women are prescribed HRT, the majority take it for less than five years. In the future, HRT may not be a routine treatment at all. However, in the interim it will have made a great deal of profit for its manufacturers.

Only one development stands out to show that there is another way. Two British scientists, Nicholas Ward and Malcolm Law from the Wolfson Institute of Preventive Medicine, are beginning trials of a daily 'polypill' which combines low doses of out-of-copyright (and thus cheap) drugs to lower cholesterol and blood pressure. Their belief is that, by making it available to all over-50s, the rate of heart attacks and strokes could be significantly reduced. The fact that there will be no profit in it, though, for anyone other than the India-based manufacturers shows why research into other uses for cheap, familiar and therefore relatively safe drugs is seldom funded.

Testing and its pressures

As we continue to demand that scientists keep on developing unnecessary drugs, the poorest members of society suffer. This is not only because of the impact on research priorities and the resulting lack of treatments for the diseases that affect them most, but also because they are forced to function as guinea pigs for the rest of us.

The search for the 'perfect' drug is, as we have seen, illusory. All drugs have side-effects, and some of these may not be apparent for many years. We may never reach a point when we have the 'perfect' drugs to treat disease, let alone to enhance the body and mind. We will also never be able to replicate in a laboratory the way in which a drug reacts within the human body, with all of its complex systems. Animal testing, meanwhile, is proving to be of little use for a new generation of drugs.

Drug trials will therefore continue to be necessary, simply in order to treat disease. If we also wish to try to develop a much wider range of drugs, in order to 'enhance' the body, far more drug trials will be needed than now. Yet today, one in ten of all patients in Britain are already participating in a drugs trial at any one time, while a much higher proportion of those receiving medical treatment in the developing world are taking experimental treatments. Related human rights abuses will inevitably increase if pressure grows to find even larger numbers of research subjects.

A huge amount of thought has already been put into how to prevent human rights abuses arising from the use of new scientific and technological developments. Britain is recognised as having led the world in examining the ethical dilemmas posed by bio-science in all of its manifestations, and in setting up regulatory bodies where these are thought to be necessary. Most importantly, the systems that have been created have been shown to be responsive to change as new developments come forward, even if responses have not always come as quickly as some might desire. To a great extent, too, the ethical debates have succeeded in including the public as a whole, even if those debates have been less than fully informed — as in the case of 'designer babies', where unnecessary concerns about the abuse of the technology have held back treatment for the tiny minority of couples who can actually benefit by it.

Why, then, should we worry about human rights abuses in the future? And why should we worry particularly about human rights abuses that arise from our body dysphoria, as opposed to those that arise from our search for better health? Well, we already know that human rights abuses are resulting from our existing research into new drug treatments.

Poverty is the key motivation for participating in drug trials in both the developed and the developing world, making this a negative rather than a positive choice. For the people participating in drug trials today the money paid may simply mean the ability to travel or to get out of debt, or it may mean the difference between life and death for an entire family.

After six people were seriously injured in a trial of a new anti-inflammatory drug in Great Britain in March 2006, pharmaceutical companies experienced a surprising surge in the number of people enquiring how they could participate in future testing. This was solely because more people had been made aware that they could earn money from volunteering for drug trials; around £1000 a week was the figure quoted. Their desperation was enough to overcome any fears at seeing the horrific injuries that the six previous 'volunteers' had suffered, effects that were expected to last a lifetime and possibly to shorten their lives. In the USA, participants who cannot afford health insurance also benefit from free health screening — something that Britons take for granted, but which many Americans lack.

Most of us accept — if we think about it at all — that some people who are already living in poverty may have been injured or killed in order to develop the drugs that treat our diseases: diseases that may be linked to our wealthier lifestyles rather than from any genetic susceptibility. In the future, if we demand that science finds ways to extend our lifespans artificially, we would have to accept that poor people have been injured or killed simply to develop drugs to improve the lives of wealthier people still further.

We may say that we are not responsible for the social inequities that drive test subjects to risk their lives; but if social inequities were addressed, it would be extremely difficult to obtain sufficient 'volunteers' to trial variations on existing drugs, let alone entirely new ones. And given the risks to life that drug trials entail, it would be virtually impossible to find enough volunteers to trial drugs to 'upgrade' the body without some form of coercion being used. This might, as in the past, involve testing drugs on prisoners, on members of the armed forces or on residents of institutions. This type of thing was kept hidden from view in the past, but new communication technologies mean that we would be unlikely to be able to avoid this uncomfortable knowledge in the future.

In the mean time, more and more drug trials are taking place in developing countries. This is partly because of the much larger numbers of poor people there, who are virtually unable to resist an offer to be paid to participate in testing. People in developing countries are also less likely to have access to health care. If they suffer from the illness that the drug being trialled is intended to treat, they are unlikely to be able to afford to opt for proven treatments instead. Drugs are also tested in the developing world because the political regimes there are more lax, and in many cases are highly corrupt. This allows pharmaceutical companies to operate without the restraints and pressures that they face in the developed world.

The profits made by pharmaceutical companies are immense — by the mid-noughties, Pfizer, the biggest drugs company in the world, made a profit of $42.7 billion in the year to April 2005. However ethical these companies' policies might be, the temptation for individual employees to commit human rights abuses is enormous when the profits are so high. It is virtually impossible for any company to have absolute control over its local operatives in the developing world, however hard they might try.

The finite availability of doctors

Aside from human rights abuses during drug testing and development, what else would result from the impact on medicine of society's continuing body dysphoria? What would happen if we continue to insist that medicine extends our lifespan through direct intervention, rather than through providing information and advice on how to achieve a healthier lifestyle? Or if we make annual cosmetic surgery routine for those who can afford it? What would happen if we do decide to attempt to 'enhance' the body through the use of surgical implants rather than continuing to extend our abilities simply by surrounding ourselves with a range of technology?

Would existing inequities simply deepen? Would society be divided into those with and those without 'enhancements'? When we look carefully at the potential future impact of our body dysphoria, it becomes obvious that the implications are far more serious than this. If unnecessary surgeries and drug therapies become common and widespread, it is inevitable that many people will be left entirely without access to basic medical treatment for disease. The reason for this is simple: the supply of doctors will always be limited.

In the developed world, we are already importing doctors from the developing world because of a shortage of doctors in our own countries. This need to import doctors is partly because every doctor who is performing unnecessary cosmetic surgeries is a doctor who has been lost to medicine — often after having their training funded by the taxpayer. In particular, patients who badly need plastic (as opposed to cosmetic) surgery, for whatever reason, are having to wait longer for treatment. Likewise, the large number of patients with illnesses that result from their lifestyle impacts on the availability of doctors for those with unavoidable health problems. This means that survival rates from conditions like cancer are much lower than they could be due to a shortage of doctors available to train in a range of related specialisms and the resulting long waiting lists.

But the importing of doctors also results from the fact that only a small proportion of the population is considered to be intelligent enough and to have the right personality to practise medicine. The numbers of doctors available will always, therefore, be finite: unlike, say, plumbers or bricklayers, medical practitioners cannot respond to the market and become more numerous as demand for their services increases. If we divert doctors on a large scale to perform cosmetic surgeries and to administer and monitor unnecessary drug therapies, then we simply cannot provide medical care for all of the world's population that needs it.

We can see this today from the example of dental care. Large numbers of people in the UK have already lost access to essential dental care because of the diversion of dentists to provide unnecessary and disfiguring cosmetic treatments. At the end of the noughties, one in four dentists had trained to offer Botox and other facial 'fillers' alongside dental treatments. Meanwhile, seven million people had failed to gain access to an NHS dentist, so three million people went without the dental treatment they needed. A growing number of people were even forced to pull out their own teeth rather than having them dealt with professionally. As few as one in ten decayed teeth among children were treated, with dentists leaving primary teeth to rot and fall out: the vast majority of affected children were from the poorest families.

The reality is that we need to tackle the main causes of ill health — pollution, war, poverty and unhealthy lifestyles — just in order to have adequate numbers of doctors and dentists to meet the world's health needs. At present, there is still a global imbalance between the number of doctors and dentists needed and the number of people who could potentially be trained to do this work and this would exist even if everyone who needed medical treatment could afford to pay.

Of course, there are two alternatives to this scenario. The first involves imagining, for a moment, that we have successfully developed relatively safe smart drugs at some point in the not-too-distant future, and that their use has been widely accepted. Then we could increase the number of doctors and dentists available by using people who have had their intelligence 'upgraded' with 'smart' drugs. At best, though, these doctors would still be less intelligent and less able than brighter and more capable people who had also had their intelligence 'upgraded': they would still be second-class.

The other alternative is to imagine increasing the part played in medicine by robots and interactive software. Robots have, after all, the potential to deliver some types of surgery more efficiently than humans so long as they remain controlled by humans. Software, too, might be more efficient than doctors in some circumstances when it comes to making a diagnosis. However, robotic developments are more likely to assist us in widening access to health care and in delivering more effective surgery than in replacing the need for doctors and dentists. Robots, after all, are really only effective in medicine when they are under the control of a human being.

How many people would really be prepared to undergo an anaesthetic and then have their breasts surgically altered if the doctors involved were only competent to perform these procedures because of the drug therapy they had received? And of those who would, how many would be happy about the same doctors inserting an implant into their jaw or brain? Would they feel better about it if these doctors were simply assisting a robot, rather than the robot assisting them? And how would they feel about a non-doctor assisting a robot to perform the same surgery? We can imagine a world where all this is happening, but it is a stretch too far to imagine it becoming a reality.

Of course, we could reassign doctors to cosmetic medical and dental surgery and drug enhancements if we had little need of them elsewhere — if we had found the cure for every disease, and only required doctors to treat the results of accidents. We have already discussed some of the reasons why this is unlikely ever to happen: disease becomes resistant to existing cures and requires new ones; new diseases take the place of diseases that have ceased to threaten our health; and experience shows us that, at its very best, no treatment is likely to be suitable for everyone. In addition to this, as lifespans increase, so do the odds of developing disease. We will never have enough doctors to go round if cosmetic surgery and other treatments become a 'normal' part of our lives.

Finite resources

The other consequence of continuing to demand that science and technology upgrade and enhance our bodies is the waste of the world's and our own resources that this involves. We may well argue that the world's resources are already being wasted in a multitude of ways, and that we are entitled to use our personal resources in any way that we wish. However, we still need to remember that we are paying the price, and that our choices involve losses for all of us.

For example, in the recent past, elective cosmetic surgery was limited to one-off procedures with a limited cost, such as reshaping the nose or pinning back the ears. This benefited those who wished to minimise the effects of minor accidents and birth conditions — many of whom were therefore able to get funding from the state; and it had very little impact on the overall picture. Breast enhancement surgery also began to be accepted for women who felt that their natural proportions were 'abnormal' — the state also funded women whose mental health was being affected by this. Meanwhile, plastic surgery continued largely to benefit those who had experienced serious accidents or were severely affected by medical conditions (including women needing reconstructive surgery after cancer operations), whether the effects were psychiatric or physical. Otherwise, facelifts were limited to ageing actors and socialites, and breast enhancements to those wishing to be 'glamour' models (i.e. to work somewhere on the pornography continuum).

Then 'nose jobs' began to be routine for a particular sub-section of society who had perfectly ordinary features, but who wished to conform to an ideal created by advertising and the media — an ideal that, as we know, is always changing. Breast enhancement surgery began to increase among those who had ordinary-sized breasts and no desire to work in the 'glamour' industry, despite the side-effects experienced by many of those who had already had the surgery. Cosmetic surgery in effect became normalised for an increasing, though still small, number of the population, especially the women in the aforementioned career groups, who have always been under great pressure to conform to an ideal.

Today, cosmetic surgery has become an ongoing process for many, involving multiple parts of the body and repeated surgeries of the same type as the years progress. As we saw at the beginning of this book, in the first years of the 21st century cosmetic surgery has become not only acceptable but also something that is viewed as being essential in order to compete in the workplace as well as to maintain relationships, and, critically, as being central to the anti-ageing process. Meanwhile, the language of the media encourages people to believe that cosmetic surgery is not only desirable in the extreme, but also will soon be an ordinary part of life. This is despite the fact that surgery can only ever be partially successful in altering the body's appearance.

Many of the people now opting for cosmetic surgery have limited financial resources. Whether they realise it or not, they may be giving up the opportunity to have access to secure housing, foreign holidays or financial security in retirement in return for the dysphoric pursuit of happiness with their bodies. They are also, of course, risking serious complications, and even death, every time that they opt for surgery. And yet it would be entirely possible for the majority of them — those who are not experiencing a psychiatric condition that is only responsive to surgery — to achieve happiness with their bodies without any surgery whatsoever.

We need to decide. Do we want to live in a world where half of us may have no access to medical care at all, while unnecessary treatment plays an increasingly dominant role in the lives of the other half? And do we really believe that it would be possible to achieve this without, ultimately, economic collapse? If so, then there is no need for us, personally or politically, to make any changes whatsoever. If not, then we need to begin to question seriously the demands that we make of our doctors and medical researchers, and the choices we make in our own lives.

17. (IN)VOLUNTARY EUTHANASIA or, Better dead than disabled?

If we removed the prejudice, the discrimination, the poverty, the stereotyping, the disabling environments and all of the other issues that disabled people face as a result of society's body dysphoria, disabled people of all age groups would still be left with their impairments. And it is impairment, rather than the barriers that create disability, that most people cite when saying that they would rather die than live if they became seriously disabled because of an accident, illness or ageing. This, rather than eugenics, is also the overwhelming reason why many people feel that it is 'unfair' to allow disabled foetuses to be born. Euthanasia would certainly reduce the need to make wholesale changes to the way in which we organise our society. But is it really better to be dead than disabled? If we are able to look at impairment without the distorting effect of our body dysphoria, we can conclude that the answer is a resounding: 'No!'

Dependency on others

The most common reason that people give for their preference for death over disability is the enforced dependence on other people that a condition such as multiple sclerosis or extreme old age is seen to create. People perceive it as being highly undesirable to have to depend on another person to carry out simple daily tasks such as opening and closing curtains, running a bath, dressing them, brushing their hair, preparing their food and so on. It is impossible in this scenario, they believe, to be happy or to have any meaningful quality of life.

In comparison, suffering pain is seen as a secondary consideration — in fact, since stoicism is generally regarded as a virtue, the capacity to endure pain is often regarded as being desirable and as a mark of strong character. But in any case, medical science has shown us the way to prevent or alleviate pain in all but a tiny minority of cases. Unfortunately, since suffering pain has been regarded for millennia as being desirable, pain relief has been stigmatised and is still widely restricted, meaning that many people believe that suffering is inevitable, based on their own or other family members' experiences. Where appropriate palliative care is available, though, the vast majority of terminally ill people do not suffer significant pain at all.

In any case, it is the thought of accepting help with personal tasks, not the idea of suffering pain, that so many people find unendurable. Although the scientific reality is that we are all inter-dependent on each other, we subscribe to the myth of the independent, isolated individual who is able to meet all of their own needs without outside assistance. As a result, many women regard it as demeaning simply to be dependent on someone else to fetch their shopping and to carry out their domestic work for them.

This attitude is clearly gender-specific: most men are already used to someone else, i.e. a woman, carrying out their domestic work and buying their shopping for them. And this is largely done not because of any impairment or incapability on men's part, but simply because our society is organised in such a way that cleaning and shopping are regarded as being 'women's work'. (In the past, men would also have admitted that they considered domestic tasks to be beneath them: carrying out your own domestic tasks has always been a sign of social inferiority.)

Men may be concerned at the impact of impairment on their sex lives, but absolutely not on their ability to clean or clear up after their children — and they are quite right. We are not defined by our ability to cook and clean. Most women, though, feel that their whole sense of identity is threatened if they can't carry out these tasks for themselves. We need to learn from men's very different attitude that there is nothing intrinsically negative about having other people carry out shopping and domestic tasks on your behalf.

Power and control

In fact, having others carry out the whole range of 'caring' tasks for you can be perceived as being highly desirable. The majority of young people now aspire to a 'celebrity' lifestyle, with tabloid newspapers and women's magazines both full of stories of the famous and wealthy. Many people spend their lives pursuing wealth, and in general the improvement of our personal financial circumstances is seen as being a sensible and desirable goal. But the very same tasks that are perceived as being so extremely demeaning that death is preferable to having other people do them on your behalf when they are associated with impairment are the ones that characterise the status of the extremely wealthy.

(In)Voluntary Euthanasia

For centuries, the very rich have relied on servants to wake them up, open their curtains, bring them breakfast, run their baths, dress them, arrange their hair and so on and so forth. Likewise, the wealthy depend on servants to clean their homes, buy and cook their food, dig their gardens, and so on. And for wealthy women, daily personal grooming from hairdressers and a wide range of beauticians is perceived to be further evidence of their high social status. As with men and housework, there is no innate reason why the very rich should not carry out their own daily and domestic tasks: they are not, by and large, incapable of doing these things for themselves, nor, by and large, do they lack the time. Rather, the fact that other people meet their needs demonstrates to others that the wealthy are elevated above the norm: they are too important to do these things themselves. No one suggests, for example, that their failure to carry out these tasks is grounds for institutionalising them. There is nothing innately undesirable or humiliating, then, about abandoning responsibility for daily tasks to others.

Similarly, wealthy women use nannies to help them to look after their children, and this, too, is seen to be desirable. No one seriously regards the use of nannies to be evidence of poor parenting: rather, these parents are widely envied. Yet disabled mothers who need help in order to look after *their* children are widely criticised, and often lose custody of their children altogether if they cannot afford to pay for this help themselves. Poverty, rather than disability, is the real issue here. Critics of disabled mothers are only really concerned when the state is asked to pay for their assistants. So long as parents can afford to pay for their own nannies — and they are described as nannies rather than care workers — no one cares about the reason why they are being employed.

The rich have secretaries, drivers, cleaners, cooks, housekeepers and, if necessary, nurses whether they could manage without them or not, and all of these helpers enhance their employer's personal status. Only the poor have care workers and are categorised as being disabled, which in turn robs them of any social status at all.

There is nothing intrinsically demeaning about relying on other people to carry out common daily tasks for you, then. Nor is this inextricably linked to a lowering of social status and a loss of power. Rather, it is more normally linked to higher social status and economic power, whether this is dictated by class or gender. We need to understand that so long as we are able to dictate what form help should take and how it should be provided, we do not have to lose control or social status by accepting it. In fact we can gain power by accepting help, rather than automatically losing it.

The development of domestic forms of technology also means that today many of these tasks can be automated and needn't involve human support at all. At the press of a button — or via voice-activated controls — curtains and doors can be opened and closed, baths can be run and emptied, heating and lighting can be switched on and off, and so on and so forth. 'Smart' homes that can do this and more are being developed for the very rich — Bill Gates was a pioneer of this kind of living. However, with wireless technology these kinds of controls are rapidly becoming cheap and widespread, and are being incorporated into modern lifestyles whether or not they are, strictly speaking, unnecessary. So there is no reason at all why people who need to use this type of technology because of impairment should feel belittled by it.

Life on wheels

Another reason commonly given for stating that death is preferable to disability is the loss of the ability to walk. But as we have seen, it is the ability to *avoid* walking, rather than the ability to walk, that attracts the higher social status: outside the home it is life on wheels, not on our feet, that is perceived to be desirable. In the course of a typical working day, many people are unlikely to have walked further than the distance that disabled people need to be able to have difficulty in walking to qualify for parking concessions, and some of this will have been to the coffee machine and back. This is despite the fact that scientists have proved walking to be the most effective way of keeping fit and reducing the risk of chronic disease, as well as boosting cognitive ability and mental health.

The reality is that we fail dismally to celebrate our ability to stand and walk. Most of us fail to take any advantage whatsoever of our ability to walk beyond the minimum required to sustain life. And this is despite the fact that walking is one of the most accessible forms of exercise, and will increase our longevity without wearing out our joints. Why, then, should the use of a wheelchair be perceived to be a tragedy, something that makes life not worth living? Why is it considered to be, on the one hand, normal to build roads and use them for even the shortest journeys, but on the other hand an expensive 'extra' to build ramps to allow wheelchair users to access buildings? Why is a car seen by many people as an essential, but a wheelchair as something to be avoided at all costs, even if this means spending a decade or more inside the home? The answer can only lie in our body dysphoria.

In fact, when wheelchairs fully meet the needs of the people using them, and our environment allows them access, then they are the most liberating, desirable means of transport for people with mobility impairments of every kind. Suddenly they can sit comfortably and move wherever they wish for as long as they wish at the touch of a button or the flick of a wheel: they are free.

Intimate assistance

Many people would argue that the main reason why they would rather die than live with serious impairments is not the need to use a wheelchair, or even to be helped with intimate tasks such dressing. Rather, it is the need to depend on others for help with bodily functions such as toileting. 'Loss of control over bodily functions' is listed by organisations that support assisted dying as being one of the key ways of determining when euthanasia is appropriate. Incontinence in particular is often seen as a reason for preferring death, and in itself is described as 'suffering'.

But all this is despite the many products that are now available to help make incontinence easy to deal with, including bladder implants for people who are paraplegic. It is also despite the testimony of disabled people who state that incontinence has not harmed the quality of their lives in any way at all, and who are horrified that incontinence is seen as a fate worse than death. Plenty of people living with total incontinence are still holding down jobs, bringing up children and living full lives.

What is particularly strange about this attitude is the fact that dealing with human faeces and urine is an integral part of life. It is not and never has been an optional life experience that can be disposed of by euthanasia. We all had our bottoms wiped for several years when we were infants, and most of us will wipe bottoms as adults when we become parents. In fact, parents will deal with their children's urine and faeces on a daily basis for several years; in larger families, parents can spend a decade or more of their lives doing this. We may not enjoy it, but bottom-wiping is part of the human condition.

It is difficult to know to what extent our disgust at dealing with faeces, in particular, is biological (i.e. we worry that infection will be spread by it) and to what extent it is cultural. Certainly, faeces provide a graphic reminder of our physical state, and as such prevent our body dysphoria from continuing while we are in contact with it. However, while many parents now prefer to use disposable nappies, there has never been a demand for technology to replace washing and changing babies by hand, despite the fact that this would be entirely possible. Nor do people give the need to change nappies as a reason for not having children. It is reasonable to assume, therefore, that having to meet someone else's continence needs is not so distasteful as to prefer that they were dead.

Is it, then, such an appalling experience to have your continence needs met by someone else? As teenagers, we may have thought that we would die from embarrassment if a lover saw us undressed. As adults, we may have worried ourselves sick about undergoing a first breast examination or a cervical smear. Many a pregnant woman has wondered if she can ever give birth when the presence of others is required. And yet somehow, all of these things quickly become an accepted part of normal life. So long as we can trust the person meeting our needs, and can dictate the means by which they are met, is incontinency really a reason to prefer to die? Younger people who are already living with incontinence say it is not.

And of course many people who are incontinent are in fact able to meet their own needs, rather than requiring any help from others. Also, incontinence affects only a minority of disabled and older people, despite perceptions that it is an inevitable part of experiencing severe levels of impairment and extreme old age. Most people who do require assistance with toileting need practical help — with getting on and off the toilet, getting clothes on and off, and, yes, having their bottom wiped. But even then there are models of toilet available that combine clean water and hot air to carry out this latter task, and these could be much more widely introduced. And, of course, there is the bidet — a rarity in Great Britain to date, but a standard fitting in many north European homes and one that could easily be introduced more widely too.

Re-examining the meaning of independence

On careful examination of our belief that we are better off dead than disabled, we realise that it has no basis in fact. If walking were intrinsic to enjoying life, there would be far fewer cars on the roads — in fact, there would be far fewer roads as well. If having other people to do our cleaning, cooking, shopping, childcare and so on made life less enjoyable, then there would be many more people out of work, and a lot more rich people down at the supermarket. There would also be far more women with time on their hands, as their male partners rushed to share the housework. And if dealing with continence issues were unbearable for us as adults, then we would certainly have invented a better way of changing nappies.

The real issues here are access to appropriate services, and power and control over them. If we believe that death is preferable to entering residential care, then we should be asking ourselves what action we need to take to improve those services, rather than accepting that residents' lives are intolerable. And we should be lobbying for increased support services in people's own homes, preventing them from needing to enter residential care in the first place.

Disabled people define 'independence' not as living without support, but as having their support needs fully met, and having choice and control over the support that they require. Control of our lives can be complete even when we have little or no physical control at all over our bodies. And it is possible even when communication needs to be facilitated, whether this is by technological means (as the example of Stephen Hawking shows us), or through low-tech aids such as communication boards, or by the use of sign language such as Makaton, or by other people.

Dementia and confusion

Of course, the other instance when people state that they would prefer death over disability is where a loss of mental faculties is involved, leading to confusion, distress and loss of identity as well as placing an enormous strain on other family members. Dementia affects one in twenty people over the age of 65, and one in five over the age of 80. As Western populations age, dementia will become more common: the number of people suffering from dementia in the UK — now 700,000 — is expected to rise by a million by 2050.

There are no easy answers here. However, what is clear is that, much of the time, the distress and the strain involved for all concerned are largely due to lack of access to appropriate health and social care, rather than to the condition itself. As for other disabled people, accepting help need not mean loss of control, for example through the actions of a family member; or via an 'advance directive', which dictates how someone wishes to live. Delivering services with the maximum dignity and respect for the person receiving them is also critical.

The continual development of new treatments, as well as aids to compensate for memory loss and confusion, also means that — if they're given access to these early enough — the outlook for people with dementia and their families will continue to improve on the current situation. Greater understanding of its causes will also improve their outlook: in 2010, a study published in the online Archives of Internal Medicine found that people smoking more than ten cigarettes a day increased their risk of developing dementia, with people smoking more than forty a day doubling their risk.

Another cause of loss of cognitive function is brain injury, also commonly used to 'prove' the benefits of using an 'advance directive' to refuse medical treatment and be allowed to die. In the UK, over a quarter of a million people are admitted to hospital with brain injuries each year, so this is not an uncommon scenario. Strokes (the third most common cause of death and the leading cause of disability in the UK), road accidents and head injuries all contribute to this figure.

However, neurological intensive care survival rates vary widely according to the type of treatment being provided: in some specialist units, people are now making a full recovery from brain injuries that would lead other hospitals to withdraw feeding and leave the victim to die. Meanwhile, according to the Royal College of Physicians, the vast majority of people who have strokes fail to receive the treatment that has been proven to have a major impact on disability and death rates. The charity Headway estimates that half a million Britons of working age have long-term impairments as a result of traumatic brain injuries. Again, the solution is in our hands.

Researchers are also finding that people in 'vegetative states' may have far more brain activity than was previously thought and are finding ways of communicating with them; there are even cases of people coming out of comas after 15 years or more. Other researchers have found that people can retrieve 'lost' memories with the use of brain implants, and that in general the brain is far more able to adapt to compensate for damaged parts of itself than was previously thought. We need to look at these facts very carefully indeed before deciding that life is not worth living after brain injury, and decide if we should instead be spending far more money on research and treatment, not to mention on providing support for patients' relatives and friends.

The right to die

Issues around assisted dying are many and complex. There are more than a few disabled people alive today who say that they have been suicidal in the past as a result of their impairment, and who would have met the conditions for being assisted to die under the terms of proposed legislation, but who are now extremely happy that no such 'right' was in place. There are well-publicised cases of people saying that they would prefer to die rather than undergo any further medical treatment, and then later changing their minds and opting for transplant surgery. There are many health workers around who are concerned that their interests are not being considered within the 'assisted dying' debate — in particular, the effects on their mental and emotional health of being involved with euthanasia.

There are also a few voices pointing out that the potential for drug therapies as an alternative to euthanasia has yet to be properly explored, and in particular the use of psychotropic drugs — in conjunction with effective pain relief — to make life more enjoyable. Meanwhile, people with dementia are often given unsuitable drugs that can hasten the progress of their condition in order to make them more compliant for care workers; and people near the end of their lives are often sedated so that food and water can be withdrawn from them to hasten their death.

The only thing that is certain is that dignity in dying depends largely on the quality of care and other support that is being provided for living — and, critically, on the control that we have over our lives — rather than on the end being hastened. It is a shame that today, owing to our body dysphoria, there are far fewer headlines and campaigns about improving care services and supporting carers than there are about 'the right to die'. Euthanasia can be very undignified indeed.

The right to life

We should be careful what we wish for. Most seriously ill patients and their families have to fight for access to the best and most appropriate medical treatments, rather than these being forced on them. We seem to believe that doctors will keep us alive unless we ask not to be resuscitated, yet resuscitation within a hospital setting only works in half of cases as it is. Certainly, only one in three of these patients survive to be discharged, but we might still be better off demanding more resources for this area of medicine, rather than dismissing its benefits so easily. Meanwhile, everyone already has the right to refuse treatment, even if refusing leads directly to their death. We often act as if the medical establishment is desperate to preserve our lives, no matter how difficult and expensive this may be. But funding is severely limited, and doctors are as affected as the rest of society by the belief that it is better to be dead than disabled.

As a result, older and disabled people are routinely denied treatments that are offered to younger non-disabled people, on the basis that their quality of life is not worth living. Other therapies, largely associated with ageing, are restricted, and people face unnecessary delays before accessing them. Doctors also have the right to refuse to provide fluids to patients who are unconscious or who are unable to swallow, and to deny treatment to those whose quality of life is judged to be too poor for them to benefit from it. As a result of all this, many older and disabled people die an earlier death than they otherwise would, as well as leading a more miserable life.

A quarter of all health care given to the average person over their lifetime is provided during the last year of their life, while there is currently a huge unmet demand for adequate and appropriate social care services for older and disabled people. By the 2020s, the Government predicts that the cost of maintaining even the current level of care services will double, as will the costs associated with supporting people with dementia, while the cost of disability benefits will rise by 50%. Although suicide prevention strategies concentrate on young men, people over the age of 65 currently have the highest suicide rate of any age group. The financial savings made would be immeasurable if everyone opted to end their life early, while they could still walk, wipe and do the crossword.

But would we really be avoiding a fate worse than death, or simply losing our last opportunity to enjoy life? It is notable that, alongside the campaign for the introduction of assisted suicide, there is at least an equally strong campaign by people living with cancer to have access to any and all drugs that may offer them a few extra months or weeks of life, even though these will not cure them. The campaigners, all of whom have a terminal diagnosis and whose quality of life is affected by their illness, are clear that the last thing they want is for the end of their life to be hastened.

Rather, they find life so worth living that they want it to continue for as long as possible, despite the effects of both their illness and the drugs that they wish to take to treat it, and they are supported in this by the same family members who meet the bulk of their care needs. In the UK, the NHS has now been forced to give in to this pressure and license some of these drugs for use, despite previously taking the position that drugs which did not offer a cure or a 'significant' lengthening of life were uneconomic and so should be denied to patients.

Of course, becoming disabled is often a life-changing experience. But change is what characterises human lives: childbirth, bereavement, marriage and divorce among others are all life-changing experiences, and all of them have their negative aspects. Ageing is also life-changing in itself: we are different people in infancy, childhood, youth, middle age and old age whether or not we are affected by disability. We need to recognise and accept this, rather than treating disability as if it is the only life-changing experience that we will ever encounter. The fact that we treat disability like this at all is only a symptom of our body dysphoria.

We need to distinguish between the effects of lack of access to appropriate services, and the effects of the condition itself, when deciding our responses to ageing and disability. We can, after all, choose whether to spend our money on war, or on life; we can actually afford to provide free social care for all if our priorities were different.

Issues around suicide/assisted suicide are complex, and in the end are highly individual: there is no absolute answer that applies to everyone. But there is the world of difference between leaving the world less consciously and perhaps a little earlier, but more comfortably than otherwise — as good hospice care already provides for; and leaving the world months, or even years, earlier than necessary, killed, not by our impairment or condition, but by our body dysphoria.

18) A DIFFERENT TOMORROW
or, How to heal and live healthily

Is it really so abnormal to want to extend our healthy lifespan? Isn't it actually quite *normal* to want to use medicine, science and fashion to get the most out of our lives? It is undoubtedly true that an extra decade or two of active life can add enormously to the richness of our life experiences. There is only so much that any of us want to do with our lives, and it does not take an infinite number of years to achieve it. Given even ten extra years, we could travel, learn new languages and subjects, develop new hobbies and interests, and form new relationships. We could even demand that fashion adapts itself to the needs of our bodies, rather than continuing to try fruitlessly to adapt our bodies to the 'standard' size range. Well, the good news is that we already have the ability to make this a reality today.

Science has shown us that there are many ways in which we can optimise our life chances. We can take regular moderate exercise (over-exercise will damage our bodies); eat a nutritious (tasty and satisfying) diet; and maintain a healthy weight — scientists believe this on its own would reduce cancer rates by a third. Then we could drink alcohol in moderation; avoid smoking; improve our working and living conditions; be careful of our own and others' health and safety; and reduce pollution. We can also try to find non-violent solutions to conflicts. And, crucially, we can tackle inaccessible environments, discriminatory attitudes to disabled and older people and policies and practices that exclude all but the young and fit, so that we can continue to use our abilities to the full for the whole of our lives.

Best of all, we are not reliant on scientists to do these things for us, but can control them ourselves — admittedly not as individuals, but certainly by working together. Science can provide us with medical care, including the prevention of some diseases and the cure of others, and can provide us with treatment and specialist aids to overcome the effects of impairments. What science cannot do, and what we should not ask it to do, is to meet the artificial needs that have been created solely by our society's body dysphoria. As we have seen, if we nonetheless insist that it tries, then the consequences will impact negatively on us all.

Why, despite knowing that all this is true, do we find it so hard to put the things that *are* under our control into practice? Why is this so difficult for us? Why did the final Health Survey for England at the end of the noughties find that two-thirds of the population were clueless as to how much exercise they should be taking, and less than a third knew how much they could drink safely? Why did less than a third of the population eat the recommended portions of fruit and vegetables each day, and why couldn't more than one in nine people identify how big said portion should be? How do we overcome our body dysphoria and create a 21st-century society that benefits from all that science and history can teach us?

Accept ourselves as we really are

First, we need to understand that accepting life as it is — letting reality in — is liberating rather than being something that will inevitably induce fear, panic and horror. Other people may benefit when we overcome our personal body dysphoria, but the principal beneficiaries are ourselves. This book is not about the benefits of altruism, but about the many gains that we ourselves will make from examining and tackling our dysphoric attitudes. And in any case, we will certainly not be able to accept other people as they are until we can first accept — and love — ourselves.

Crucially, we need to recognise that there is no such thing as a 'standard' human being: that emotionally, physically and intellectually we are all a unique mixture of vulnerabilities, fragilities and strengths. Similarly, we need to accept that these elements are not static, but will vary considerably over our lifetime. And we need to recognise that they will also be affected by our environment, our clothing, our aids and equipment — and by our confidence and fears. We also need to accept that we all suffer from physical and emotional pain at times; that all intelligence and ability to learn is on a continuum; that the border between sanity and insanity cannot be drawn; and that no one can live without physical and emotional support for the whole of their lifespan — we need to recognise that divisions between disabled and non-disabled people can only ever be artificial. Most importantly, we need to accept that our bodies are perfectly 'normal' already. Once we understand all this, we may be able to reject the voices that tell us we will only be valid with the help of surgery, drugs or cosmetics.

As we have seen, advertising has always depended on creating an artificial need and then meeting it; on convincing us that our lives are in some way defective and then offering us a solution. This has caused us to learn to develop dysphoric attitudes towards the body. But advertising and product development only follow trends that already exist, and encourage demands that are already being created by other means. Challenging the advertisers will not lead to the downfall of our economy; it will simply result in different products being targeted at us — and hopefully help to reverse the sexualisation of our children at the same time. In the process, we will all become happier: feeling ashamed and invalid because we are not perfect currently affects every part of our lives.

Of course, there will always be a small group for whom apparently unnecessary cosmetic treatments will be necessary, because they will be unable to achieve self-acceptance otherwise, and they should receive the support that they need and deserve when undergoing them. Someone who looks completely ordinary to the rest of us may still be extremely self-conscious — body dysphoric. But we need to recognise these people as experiencing psychiatric medical conditions, rather than viewing the treatment that they receive as routine 'self-improvement' to which anyone in a similar situation should aspire. Given the risks, pain and scarring that surgery entails, people should never be made to feel that surgery is a more straightforward, 'normalised' route to self-acceptance than counselling.

Critically, we need to recognise that we have no right to dictate what other bodies should look like — this is absolutely not the intention of this book. Scars from accidents or assaults may be regarded by their bearers as proud signs of survival, or as continual reminders of past trauma that prevent them from moving on. Someone whose features have been changed by illness or injury may experience deep identity problems without cosmetic surgery, or may find the thought of further medical intervention unbearable. As with people who have been born with unusual features or with bodies that they feel don't reflect their innate gender, they need to be supported to decide what is best for *them* — surgery, or the status quo — rather than being expected to conform to the expectations of the rest of us.

Accept that impairment is normal

Once we recognise that science is not magic, we will find it easier to accept that impairment is a normal part of the human experience that cannot be selectively removed from life. The principal beneficiaries of this change of attitude will be ourselves: the vast majority of us will experience impairment at some point in our lives; and those who escape it will have done so only because they have died prematurely. With the majority of the Western population soon to be over the age of 40, this is not an issue that we can ignore for much longer in any case. But while we continue to do so, we contribute to creating a society that at some point will discriminate against or exclude us all. We will only be able to enjoy our extra decade or so of active life once we accept that physical, emotional and intellectual diversity needs to be mainstreamed.

We also need to think about what really makes us human. People who have been segregated from disabled people with profound and severe learning difficulties are frequently surprised to find that this group still have strong personalities and emotions: being human has little, if anything, to do with intelligence. Similarly, people who become severely ill or impaired are often surprised to find how much pleasure they receive simply from enjoying the feel of the sun on their skin or the wind in their face: we do not need to enjoy sophisticated pleasures in order to be fully human. Quality of life is not determined by our ability to read the paper, or to remember what we were doing 20 years previously. Meanwhile, sex can be fun however impaired we become; whatever the belief to the contrary, it is not solely the province of the young, healthy and fit.

As we have seen, many of our attitudes to impairment are related to economics. We have learnt to value people for the contribution that they can make in the present to the (paid) workforce, rather than for any other quality, or for any contribution that they might have made in the past or be able to make in the future. As a result, we have learnt to devalue children, disabled people, older people, women and anyone who is not currently in paid employment. We may only be able to accept that impairment is normal when we also accept that the way in which we place value on human beings needs to change too.

Recognise that impairment has never been less important

In any case, we live in a society in which — in every way that counts — impairment has never been less important. This is despite our distorted perception that it has never been *more* important. Recognising this is crucial to being able to tackle our body dysphoria. If we understand that our quality of life need not be lessened when we are impaired, we might be able to overcome our panic at the very thought of disability, and thus also overcome our denial of reality.

A Different Tomorrow

Without wishing to minimise the impact of ongoing development of medical treatments, for most of us it is in fact the technological and social developments that will contribute most to maximising our quality of life in the future. For example, visual problems become more common with ageing, and in any case are now affecting a younger and larger proportion of the population than previously. However, the majority of visual problems can now be alleviated with spectacles, contact lenses, or, in many cases, laser surgery. Meanwhile, everything from speaking clocks and microwaves to canes that can feed back information on the user's surrounding environment are now available for people who have serious visual impairments.

Further developments may mean that blind people will also be able to have visual information provided electronically to their brains via their visual cortexes (although, despite the media hype, this will be a mobility aid rather than a 'cure'). In the mean time, the move to electronic communications has also meant that information now has the potential to be accessed in a wide variety of formats — written information including websites can be viewed in a wide range of fonts and text sizes, can be translated into audio and read aloud by a computer, or can be printed out in Braille. And the advent of digital television has meant that audio descriptions of films and television programmes are provided which can be easily accessed by those who require them.

Similarly, digital hearing aids, which enable users to focus on a particular sound, now offer a means of enhancing hearing that is far superior to the old analogue models, which simply amplified sound; while digital implants can also be used to carry sound directly to the brain. Public buildings now routinely have induction loops built in to improve the function of hearing aids still further. There is also a wide variety of technology available that substitutes visual cues and alarms for aural ones. Meanwhile, captions are now routinely created for films and television programmes and can be accessed on standard TV sets, and written information can be automatically translated into British Sign Language (BSL) video. Hearing impairments have never had less of an impact than they do now.

Predictive text has made keyboard use much easier for people who have difficulties in using one. For those who are unable to operate a keyboard because of lack of control over their arms, computers can now be controlled by voice commands. In all, there are a wide range of adaptations to enable just about anyone to use a computer. Voice synthesisers, famously used by Professor Stephen Hawking, also make it easier for people with speech impairments to communicate, as do a range of other communication aids.

Abnormal

Meanwhile, as we have seen, wheelchair technology has advanced to the point where there is a model available that just about anyone can operate, including chairs that will stand you up. Sip/puff controls enable anyone who can breath unaided to control not only a wheelchair but a wide range of technology. A British sailor, Hilary Lister, even crossed the Channel and sailed solo around the British Isles using a boat that was adapted to sip/puff controls, and she is currently planning longer voyages.

Defence technologies already exist whereby pilots are able to control, for example, the direction of fighter planes by eye movement, and there are many potential domestic uses for this type of technology. Gaming technologies available for just a few hundred pounds have introduced software that can be controlled by the subtlest of body movements, and the uses of this will continue to expand exponentially over the next decade. Further understanding of how the brain operates should also lead to technologies whereby people can control wheelchairs, artificial limbs and computers by thought alone. Games manufacturers have already started trials using electrodes attached to the head that enable someone to control their direction in virtual environments just by thinking about it.

A wide range of more domestic technologies are also available, controlled by voice, computer, movement or remote control. As we have discussed in the previous chapter, curtains and doors can be opened and closed automatically; lights and other electrical appliances including heating can be switched on and off; and there are even robotic carpet cleaners available. Baths can come with built-in lifts, and toilets are easily available which can wash and dry the user's bottom and which have a lid that closes automatically. And, of course, common domestic technologies already make it far easier than it was a century ago for people with conditions that limit their energy to carry out a wide range of domestic tasks for themselves. Already, too, portable medical technology enables many people to self-monitor their condition at home with the support of doctors at a remote location, rather than them needing to enter institutions.

The fact that (apart from gaming machines) not all of these technologies have yet become 'normalised' and part of the mainstream is due solely to our body dysphoria — to our denial of the fact that we can all benefit from them. Instead, we either have regarded them as being the province of an elite, or have stigmatised them and viewed them as only meeting the needs of a minority who should not exist at all, and who will cease to exist in the future. In fact, all we need to do to make these technologies a normal part of our lives is to recognise that it is normal to use them. As with all technologies, they will become much cheaper and more efficient to use when their supply is no longer restricted to 'special' manufacturers and retail outlets, and when other technologies are routinely designed to interact with them. Once this happens, impairment will become even less significant than it is now.

In the meantime, while we may not be about to become 'silicon humans' any time soon (if at all), the rapid rise of the internet means that we can carry out a wide range of activities without moving from our homes, or indeed our beds. We can work online, shop online, watch films and listen to music online, meet people online, participate in our communities online, watch remote parts of the world online, and indeed have (some sort of) sex online. However impaired we might be, our potential quality of life is far, far greater than it was even a decade ago. All we need to do is to ensure that the internet is genuinely accessible to us all.

Recognise that we are already 'superhuman'

However slow we are to recognise it, technology is already enhancing all of our bodies in a wide range of ways, whether we have impairments or not. We can see objects much further away than the human eye will normally allow through the use of telescopes, binoculars and remote cameras. Similarly, we can see objects in much more detail through the use of microscopes, and we can see in the dark through the use of infrared night scopes. We do not need implants in order to achieve this. In the same way, our hearing is already being enhanced through the use of headphones and telephones, as well as by amplifying sound from a wide variety of sources. Meanwhile, our memories and cognitive abilities are enhanced by electronic organisers, calculators and computers; our ability to communicate is enhanced by telephones and the internet; and our movement is enhanced by everything from skates and bicycles to cars and aeroplanes.

Within the developed world, body enhancement technology has already become normalised, and is readily available to the majority of the population. Where we have gone wrong is in imagining technology that enhances the body as being an endo-technology (something that is internal to us) rather than an exo-technology (something that is external to ourselves). Exo-technologies are, in fact, vastly superior to endo-technologies. No surgery or other procedures are necessary to connect us to them, while we are free to decide whether to commit to them for a lifetime or simply for a matter of seconds. They have few or no known side-effects, and cause only psychological dependence. And they can be replaced, both temporarily and permanently, without causing damage to anything other than our finances.

In every way that matters, we are already 'cyborgs'; we have simply failed to recognise this. We have already quietly accepted the fact that we live without hover cars and anti-gravity shoes and continue to occupy Planet Earth, although 20th-century science and science-fiction writers predicted that we would by now be using such products daily and be living across the universe. Once we can and do recognise the reality of our already enhanced lives, we might also be able to abandon our vision of the human body that is routinely 'upgraded' by implants, and accept that implants are only really of use within medical technologies. This in turn might bring us closer to being able to accept our bodies as they are.

Improve conditions for all pregnant women and mothers

Providing much better care and support for pregnant women and mothers is, of course, the best way to ensure that our children are as healthy as possible, and to optimise their genetic inheritance, whatever that might be. As we have seen, the most important factor in foetal development will always be the welfare of the pregnant woman, not the genetic status of the foetus. Poverty, not genetics, is the single biggest factor influencing the health of unborn children and infants. For example, research by the Perinatal Institute shows that women living in the most deprived areas of Britain are twice as likely to have a stillbirth as women in the richest areas, and their children are also twice as likely to die in the first month of life. As a result, Britain has the highest number of deaths per 1000 live births in western Europe, and its stillbirth rate has not declined significantly since the early 1990s.

Among the 24 richest countries in the world, Britain also has the second highest child death rate, with children in the UK being twice as likely to die before the age of five than children in Sweden. According to the Audit Commission, children in poorer areas of Britain are 9% more likely to have been underweight at birth: inequality between the richest 20% of the population and the poorest 40% is only higher in the USA. Overall, researchers have found a very high correlation between income inequality and mortality among the under-fives in the wealthiest countries, and it is highly probable that the same link exists between inequality and impairment levels.

Meanwhile, at the end of the noughties the number of British women dying in childbirth remained the same as it had been 20 years previously. In 2010 The Lancet reported that Italy had the lowest maternal mortality rate in the world with just 3.9 deaths per 100,000 live births, and that the UK came 23rd, with 8.2 deaths. There is a huge amount that we could do to improve this shameful statistic, as well as improving the experience that British women have of pregnancy and childbirth.

However, we have the power to reduce death and impairment among children and pregnant women on a global, not just a national, scale by improving the welfare of women worldwide. At the end of the noughties, over half a million women died in developing countries each year during pregnancy or childbirth, and a million babies died during their first month of birth. Many other women and children were left needlessly impaired.

In order to change this we first have to recognise that, wherever they live, women have the right to parent and that it is impossible to plan for every pregnancy; we must do this rather than place the blame on poor women for having children at all. We also have to recognise that many women currently have no access to contraception, and in general have little right to choose whether or not to get pregnant, and tackle the difficult issues that this raises, too. If we really care about reducing death and impairment levels, then we cannot simply shrug our shoulders and leave women to get on with it.

Examine our attitudes to food

Examining the relationship between food, impairment, social attitudes and quality of life is enough to fill a book on its own; however, it is impossible to write a book about the body without at least mentioning it.

On the one hand, the rise of the processed food industry has reduced the workload for a huge number of people — not just within the home, but also within food and related industries. (It has also been extremely convenient for men, coming in tandem with the rise of feminism — which would otherwise have seen the male of the species spending far longer in the kitchen.) On the other hand, the need to make processed food palatable by adding sugar and appetite stimulants and other chemicals has dramatically increased the impact and rate of food cravings and food addiction; the brain responds even to substances such as sugar and carbohydrates by releasing 'feel good' neuro-transmitters. More worrying still are recent findings that toddlers eating diets high in processed foods have measurably lower IQs than others by the age of eight.

In addition, the development of the multinational food industry has worked against the fact that, actually, we need to eat far less than our ancestors because of our far more sedentary lifestyle. However much we aim to burn off calories in sporting activities, we cannot alter the reality that whereas in the mid-20th century both children and adults commonly walked several miles a day, today we are lucky if we walk several hundred yards in a day.

Larger people are commonly stigmatised as being lazy, lacking self-discipline and having personality disorders. We do not want to accept the fact that they are simply more susceptible to the pressures of advertising, the effects of food additives, and the convenience of buying ready-made food than we may be ourselves. Or that their economic status means that cheap food, high in fat and sugar, is all they can afford. Or, of course, that they may have put on weight simply because impairment means they are unable to exercise as much as they previously did — something that could happen to any of us at any time. It is easier to blame the victim, and to continue to use 'fat' as a term of abuse, than it is to provide help or to take other positive forms of action.

Certainly we need far more state support for both children and adults to relearn their eating habits and lose weight, instead of simply returning to an ethos of 'individual responsibility'. We also need to consider the previously unthinkable, including raising taxes on food containing excessively high proportions of fat and sugar, and restricting advertising. No more than pharmaceutical companies are food industries there to promote the health of the nation; they exist simply to make profits. It is perfectly possible to produce pre-packaged convenience food that also meets the highest nutritional standards, and we need to make it more profitable to do so.

It is hardly surprising that after the food shortages of the Second World War and the rationing of the late 1940s, Britons greeted US-style processed food with enthusiasm. It is also unsurprising that the glamour attached to American food and restaurant brands was enough to associate eating the products with conveying glamour on ourselves too. But this is the 21st century, and we need to grow up if we are not to continue growing outwards at a rate that may take decades off our potential lifespans. More than half of us are already overweight; this is not simply a problem that affects other people.

Change our approach to social care

As discussed earlier, we currently regard people as being of a lower social status if they require assistance with personal care and domestic and business activities, yet at the same time we regard people as being of a higher social status if they accept assistance with these activities despite not actually requiring it. Crucially, people who actually require assistance are often unable to pay for it themselves, whereas people who use assistance without requiring it are always able to pay for it. Before we can move forwards, we need to recognise that our current attitudes towards social care are illogical and are based on economic values.

We also need to recognise that there is nothing inherently low-status or undesirable about people *providing* social care, whether this is paid or unpaid. We also must recognise that caring is a 'proper job', rather than dismissing it as more properly done on an unpaid basis because it has traditionally been women's work — which in turn leads to the insidious concept of the 'young carer', the child who cares for a sibling or a parent who is in some way incapacitated, by helping with tasks such as washing and dressing.

While we continue to fail to recognise social care as being a profession in its own right, we continue to allow the authorities to take the contribution of children as young as eight years old into account when deciding whether or not to fund outside support. Providing breaks and 'young carers' clubs' is not enough, and indeed piles on the pressure for children and young people to continue in their caring roles. Rather, we need to ensure that local authority and benefit assessment procedures are changed so that the presence of under-18s within households containing disabled and older people is ignored when assessing the need for outside help.

We also need to recognise that there is nothing inherently undesirable about paying people for domestic work, whether this is carried out in the home or elsewhere. Throughout history, society has only been able to function because some people have assisted with other people's housework, shopping and childcare. Rather than believing that we should all be able to function without assistance, we need to tackle the issues of domestic workers' low pay and low status. This is also true, of course, for workers who carry out these tasks in business or institutional settings.

What we may need to do is to look at supply issues when deciding whether access to assistance is based on personal need or on personal wealth. If the domestic labour force is limited, then we may need to accept that we must all carry out our own domestic work at the times of our lives when we are able to do so, in order to be able to have access to assistance at the times of our lives when we most need it. We might also wish to look at ways of increasing the social care labour force, not only by offering better pay and conditions, but also by encouraging people to spend a year or two of their lives offering service to the rest of the community and developing incentives for this. For instance, we might offer young people financial support during their studies in return for spending a 'gap year' working within the community. Or we might change our value system to encourage people to contribute a year or two of community service at times in their lives when they are able to do so. Other countries have already begun to trial these options.

We need to adopt anything but the status quo, when people are either left to manage without the support that they desperately need, or are forced to provide unpaid support to others at times when they have no real ability to do so. The majority of developed countries manage to provide free access to health care without this having anything but a beneficial effect on the economy. Ensuring that people also have free access to social care would equally benefit us all, rather than only benefiting those who are unable to pay for it themselves.

Change the way in which we design and build our environment

Our body dysphoria has resulted in us creating a built environment that takes no account of the needs of the majority of the population. Mothers, children, disabled people, older people, fat people and short people all have to contend with a built environment that takes little or no account of their needs. As a result, many people are excluded from participating in a wide range of activities that they should be able to take for granted, from working, to shopping, to using public transport, to participating in leisure and community activities and public life.

This is despite the fact that an environment that is accessible to all benefits everyone, and not just at the times of our lives when we fall into one of the groups listed above. Accessible environments have been proven time and again to be far more comfortable and stress-free for everyone who uses them, while environments that are inaccessible to some are usually accessible only with difficulty to everyone else. Poor access, for example, not only bars some people from working, but also creates an atmosphere where all workers are more stressed and less productive than otherwise.

A Different Tomorrow

Meanwhile, leisure facilities are less of a break and more of a headache for everyone when they are badly designed.

As we have seen, recent experience has taught us that it is not enough to understand what makes an environment accessible and to have laws that insist we do this. Time and again, new public buildings that are supposed to comply in full with accessibility regulations turn out to have just as many access problems as older buildings. There seem to be several reasons for this inability to implement the expertise that we already have.

First, our body dysphoria does not allow the people commissioning and creating the buildings to believe that disabled people and older people will really want to use them. Second, the fact that the commissioners and builders are overwhelmingly male seems to make them overlook the needs of mothers and children. In addition, the lack of awareness of how groups like mothers, children, older people and disabled people use buildings means that construction workers find it virtually impossible to understand how to implement the regulations in practice. Finally, the checking of accessibility compliance is not prioritised when ensuring that the building is being created as it was originally designed.

Both legislators and the construction industry have been aware for some time of the need to build homes for 'lifetime' use. This means building homes with doorways and corridors that are wide enough for pushchairs, wheelchairs and larger people to move through easily. It means building homes with level access, and with stairways that can be adapted to fit a stairlift. It means setting windows low enough for children and seated people to see out of. It means installing kitchens and bathrooms that can be accessed by people of different heights (including children), and by people using wheelchairs. And it means a host of other common-sense measures that would allow all of us to enjoy our homes in full throughout our lifetimes.

After all, no one wants to have to move or be trapped in their home whenever they develop an impairment, let alone simply because they have had children, or have put on weight, or are temporarily unwell. And no one wants to live in a home that only the fittest members of their family and circle of friends can visit. However, today even the newest homes are only required to be partially accessible, and only a minority of new homes are designed so that they can be converted to wheelchair use. We now demand at least two bathrooms as standard, with at least one en suite, but we never think to ask that a property is designed so that it can easily be converted to include a lift.

Perhaps we are so prepared to put up with inaccessible new homes because we have become so used to inaccessible old ones. We have also learned to regard domestic property as an 'investment' rather than as being the place where we spend a significant amount of our lives. But, as with the brand new non-accessible 'accessible' public buildings, we are storing up several lifetimes of difficulties as a result of our failure to change. We will only be able to enjoy our extra decade of active life once we start to use our expertise — not only to build new homes and public buildings that actually meet our needs, but also to adapt our old ones.

Change our attitude to ageing

We need to accept that our attitudes to ageing are cultural rather than innate before we can change them. We can see that our attitudes are cultural quite simply by recognising that older people are respected and valued much more highly in some other cultures than they are in the West. This is not to say that we should adopt other people's cultural attitudes wholesale; rather, it is to point out that we can easily change our own. Again, since we will all — unless we die prematurely — become old, the people who have most to gain from this are ourselves.

First, we need to appreciate the gains of old age, rather than simply focusing on the losses. In our overvaluing of youth as a time when workers are most able to be fit enough to work long hours, we undervalue experience. But this has not always been the case. Rather, it resulted from a major attitudinal change in the 20th century, when the introduction of industrial techniques based on Fordism meant that apprenticeships and lengthy training periods became less and less necessary. Prior to this, workers with training and experience were highly valued, but after Ford, manufacturing tasks were broken down into smaller ones that required far less skill. By the end of the 20th century, computerisation had increased this devaluing of skill and experience still further, particularly as individual knowledge could be supplemented and replaced by the computer's knowledge.

In reality, however, Fordism has long had its day. Experience is highly beneficial to the modern way in which we do business, whereas the physical strength offered by youth has never been less important to our contemporary industries. Science has shown us that, while younger brains are better at remembering 'lists', older brains are better at contextualisation, categorisation, inductive reasoning and debating, and that generally older people have a better understanding of how the world works. So our economy suffers daily because businesses fear that their image will be damaged if they are represented by older workers, without their gaining anything whatsoever by only employing younger workers. Our body dysphoria means that companies feel forced to deny themselves the benefits of age and experience, even though many actually recognise these benefits.

We will not make any real progress in dismantling our body dysphoria, though, while we continue to operate a value system based around the ability to work. Our elders can in fact offer us a wide range of other experiences that we can learn from and respect, and their continued contribution to society would be much greater if only they were enabled to participate. Most importantly, though, we can value older people for their past achievements and contributions, rather than demanding that they make a contribution now or be regarded as worthless. We can value and respect our older people simply for surviving.

As we have already seen, the impact of impairments associated with ageing has never been less, while there is nothing inherently negative about making use of social care and domestic support services. But we will never be able to lose our fear of ageing until we know that we will not lose our social status simply by growing old. When this happens, we can welcome our wrinkles and liver spots as a sign of reaching a stage in our lives when we will be highly respected, rather than believing that cosmetic surgery and laser treatment are necessary in order for us to remain valid.

After all, the only thing that youth really denotes is (probable) fertility, and, even then, men remain fertile into old age, and reproductive technologies are beginning to offer a longer period of fertility to women, too. At the same time, pregnancy and motherhood have never given women social status; fertility in women has never been as prized as it might appear. In reality, many women feel more powerful and in control of their lives after the age of 35, and the majority do not even begin to reach their sexual peak until then.

A detailed look at the history of cosmetics before the 19th century shows that products were once developed which exaggerated, rather than hid, the signs of ageing. So a radical change in our attitudes is not as impossible as it might seem. We could, after all, decide that old age is a time for celebration, a real 'coming of age'. We could decide that we will provide our old people with the best that life has to offer, and ensure that every day for them is as full and as rich as possible. We could all look forward to 'the time of our life' as something worth achieving, worth staying alive for. We could 'keep the best for last'.

Change our attitude to death

Fear of death lies at the root of our body dysphoria. Since we can't face dying, we credit science with having — and expect science to have — the power of ensuring that death is impossible. Because we can't accept the inevitability of our death, our denial leads us to create a world rooted on the hopeless expectation of our immortality. And even when we do accept that we will nonetheless die, we focus on finding ways of hastening this through euthanasia and 'assisted suicide', rather than undergoing it as a natural, potentially pleasurable process. Changing our attitude to death is therefore essential to the process of eliminating our body dysphoria.

If we go into any bookshop in the developed world — or search an online bookstore — we can find far, far more books related to birth than we can find books dealing with death. Of the books that do exist about death, the vast majority either are religious, or describe how Eastern and historic cultures deal with mortality. Most of the rest deal with bereavement and grieving, rather than examining how an individual, their family and their friends can approach death in a way that fully meets their needs and gives them the maximum comfort and support. As a result, the majority of people are forced to find their own path at a time when they may already feel isolated and alone. It is unsurprising that we fear a death like this, but it is our fears that are causing the isolation of the dying in the first place.

Similarly, most of our rituals relating to death are confined to what happens afterwards. Only the religious have access to rituals that deal with dying itself, and these relate to the final hours rather than encompassing the final months and weeks of life. We urgently need to share our experiences and develop ways of dealing with death and dying, rather than continuing to pretend that it will never happen to us. Only then can we also provide support to others facing death and bereavement.

To date, the hospice movement has been alone in developing innovative ways of coming to terms with death, as well as developing rituals and providing practical support and advice about the legal and other issues involved. Research has shown that our hospices lead the world in providing end-of-life care — ensuring that people in the last stages of terminal illness do not suffer pain or lack of dignity. Although hospices are popularly believed to provide inpatient care only, they also provide a variety of home-based and outreach services.

At the end of the noughties, three quarters of Britons died in hospitals or care homes, and only 4% were admitted to a hospice. Less than one in ten died at home, although this is most people's preferred choice and costs no more than hospital provision. We need to ensure better awareness of the hospices' experiences and knowledge, and vastly increase their funding so that everyone who wishes to can have access to their services. Only then will we be able to face death without fear, and only then will the dying and bereaved receive support from their community rather than being shunned.

We also need to make vast improvements to the way in which we care for people in the last years of their lives. Repeated research has found that older people receive a poorer service from the NHS, and this is exacerbated by the fact that we expect all of our doctors to be generalists rather than having geriatricians. Then thousands of people with conditions that cause dementia are being prescribed drugs that double their risk of suffering a stroke, a fall or a chest infection, and which cause a worse as well as an earlier death than would otherwise have occurred, simply to make them more compliant. These so-called neuroleptic drugs are not licensed for use by anyone other than schizophrenics, but are widely prescribed for people with dementia, including those with mild symptoms, despite there being alternatives. In 2005 the Alzheimer's Society presented evidence that over 100,000 people with dementia were being prescribed neuroleptics in the UK, with nearly half of people with dementia who live in care homes receiving them.

Meanwhile, research carried out in 2006 found that nearly two-fifths of people in nursing homes are suffering from constant pain, with the majority receiving no medical advice or medication to relieve it. Ninety per cent of this group felt that their quality of life was reduced as a result, and a third suffered related depression. Yet pain can almost always be relieved completely with medical help. When we believe that euthanasia is preferable to a slow death, we are often basing our decision on the example of this entirely unnecessary suffering.

Fear of dying needs to be tackled on both the metaphysical and the purely practical levels. We cannot relieve our fear of the unknown, of the fact that we will no longer exist (at the very least, in this form), without relieving our fear of the physical process of death. Rituals and roses are all very well, but the provision of practical and appropriate support services are critical.

Change our attitude to medical research science

The knock-on effect of our body dysphoria is actually to hamper medical or bio-scientists in carrying out their research. First, we credit them with being godlike, all-powerful figures, because anything else exposes our dysphoria for what it is. Alongside this we continue to believe, as the Victorians did, that everything about the world in which we live can first be discovered, and then be controlled. We are able to believe this by ignoring the fact that science continues to show us a world that is infinitely more complex and unpredictable than we could have believed when we had only the knowledge of the 19th century to rely on. Then we create both utopian and dystopian visions of what will result from medical researchers' work.

In our dystopian visions we imagine a world where, for example, we will be able to 'design' our children. As a result, we put as many measures in place as possible to ensure that this will not happen without, at least, the approval of the majority. In fact, as we have seen, this is an impossible scenario; so many of these measures are unnecessary. Stem cell research is similarly hampered by dystopian concerns about human–animal hybrids and the use of foetal tissue from abortions. Overall, our failure to recognise the reality of the limitations of medical science means that we put unnecessary prohibitions on the research that medical scientists may and may not do, with the result that research is slowed down or even halted.

In our utopian visions we also imagine a world where medical scientists can do anything. As a result, we demand that medical researchers come up with not only treatments but also cures for every disease that afflicts humanity. We refuse to accept that anything might eventually turn out to be impossible; instead we believe — in the face of all scientific evidence to the contrary — that it is simply a matter of allowing enough time and resources for something to happen.

Consequently, we expect that if we provide medical researchers with the resources they ask for, they will in turn provide us with treatments and cures in whatever area they are working in. We accept that not all avenues of research will prove to be fruitful, but we refuse to accept that the vast majority of research may not result in anything more concrete than increased knowledge. We certainly refuse to accept that in order to make further advances on the many discoveries of the past, it may cost us far more and take us far longer than it did then. Instead, we firmly believe that, 'just around the corner', we will be able to do everything that we ever dreamed of.

Increasingly, we vent our frustrations at the realities of life on the scientists whom we expect to be able to change reality for us. We believe that they are not sufficiently driven by the market, or that they are motivated too much by intellectual curiosity and are wilfully refusing to produce cures. We certainly believe we have a 'right' to expect that, in return for resources, we will be presented with practical applications of their work.

Moreover, we expect this in the short rather than the long term: we demand that scientists promise us the moon as a pre-condition of their work being funded at all. And when the moon is not forthcoming, we withdraw their resources and/or change their working conditions in the hope that this will bring them to heel. Unless and until we accept reality instead, the very research that may one day produce the most benefit to the human race may be stymied for lack of immediate and practical application.

Change the way that we fund medical research

As we have seen, 90% of the money that is currently being spent on medical research goes towards researching treatments for the diseases that cause 10% of the world's health problems. And in many cases this research is being carried out to develop alternative treatments for illnesses where effective treatments already exist today. There is often little or no research at all being carried out into the treatment of diseases for which existing treatments are only partially effective or cause serious side-effects, because the majority of medical research is funded by the pharmaceutical companies and they exist to make a profit. Since it is much more expensive and difficult to make completely new discoveries today than it was in the past, it is most profitable to tinker with existing drugs in order to extend their patents and thus their profitability.

Meanwhile, the number of new drugs being registered each year has fallen from around 50 in the 1990s to around 20 in the teens. Whatever our beliefs and expectations, the reality is that medical research is producing fewer and fewer results each year. New drugs, too, are increasingly expensive to buy. Investors rightly argue that when they fund millions of pounds' worth of research that does not result in a product, they should be able to recoup this investment and more from the minority of products that are released successfully on to the market.

However, this creates massive inequities on a worldwide scale, and in turn has horrendous implications for the world economy. On a worldwide basis, the majority of illness is suffered by people who are too poor to pay for their medications. As we have seen, HIV and malaria in particular have decimated whole populations because of lack of access to affordable medication. This economic instability also creates the unrest that leads to wars and armed conflicts. There has to be a better way.

Another problem with leaving research to the private sector is that information usually cannot be shared, because other researchers are viewed as being competitors rather than collaborators. Recent attempts by one or two long-established pharmaceutical companies to share information show that they are now recognising the importance of information-sharing for themselves. However, this could not happen where the research is being funded by individual investors, as happens with so much biotech research today.

Perhaps we need to separate medical research from pharmaceutical production, and to fund medical research primarily from the state? Then pharmaceutical companies could concentrate on bidding to produce drugs as cheaply and efficiently as possible, rather than on developing drugs for the market place. Resources could be diverted away from tinkering with existing drugs into entirely new areas of research; and there would be far less pressure to bring a drug to market when it was known to be no more effective than existing treatments, or, indeed, than a placebo. And with international cooperation over research, medical research could move forward far more quickly and cheaply than it does now.

An impossible dream, perhaps — but only when we change the way in which we fund medical research can we live in a world where its priorities are determined by need, whether that need is local or international. And only then would we have access to medications that are more effective and cause fewer side-effects, as well as being affordable to all. Yes, the benefits would be felt most in the developing world, but there would still be considerable benefits for the rest of us.

Change our pace of life

By the end of the 20th century, we had accelerated the pace at which we live to one that would have been unrecognisable in many of the centuries that preceded it. If we slowed life down again just a bit, then the very old, the very young and the disabled would become much more able to participate. In particular, it would be much easier to enjoy our extra decade of active life if that life were organised in a way that took account of our needs.

Of course, working hours have always been dictated by class, with the poorest people working longer hours and for more of their lives than the richest. Working hours have also been affected by gender, since women have traditionally been expected to carry out the bulk of domestic labour and childcare on a voluntary basis, while the poorest women have always had to carry out paid work alongside this and middle-class women now have the 'right' to do this as well. But overall, we still work longer hours than our ancestors, with the British now only behind the Turkish in working the longest hours in Europe and taking the fewest breaks during their working day.

This acceleration of pace has in itself contributed to the rising level of impairment among people of working age. In Britain, there has been an epidemic of mental illness and back injury because of the 'long hours, short breaks' culture, ending many people's working lives prematurely because recovery from these conditions is usually only partial. At the same time, Britain's stressful working culture has excluded many people from the workplace who would previously have been able to participate, including people with all kinds of 'non-standard' bodies (whether the system recognises them as being disabled, or simply as being 'long-term unemployed'). People who could manage a strict 35-hour week with regular breaks may well not be able to manage a working week that is even slightly longer, particularly those who experience back problems or stress and depression.

Slowing our pace down would enable many more people to enter the workplace, as well as protecting the health of those already there. This is essential if we are to achieve our goal of enabling people to work up to the age of 70 in a society where the majority will soon be over the age of 40 — something that is necessary to benefit our economy as well as the individuals concerned. But it would also impact on every other area of our lives. Longer working hours leave us less able to parent; less able to see our families and friends; less able to care for our elders; less able to exercise; less able to prepare healthy food; and, in general, with less time to look after ourselves. Our current workplace culture not only makes it harder for us to enjoy real quality of life; it also contributes to our premature deaths.

Gain a global perspective

A sure way to gain a saner, more realistic view of our own situation is to take a global perspective, rather than limiting ourselves both socially and geographically. For example, it is hard for anyone living in a wealthy, developed country to view themselves as a victim of circumstance simply because they have an impairment, when we compare our lives to the daily struggle that the bulk of the world's population faces. (This is not, of course, to deny that deep poverty exists within the developed world, too, on a much greater scale than we usually admit, and that this affects a disproportionate number of older and disabled people.)

One benefit of living in an age of electronic communication and cheap international travel is that it is now much easier than it used to be to think globally. Science has also taught us that we are all descendants of the same small group of Africans. We can no longer distance ourselves from the situations in which other human beings find themselves by believing that these other people are not part of the same tribe or family as us. Whether people come from minority ethnic groups within our own country or live on the other side of the planet, we are all related.

Taking a global perspective also enables us to realise just how much power we have to reduce impairment levels across the world. Enabling everyone to have access to clean drinking water and sanitation would save the lives of over two million children a year, as well as reducing impairment among those who currently survive. At present, more than a billion people do not have access to clean drinking water, and more than 2.5 billion people do not have access to adequate sewerage, solely because of poverty. The United Nations Development Programme estimates that at any one time almost half of everyone living in the developing world is suffering from a related illness, including blindness. The fact that, worldwide, a billion people are now undernourished increases this impact.

The extension of basic health care would also have a major impact on impairment levels in the developing world. Malaria, for example, kills more than a million people a year, 90% of whom are under the age of five. Although drug treatments are not completely effective, access to drugs would make a vast difference to the survival rate. (So would access to mosquito nets: in the late noughties, the child death rate from malaria in Kenya was halved after nets were given away free.) Meanwhile, more than two million children under the age of five die each year from diseases such as measles, polio, diphtheria and hepatitis, while others are permanently impaired by these. Effective vaccines are available, but poverty prevents access to them.

Likewise, the majority of women in the world who are living with HIV do not receive anti-retroviral drugs in pregnancy, meaning that millions of babies contract the disease unnecessarily. Basic disability aids are absent across the world, too; in addition to a huge unmet demand for prosthetic feet and legs, two billion people do not have the spectacles that would enable them to see properly. We all have an amazing ability to save life, simply by helping to widen access to food and water, sanitation, health care and basic aids and equipment.

It is also important to remember that people in the developed world, too, are often denied access to medical care because of their income or nationality. In the noughties in the USA, the richest country in the world, almost 44 million people (or 15% of the population) were without health insurance and had little or no ability to pay for medical care. And in western Europe, migrant workers and asylum seekers were routinely denied medical treatment because they lacked the correct paperwork. If we wish to reduce impairment levels in the developed world, then there is an easy solution: universal access to health care. Even the USA is now moving — albeit slowly — in this direction.

Extending Western health and safety standards to the countries that provide most of our imports would reduce impairment further still. Workplace accidents will always happen, but many of those that take place today in the developing world are easily preventable. So are many in the UK. We need to abandon, once and for all, ancient beliefs that accident victims have only themselves to blame, and ensure that changing health and safety legislation to make it less complex does not make it less stringent. It is, after all, society that picks up the resulting medical and benefit bills.

Pollution, another major cause of impairment worldwide (including Britain itself), is also closely linked to industries that are providing goods for the developed world. We need to accept that part of the price we pay for cheap goods is other people's impairment, and ask ourselves whether we are prepared for this to continue rather than working to improve factory conditions in developing countries. We also need to continue to reduce pollution on our own doorstep. In 2010, a report to Parliament showed that air pollution alone causes 50,000 premature deaths each year in the UK.

War, of course, is also a major cause of impairment, among both the armed forces and civilians. Even after war ends it leaves a legacy of continuing impairment, both as a result of the landmines and other ammunition that are left behind and because of the poverty it brings with it. Outside the USA and Great Britain, very few people living in the developed world believe that they have any relationship with armed struggles. However, the vast majority of countries within the developed world contribute to creating wars in the developing world through trading arms, while instability is often the legacy of their historical colonial activity. Prioritising social care over armed aggression would have a significant impact on worldwide impairment levels, too.

Recognise the importance of politics

If we really want to create a world without disability and premature death, and without disabling barriers in every area of our lives, then it is to politicians, not the men in white coats, that we need to look once we have cured ourselves of our body dysphoria. Politics, not science, is where the fundamental ability to prevent impairment and death on a global scale lies. Closer to home, it is politics that can give us all an additional decade — or more — of active life.

In the noughties, people living in Britain's poorest communities died on average seven years earlier than those living in the richest; while homeless people had a life expectation that was in the low 40s. When smaller areas of the country were compared, gaps in life expectancy were as big as 28 years between rich and poor neighbourhoods. Poor people were also more likely to die than rich people following heart surgery and other operations, and more than 25,000 older people died unnecessarily each year because they could not afford to heat their homes.

The relative difference in rich and poor people's health while they were still alive was even more extreme. On average, the difference in 'disability-free life expectancy' in the noughties between those at the top and bottom of the wealth spectrum was 17 years. Meanwhile, poor people were more likely than richer people to suffer from impairments associated with ageing, showing that the links between illness and age are as much to do with economics as they are with years lived.

Rather than decreasing as time has gone on, the gap in living standards between rich and poor Britons was wider at the end of the noughties than it had been three decades earlier. Overall, inequality was officially deemed to be 40% higher than it had been in 1974. We cannot leave it to 'progress', then, to solve our social problems, and we need to do far more than channel more of our resources into health and social care if we are to create a society that takes account of the scientific realities of our lives. Rather we have other, more fundamental changes that we need to make — changes that will ultimately improve life for us all.

We have everything to gain, and only our dysphoria to lose…